The Genealogy Sourcebook

ALSO BY SHARON DEBARTOLO CARMACK:

Italian-American Family History:
A Guide to Researching and Writing About Your Heritage

A Genealogist's Guide to Discovering Your Female Ancestors

The Genealogy Sourcebook

BY

SHARON DEBARTOLO CARMACK, CGRS

Foreword by Marsha Hoffman Rising, CG, CGL, FASG

LOWELL HOUSE

LOS ANGELES

CONTEMPORARY BOOKS

CHICAGO

Library of Congress Cataloging in Publication Data

Carmack, Sharon DeBartolo, 1956–
    The genealogy sourcebook / by Sharon DeBartolo Carmack ; foreword by Marsha Hoffman Rising.
       p.   cm.
    Includes Bibliographical references and index.
    ISBN 1-56565-794-2
    ISBN 0-7373-0007-8 (paper)
    1. United States—Genealogy—Handbooks, manuals, etc.
2. Genealogy.   I. Title.
CS44.C39 1997
929'.1' 072073—dc21

Requests for such permissions should be addressed to:
Lowell House
2020 Avenue of the Stars, Suite 300
Los Angeles, CA 90067

Lowell House books can be purchased at special discounts when ordered in bulk for premiums and special sales.

Publisher: Jack Artenstein
Associate Publisher, Lowell House Adult: Bud Sperry
Director of Publishing Services: Rena Copperman
Managing Editor: Maria Magallanes
Text design: Laurie Young

Manufactured in the United States of America
10 9 8 7 6 5 4 3 2

For my husband, Steve, who encouraged me to follow my dream.

Contents

Permissions

Revisions of Sharon DeBartolo Carmack's "Branch Office" columns, 1991 to 1996, are reprinted with permission from *Reunions Magazine,* P.O. Box 11727, Milwaukee, WI 53211-0727.

Ancestor chart (Figures 1.1 and 1.2) courtesy of National Genealogical Society, 4527 17th St. N., Arlington, VA 22207-2399.

Family group sheet (Figure 1.3) courtesy of Genealogical Books in Print, 6818 Lois Dr., Springfield, VA 22150.

Permission to reprint the Association of Professional Genealogists Code of Ethics granted by APG, P.O. Box 40393, Denver, CO 80204-0393.

Permission to reprint portions of "Genealogical Certification: Who? What? Why? How?" granted by the Board for Certification of Genealogists, P.O. Box 14291, Washington, DC 20044.

Foreword

Genealogy is rapidly becoming the most popular hobby in America. If you pose the question "why?" to scholars, it may lead to a discussion of demographics, the weakening family structure, or the desire for each of us to find where we fit in the world. Psychologists might tell us that it is important to feel a link with the past and the future. The true answer is more simple: Genealogy is fun, it's flexible, and it's important.

You can work as diligently or casually as you wish. You can travel the country (or the world), ferreting out farms where your family lived, courthouses where their records are stored, churches they attended, and cemeteries where they are buried. Or you can search from the comfort of your home. You can write letters, rent microfilmed records and books, subscribe to periodicals, and communicate through a computer modem. If you tire of your ancestors or other demands are made on your time, you can put the dead folks away and take them out some other time. One of the best-known genealogists of the past, John I. Coddington, once said, "After a while, ancestors can become a bit of a bore. You simply put them in a drawer and you study your cousins." He was right. When researching cousins, you can change the geographic area of interest, shift the time period you are researching, and make different and exciting discoveries that would have eluded you if you had kept your family study too narrow.

Genealogy can become an expensive hobby or it can remain inexpensive. It all depends on how obsessed you become and how much discretionary funds you have. Hobbies such as golf, fishing, hunting, and skiing require the purchase or rental of expensive equipment. A computer is the most expensive piece of equipment a genealogist is likely to need, and it can be used for a myriad of other activities. Hobbies such as stamp collecting, coin collecting, and bird-watching may require less travel and less physical exertion than athletic pursuits, but if you are serious about these hobbies, they, too, require an investment of time and money. By reading *The Genealogy Sourcebook*, you will find new ways to dispose of your money that you never dreamed about. At the same time, you will learn how to spend many interesting hours at libraries and courthouses—neither of which charge an admission or a fee for using their materials.

Many people are searching for their ancestry. Some have been engaged in the process for twenty years; others are just beginning. Yet few will reach their potential as genealogists without making a simple investment in a book like this. They believe the first step is to go to the courthouse or the library. The result is that they usually become overwhelmed or frustrated. Your quest will be easier, more successful, and create better relationships with professional records staff if you first read *The Genealogy Sourcebook*.

Sharon DeBartolo Carmack takes a unique approach with this basic methodology book. Rather than devoting a Chapter to each of the commonly used genealogical records, she takes a personal, direct, and practical approach to getting organized, interviewing family members, and planning research. Even if a researcher has read several beginning texts, Carmack's reference work includes essential material often neglected. She discusses the importance of education in genealogy. She emphasizes the value of joining genealogical societies, both small and large ones, locally and in the area where your ancestors lived, and national societies, which offer a different but equally important focus.

When one starts searching for family information, the first thought is to uncover what the family has kept. Most of us assume that the vast majority of what we will find about our family will come from within the family. What a surprise to find the vast assortment of public records (local, state, and federal), journals, bibliographies, source books, published abstracts, and local genealogical periodicals that have the potential for providing much more information. No genealogist ever forgets the first time they found the person they were looking for on the federal census; or the first time a newly discovered cousin mailed a large packet of public and private records collected over the years. Within this book, you will learn the best ways to find both family and public records. You will also learn to maximize what you obtain from them once they are located. These two completely different skills are both essential.

When Carmack begins the Chapter on genealogical records, she becomes a teacher standing by your side. She shares her knowledge by using her own family examples as case studies. She takes a progressive approach to the research process rather than expecting the reader to absorb a plethora of data. Through her hands-on approach to using the records, she brings the reader directly into the research process even though working from between the covers of a book. She shares her own frustrations, successes, and knowledge in such a way that the reader gets to know her as an interesting and vital person, not just as "an expert."

Unquestionably, those who not only read but *use* this book will become better researchers no matter when they began their initial pursuit of their ancestry. This book, however, offers more than advice on how to become a better researcher. The reader will become familiar with the jargon and "alphabet soup" that have proliferated within the field of genealogy as they have in all fields of endeavor. There was a time when I would have felt completely excluded by listening to genealogists at society meetings or at conferences. Ms. Carmack makes sure that doesn't happen to new genealogists today.

She also includes a discussion of how to find a professional genealogist or become a professional genealogist yourself. You probably don't think your interest in genealogy will ever lead beyond finding your own ancestors. Wasn't it because of this interest alone that you picked up this book? Good. Have fun. You will learn new sources, explore educational opportunities, and develop better research techniques. In a couple of years, however, you will need a professional or wonder how you can become one. You can then pick up this book again.

MARSHA HOFFMAN RISING, CG, CGL, FASG

Preface

There is something that draws people to the past,
a delicate thread of spirit and soul that binds us with
our past. This is the essence of our ancestors that does not die
when they do. It is a persistent part of their life's force
that waits quietly for someone to listen.

—BECKY SHY

ecky Shy, one of the non-genealogists I asked to review this book in manuscript form, eloquently summed up in three sentences what has taken me a whole book to say. Genealogy is about our past, our present, and our future. Unfortunately, many people have no desire to know about their ancestors—the people who made life possible for them, the people whose genetic makeup they carry, the people who made history. As Cicero (106–43 B.C.) said:

> To be ignorant of what occurred before you were born is to remain always a child. For what is the worth of human life unless it is woven into the life of our ancestors by the records of history?

Can we truly know ourselves if we do not know our ancestors? I don't think so. But then, I'm a genealogist who believes that researching one's ancestry is a worthwhile personal endeavor. For those of you who have the desire to learn about your forebears, I hope to guide you to the right places to begin a most interesting journey.

SDC

Acknowledgments

Many teachers of genealogy think about writing their own instructional guide for beginners, and I was certainly no different. When my publisher asked if I wanted to write one for their *Sourcebook* line, I agreed—but not without some reservations. I didn't want this to be a traditional "how-to" book, naming one record source after another. I wanted it to complement these types of guides; and Suzanne McVetty, CG, was instrumental in helping me develop the concept for this book.

I also owe appreciation to many other people. I coerced several friends and colleagues to read drafts of this book: Becky Shy; Jacqua Lee Swennes; Marcia K. Wyett, CGRS; Roger D. Joslyn, CG, FASG; Ruth Herlacher Christian; and Marsha Hoffman Rising, CG, FASG, who also graciously agreed to write the Foreword.

Then there are my genealogical instructors, two women who made a strong impression on me during my formidable years as a baby genealogist: Sandra Hargreaves Luebking and Anne Dallas Budd.

I also owe a great deal of gratitude to a fellow genealogist who introduced me to the world of genealogy as I am now doing for others through this work: Barbara W. Winge.

Although my husband Steve and daughter Laurie—and anyone else in my extended family, now that I think about it—do not share my interest in genealogy, they have nonetheless supported me in my never-ending search for all those ancestors who are waiting quietly for me to listen.

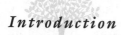
What Is Genealogy?

At some point in life, everyone wonders, "Where did I come from?" As a child, this meant, "So if I was in Mommy's tummy, exactly how did I get *in* there and how did I get *out*?" As an adolescent or an adult, the question of origin takes on a new, almost philosophical, significance: "My parents had parents, and their parents had parents, and their parents had parents . . . so how did we all come about, and how does this affect *me* and who I am?"

TAKING AN INTEREST IN YOUR ANCESTRY

As a child, were you bored out of your mind when Grandma decided to share, once again, the story of her childhood, or how her parents lived, or what crazy Uncle John did in his youth? As an adult, with Grandma now resting in peace, are you craving the sound of her voice as she told those stories, regretting that you never asked questions that would have helped add flavor to the family history you want to write?

Or perhaps you were the only grandchild who loved hearing Grandpa talk about life during the Depression, a time when everything was so different from your own experiences. His war stories came to life for you, sparking a lifelong interest and love of history. In high school history class, while everyone else was daydreaming, you sat on the edge of your seat during lectures and discussions on the early twentieth century, taking in every detail because you knew your grandfather had been a part of that history.

Not everyone becomes interested in pursuing their family history. Budding genealogists are the ones who are fascinated with old family memorabilia and artifacts, who constantly want to hear stories about the origins of the family, and seem to be the ones to whom everyone in the family donates old family photographs. Genealogists are almost obsessive-compulsive in their need to know about past generations.

For every person who climbs a family tree, there is a different reason, a different catalyst, that created an interest in discovering "Where did I come from?" In my case, I had heard that my family was related to Robert E. Lee on my mother's side. I wanted to find out if this was true. But as an adolescent, I didn't have the maturity or know-how to go about researching the answer. And besides, boys were becoming just a bit more fascinating than dead relatives. After I married and gave birth to a new generation, my interest in the past revived, leading me on an addicting and captivating journey that has become my passion and my career.

THE ORIGINS OF GENEALOGY

Genealogy, tracing one's ancestry or lineage, and *family history,* looking at a family as a whole and then placing that family into historical perspective, are popular pastimes for many people. Statisticians say that genealogy is the third most popular hobby in America, ranking behind stamp and coin collecting. A survey published in *American Demographics* in 1995 estimated that about 19 million Americans are involved in tracing their lineage. One has only to walk into a research repository and find every microfilm reader in the room occupied to agree with this figure.

The quest for an individual past has interested people since biblical times. From Genesis 5 to Matthew 1, many of us learned in Sunday school classes who begot whom and that someone thought this information was important enough to record it in the most widely read book of all time. Landowners throughout history have passed inheritances to sons through several generations, making somewhat of a record of descendants. Churches in medieval times began keeping track of family relationships in order to determine the degree of consanguinity between marriage partners. At the centennial of our nation, 1876, many counties and states undertook projects to chronicle their history, recording names and biographies of the early settlers in the area. When this nation saw an influx of eastern European immigrants in the late nineteenth and early twentieth centuries, many patriotic and lineage societies, such as the Daughters of the American Revolution and the Sons of the American Revolution, were formed to honor and boast of early American heritage. In 1976, the year of our bicentennial, Alex Haley wrote a best-selling fictional account of his family history titled *Roots*. This novel sparked a phenomenal interest in genealogy. For the first time, individuals belonging to minority ethnic groups saw the importance of researching and preserving their heritage. And in 1997, genealogy made its national television debut with a ten-part PBS series called *Ancestors*. Between this widely televised attention and the ability to connect with other genealogists across the world via the Internet, genealogy is having another boost in popularity.

MAKING FAMILY HISTORY INTERESTING

Regardless of your reason for wanting to trace your ancestry, there is nothing more thrilling than hearing stories from relatives about your forebears and subsequently finding those names in historical documents. These people really did exist. They really were thinking, feeling human beings. They really were a part of our nation's history. Keep in mind that history is not just the famous names and events that we all had to memorize in high school. Our country's history is also the history of everyday people and their lifestyles. It's about the common folk, the people who didn't make it to the pages of the history books, but who made our country what it is today. My great-grandfather, Albino DeBartolo, never did anything to make him famous enough to be in a history book; yet he was one of millions of southern Italians who came to this country through Ellis Island. He was a small part of an important segment of immigration history. Without him, his compatriots, and other immigrants, there would have been no need for an Ellis Island.

FAMILY SKELETONS

Along with finding interesting information on your ancestors, you may also open the door to family skeletons. Perhaps it is that possibility that has piqued your curiosity about your family. All families have skeletons rattling in the closet. Along with other family stories, this is what makes family history flavorful, adding spice to otherwise tasteless names and dates. I love skeletons; I wish my family had more of them. Instead, I must be content with other people's skeletons.

One of the problems I have—and other genealogists have also confessed to this—is getting sidetracked while looking for my own ancestors. People are so fascinating—especially the dead ones. You may be looking for your ancestor in a newspaper or in court records and someone else's misdeeds catch your eye. Then you want to know more about that person. This happens to me often. That's when you know you're hooked on history and genealogy.

Let me share with you an ancestor who doesn't belong to me but whom I find intriguing. The descendants, however, may find this man appalling, so I've changed the names and eliminated the location. Found among divorce records were Polly and Samuel Goodman. Polly left her husband in the 1870s and petitioned for divorce. She stated that her husband, the defendant,

> has been guilty of extreme and repeated cruelty towards her, that is to say that the said defendant, on difer. [*sic*] days and times since said marriage has beaten, struck, pinched, choked and kicked your complainant, and pulled her hair out in large quantities, and has so beaten, abused and maltreated her during periods of pregnancy as to produce miscarriage and severe and dangerous illness on the part of your complainant, and to greatly endanger her life; and has further imposed heavy tasks and burdens upon her to the imminent [danger] of her health and life; and that defendant has ever since said marriage used towards your complainant the most [unreadable] and abusive language and has frequently threatened her life, so that her life has been rendered miserable; and that on or about the first day of May 187—, defendant so beat, choked, bruised and whipped your complainant with an ox whip as to endanger her life, and did then and there threaten to chop your complainant's head in two, and said he was bound to get rid of her in same way; and your complainant, for fear that the defendant would execute said threats, was compelled to and did leave her home and defendant, and seek shelter and protection among strangers, and has not since returned to live with defendant nor could she any longer live with defendant without being in imminent danger of losing her life.
>
> The complainant further represents unto your honor that the said Samuel Goodman is a man of low, vulgar and vicious habits, and is addicted to the use of obscene and profane language towards the complainant and the said children, in the presence and hearing

of the said children, and is a person wholly unfit to be intrusted with the care and custody of children. . . .

A newspaper editorial was published the same year Polly filed for divorce:

> Our readers will recall a brutal outrage, an account of which was given in our columns by a correspondent of——, in March last, perpetrated by one Goodman, who secretly arranged a spring gun in his stable to be discharged by the touching of a wire, by which one Stevenson, who sought shelter in the stable from the storm, shot himself, severely shattering his leg, and nearly died before he was found by Mr. Weathersby and brought here for treatment. It was a murderous business on the part of Goodman, and justly brought down upon him the indignation of the public, who were surprised to find the law so ineffectual to punish an offense so vile.
>
> Stevenson suffered everything but death. He was just able to speak and barely alive when found by the humane Weathersby. His feet had been badly frozen by the exposure, and all his toes were amputated soon after. The shattered leg grew worse, and last week it was amputated by Drs. Lawrence and Pickney, of this city. In this maimed condition, it is hoped that he may survive his injuries. But crippled as he is for life, how much more to be envied than the inhuman Goodman, the unrelenting author of all his suffering.

In another edition of the newspaper:

> Samuel Goodman, who lives somewhere in the neighborhood of ——, and whose nature, we fear, is far from befitting his name, advertises in our columns that he will not be responsible for any of his wife's debts, she having left his bed and board. Mrs. Goodman alleges that she had too much reason for her departure, having made complaint before Justice Bergen, on Tuesday last, that her husband was in the habit of thrashing her instead of cherishing her. The case was dismissed, on account of an informality in the complaint, and Goodman was set at liberty.

Perhaps it would disturb you to find accounts like this for your great-grandparents. Granted, even today we are not understanding nor forgiving of domestic violence. But it did and still does happen. You never know what you will turn up when you start researching in historical documents.

Along with tragic events, you will also find humorous ones. The following document was found by Mary McCampbell Bell and Mary Leigh Boisseau among the Loose Marriage Bonds, Consents, and Licenses in the Circuit Clerk's Office, Pittsylvania County, Virginia. It was published in the *National Genealogical Society Quarterly* in March 1993:

> License granted 30 January 1823: Samuel Hall & Mary Hoskins Text of undated consent [italicized words are underlined in the original]:
>
> "I do certify unto all whom it may concern that I am most despereately [*sic*] in love with Mr. Samuel Hall of Pittsylvania County, Vᵃ, *that* I have arrived to years of maturity and am marriageable, and *therefore wish to be married*; and to be married to the said Samuel Hall aforesaid. I do now give my free consent to the clerk of Pittsylvania County, or of any other County on the face of the globe to issue a Legal License for the *inter*marriage of the aforesaid *tight* little, *sweet* little, beautiful Samuel Hall and *myself*." Signed Mary (X) Hoskins; witnesses: Richard (X) Hoskins; James (X) Hoskins.

As you embark upon your journey to the past, keep in mind that your ancestors were human, with flaws and failings. Most of our ancestors made the best choices they could for their situations—choices we might not make given similar circumstances, mainly because we have different options open to us today. But through researching the history of our ancestors' times, perhaps we can learn to understand and empathize with our forebears. With this knowledge, it becomes difficult to judge our ancestors for their actions. Given the time, place, and situation, we very well might have made the same decision. If, however, you are fearful of opening the closet door and having a skeleton jump out at you, then you may want to contact the local stamp or coin collectors' societies.

YOUR MEDICAL FAMILY HISTORY

Some genealogists become interested in their family history because they want to learn more about their own and their family's health. How many times have you gone to a doctor's office and been asked if you have any family history of diabetes, heart disease, or cancer? The vast majority of people cannot answer this question beyond their parents and siblings. The predominant causes of death for twelve of my ancestors were heart disease and stroke. Of course, we would also have to examine siblings, cousins, aunts, and uncles to see any significant patterns, but here is a sampling of a medical family history:

TABLE 1   CAUSES OF DEATH

Paternal Grandparents

Name	Age at Death	Cause of Death
Joseph DeBartolo	33	accidental—fractured skull
Stella (Ebetino) DeBartolo	76	congestive heart failure

Paternal Great-Grandparents

Name	Age at Death	Cause of Death
Albino DeBartolo	80	respiratory illness/colon cancer
Lucia (Vallarelli) DeBartolo	69	bronchopneumonia/influenza
Salvatore Ebetino	82	cerebral thrombosis and arteriosclerosis/diabetes
Angelina (Vallarelli) Ebetino	60	chronic myocarditis/chronic endocarditis

Maternal Grandparents

Name	Age at Death	Cause of Death
Pressley Medlin Fitzhugh	52	pulmonary infarction/coronary sclerosis
Rose (Norris) Fitzhugh	61	coronary occlusion

Maternal Great-Grandparents

Name	Age at Death	Cause of Death
Sidney Wallace Fitzhugh	56	carcinoma of the stomach
Kathryn (Rhodes) Fitzhugh	86	gastroenteritis
David Norris	42	heart disease
Delia (Gordon) Norris	58	endocarditis

Many genealogists, when they discover a medical condition in themselves, start looking at the past for how it might have been prevented. Many diseases, such as sickle cell anemia, are passed from one generation to the next, so genealogical research may uncover these inherited diseases. Anita A. Lustenberger wrote an excellent article that was published in the June 1994 issue of the *National Genealogical Society Quarterly*'s special issue *Your Family's Health History: An Introduction*. It's titled "How to Be a Family Health Historian." If this aspect of genealogy intrigues you, her article would be a good starting place.

WHAT IF YOU'RE ADOPTED?

People who are adopted are in a unique position when it comes to genealogical research. They may trace either their adoptive parents' ancestry or, if known, their biological parents' ancestry. If you were adopted and you do not know the names of your biological parents, a helpful guide is Mary Jo Rillera's *The Adoption Searchbook*. Adoption records in most states are closed to public access, so you may have to do some creative researching. There is a National Adoption Information Clearinghouse, 5640 Nicholson Lane, Suite 300, Rockville, MD 20852. This organization registers those seeking children given up for adoption and those seeking biological parents. When a match is made, they inform the registrants. Other adoption search and support organizations may be found in the classified section of *Reunions Magazine* along with a regular column focusing on adoption search cases called "Origins." (See the Appendix of Addresses.)

WHAT GENEALOGY IS AND WHAT IT ISN'T

GENEALOGY IS ADDICTING.

Once you begin searching for your ancestors, you'll be hooked. You'll think about it night and day. It will become your reason for living. You will begin to bore your friends, neighbors, relatives, and other genealogists with stories of your dead relatives. But don't worry; all genealogists have done this. At first, the challenge will be to see how far back you can trace a lineage. Then that will no longer be enough. You'll take a new path and want to learn what life was like in your ancestors' days: how they dressed, what kind of houses they lived in, what they ate.

GENEALOGY ISN'T ALWAYS CHEAP.

One of the first books I read on how to "do" genealogy was Gilbert H. Doane's *Searching for Your Ancestors*. I opened the cover and read, "All you need is a notebook, a few pencils, an inquisitive mind, a willingness to ask questions and dig for facts and . . . This Book!" Doane was right to a degree, but he left out one important requisite: money. In 1974 when Doane's book was published, the cost to obtain a copy of a birth or death certificate was about $1 to $3. Today, it may cost as much as $15. Then you might discover books you want to buy, research trips you want to take, computer and office equipment you want to purchase, classes, institutes, and conferences you want to attend. . . . Though I place genealogical spending at a higher priority than some, there are people who manage to trace their family tree on a tight budget. I remember one of my teachers of genealogy telling our class that she was appalled at the amount of money some people spend on genealogy. I felt guilty, until she added, "Although, there are people who would be appalled at what I spend on genealogy." Then I felt better. In short, you can make genealogy as expensive or inexpensive as you want.

GENEALOGY IS TIME-CONSUMING.

Tracing your ancestry to colonial America is not something you'll complete on one rainy Saturday afternoon. You'll wait weeks for a response from a vital records office for the death certificate you requested; you'll wait days for a roll of microfilm you ordered to arrive at the library; you'll wait months to visit a distant research repository to look for a will; you'll spend hours cranking the handle of a microfilm reader to find your great-grandfather on a census.

GENEALOGY IS A NEVER-ENDING HOBBY.

There will always be a new line to trace or a new problem to solve. Think about it: You have two parents; your parents had two parents, giving you four grandparents; they each had two parents, giving you eight great-grandparents; so that by the time you reach the tenth generation, your eighth great-grandparents, you will have 1,024 ancestors! Each generation doubles the number of parents. So there's always something to do; you will never live long enough to trace all of your ancestors. Usually, one family branch or one individual will grab your interest or prove more challenging, and you will find that you are spending most of your research time on this.

GENEALOGY ISN'T MERELY COLLECTING NAMES AND DATES.

Your initial goal may be to trace your lineage back to an immigrant ancestor or to see how far back in time you can take a line. But let's face it, even to another genealogist, names and dates on a chart are boring. Adding "flesh to the bones"—the family stories, and traditions, and putting your ancestors into historical perspective—is what makes genealogy interesting. I cringe every time I teach a genealogy class and a few novice students boast about the number of names they have entered into their computer. If that's the kind of legacy you want to leave, you'll have a lot of disappointed descendants. That's not genealogy—that's name gathering.

GENEALOGY IS DOCUMENTED RESEARCH.

The professionals and scholars in the field of genealogy have established standards. Though you may be tracing your ancestry only as a hobby with no intention of becoming a professional or a scholar, you will still want to follow the criteria already in place. Why reinvent the wheel? Part of genealogy is sharing your research—with family and with other genealogists—whether through correspondence, writing a family history, or having an article published in a genealogical journal. When you share your knowledge, it has to be in a format that all researchers understand. The format includes numbering systems and styles for citing sources of information. It does not help another researcher to know that the data on your Great-Uncle Harry came from "the census." Which census? What state? What county? What town? Because some genealogies in the past were fabricated so that a person could join a lineage society or make claim to an inheritance, documented research has become important.

GENEALOGY ISN'T ALWAYS EASY.

Genealogy requires research in historical documents such as censuses, probates, deeds, military records, immigration papers, ships' passenger lists, and photographs, to name a few. You won't be typing your family name into a computer database and having your lineage pop up on the screen. Each generation must be thoroughly researched and connected to the next generation. You certainly don't want to be tracing the wrong ancestors! I've talked to genealogists who have searched for twenty years just to discover the maiden name of one of their female ancestors. Granted, they are not spending every hour of every day for twenty years poring over documents. But they are taking the time and exerting the patience to look at every document that could have been created by or about that ancestor.

GENEALOGY IS FRUSTRATING, BUT ALSO FUN AND CHALLENGING.

While it seems like some lineages just fall into place in the course of research, others require more diligence. Historical documents weren't created with genealogists in mind. You may get only one tiny piece of information from a record that you've been waiting for weeks to arrive in your mailbox, or it may not tell you anything you didn't already know. Some records, like the 1920 federal census, contain extensive data on people; others, like the 1790 federal census, contain only scanty information. Some records have been inadvertently destroyed from neglect, in fires and floods, and through other natural disasters. The 1890 federal census, for example, was virtually destroyed in a fire, and only a small portion remains. Another obstacle is that you may not find your ancestor in certain records at all. You have to learn how to become creative and find other records that may include your ancestor. It's like putting together a jigsaw puzzle: when all the pieces fit and come together, you feel you have accomplished something. But when they don't fit, though you may be frustrated, you keep at it until it blends to make a pretty farm scene. Though it may not be easy to complete the puzzle, you can more easily see what probably goes into the spaces as you progress.

BUYER BEWARE

Genealogy isn't going to arrive already completed in your mailbox. You may have received postcards or letters advertising a book titled something like The [insert your surname] Family Across America. The advertisement claims that the publication lists everyone with your surname in the United States. It does: The compilers have extracted everyone with your last name from telephone directories. And now, with the speed of CD-ROM and directories available in that medium, it's even easier to find People with Your Surname Across America. (Notice, ladies, that you won't receive any postcards about your maiden name. That's because you aren't listed in the phone directory by your maiden name.)

Another selling point of these books is an offer to "educate you in the fundamentals of genealogical researching by describing (1) the history of American origins, (2) the development of family crests, (3) the origin of family names, and (4) the recording and documenting of family heritage." Two friends mailed their $29.95 plus $4 shipping; then, utterly disappointed, they donated their books to me to use as examples in my classes. The two books, supposedly written by two different women, remarkably contained chapters word-for-word identical and general in nature. The center insert pages contained the surname listings from the telephone directories.

Perhaps you've also received postcards or letters advertising your family coat of arms. An important fact to keep in mind is that coats of arms are not (and never have been) granted to families. They are granted to individuals and are inherited by individuals. According to an informational brochure, "Heraldry for United States Citizens," published by the Board for Certification of Genealogists (BCG),

- Anyone whose uninterrupted male-line immigrant ancestor was entitled to use a coat of arms has the right to use this same coat of arms.

- If the uninterrupted male-line immigrant ancestor has no such right, then neither does the descendant.

- Anyone who claims the right to arms under European laws must prove the uninterrupted male-line descent.

- As an exception, United States citizens can obtain a grant or confirmation of their arms—from the College of Arms in England or other appropriate national heraldic authority in other countries—by payment of required fees.

The BCG, as well as many members of the genealogical community, take a strong stand about the misinformation consumers have received on bogus family history offers. The BCG brochure further states, "Commercial firms that purport to research and identify coats of arms for surnames or family names—and sell descriptions thereof under the guise of a 'family crest'— are engaged in fraudulent and deceptive marketing. The consumer's best defense is a proper knowledge of the laws of heraldry." As in any field of endeavor, there are always going to be frauds.

ABOUT THIS BOOK

There are many excellent genealogy "how-to" books readily available and written by reputable genealogists. Basic instructional guidebooks will be discussed in Chapter 4. This book is not your ordinary how-to book. While it does offer some of the basics in the first two chapters, such as how to get started and, in Chapters 8 and 9, the different types of historical documents you'll consult, it differs from traditional beginners' guides in that it provides novice researchers with the knowledge for gaining access into the world of genealogy in order to successfully research one's heritage. The topics covered in this book contain information that most genealogists learn through conversations with seasoned genealogists as they become more and more involved in climbing their family tree.

Genealogy is an individual hobby. No two people, except biological siblings, have the same ancestry. Genealogy is also a personal hobby; everyone who engages in it has different reasons for doing so. But genealogy can also be a lonely hobby if you let it. While you won't find someone tracing exactly the same lineage as you, you will find "genealogy cousins" who may connect with your ancestry in the eighteenth or seventeenth centuries. But how do you find these cousins? Chapter 3 shows you how to network, the importance of joining genealogical and lineage societies, and how to find other genealogists with the same passion for tracing their ancestry via the Internet and other avenues.

Everyone is born with ancestors, but no one is born knowing who these people were and how to find out about them. Chapter 4 explores the importance of genealogical education. You need to know the methods and sources of genealogy that are available. Whether you are a self-learner who prefers to study genealogical how-to books or you prefer to learn in a classroom situation, this chapter will help you find educational opportunities to further your genealogical research.

When you first step into a large genealogical library, you might feel overwhelmed at all the books and magazines that line the shelves. There are many different types of published sources that will help you search for your ancestors: record abstracts; cemetery/tombstone transcriptions; guidebooks on record sources and repositories; family, county, and town histories; and many more. In Chapter 5 you'll learn about these published sources. Most genealogists love to buy books. Learn what basic guidebooks are on every genealogist's shelf and how to start your own genealogical library.

Genealogists find information on their ancestors in libraries, courthouses, archives, and cemeteries. But whether the research repository is an hour away or several days away, it is important to prepare for the trip to make your time there worthwhile. In Chapter 6 you will learn what to take with you on a research trip to help you use your time efficiently.

What can you expect when you get to a record repository? There are research institutions in almost every locality. Chapter 7 will highlight local, county, state, and national research centers and the types of records found there. This chapter also details research in the world's largest genealogical library, the Church of Jesus Christ of Latter-day Saints' famous Family History Library in Salt Lake City, Utah, and its worldwide branch centers.

Once you get to the repository, you will be conducting research in historical documents. Through two case studies, Chapters 8 and 9 give a brief description of many types of records, what record groups are likely to have indexes, the usual order in which you will examine each type of document, and the guidebooks that will give you in-depth methods for using historical documents.

Another part of genealogical research is knowing how to obtain documents and information by mail when you cannot make a trip to a record repository. Chapter 10 discusses researching from a distance, focusing on writing letters that get responses. There are also methods to obtain genealogical books and microfilmed records by mail from lending libraries. This chapter also discusses resources available on the Internet.

There comes a time during the course of a genealogical research project when nearly everyone (the professionals included) needs to hire a professional genealogist. Sometimes you just cannot make a trip to the locality where your ancestors lived, or you have hit a brick wall with a problem you cannot solve. Chapter 11 explains how to know when it's time to hire a pro, how to find and hire one, and what to expect in terms of fees and reports.

For those who get bitten by the genealogy bug and develop an interest beyond personal family history, Chapter 12 explains how to become a professional genealogist. It details what kind of education you need, how to become certified or accredited, and how to find clients.

Your family history will be incomplete if you spend hours finding records but you leave for your descendants nothing but file cabinets of jumbled notes and charts. Chapter 13 explains ways to bring all of your research together in order to leave your research as a legacy, whether it's writing and publishing a book, writing an article for a genealogical magazine, or compiling charts, documents, and photographs in a treasured family album.

The last chapter discusses the importance of leaving your own legacy: *your* life story. It is likely that someday you, too, will be an ancestor, and some crazed genealogist is going to want to know what your life was like. While the search for ancestors' documents is one of the fun parts of genealogy, you also need to follow the Golden Rule of Genealogy by leaving for your descendants what you wish your ancestors had left for you.

Finally, *genealogy is worthwhile* for you and for your descendants. On the back cover of the *National Genealogical Society Quarterly* there is a familiar quote:

> *Two things a parent must give a child:*
> *One is roots.*
> *The other is wings.*

If you don't know where you came from, it will be harder to figure out who you are and even harder for future generations. Millions of people inhabit this earth, each one with a unique ancestry. As individuals, we can get lost in the crowd; yet each of us is the by-product of more than 1,024 people! Who *were* they? Start the climb up your family tree, and I'll show you how to find out.

Chapter 1

Getting Started: Charts, Forms, and Organization

Recording names, dates, and places on charts—whether on paper or typed into a computer—can be the most uninteresting part of genealogy. But it has to be done. That's the only way to see what you know and what you don't know. Recording family information on charts and forms also lets you see where you need to start your research—the interesting part of genealogy.

You might be surprised at how much you already know about your family history. To get started on the climb up your family tree, the first step is to record details that you know from personal knowledge, like the date and place of your birth. Genealogists use charts and forms for this information; some start off using the charts and forms provided on computer software programs (which will be discussed later).

PEDIGREE/ANCESTOR CHART

One chart used by all genealogists is called a *pedigree* or *ancestor chart*. The purpose of this chart is to keep track of your ancestors (your lineage or the people from whom you descend): your parents, grandparents, great-grandparents, and so on. This is not the chart to use to record cousins, aunts,

FIGURE 1.1   PEDIGREE CHART

Compiler __S.D. Carmack__

Address __P.O. Box 338,__

__Simla, CO 80835__

Date __5 Feb 1996__

CHART NO. (1)

KEY:
ca.	about
cont.	continuation
b.	date of birth
p.b.	place of birth
m.	date of marriage
p.m.	place of marriage
d.	date of death
p.d.	place of death

Record dates as day, month, year:
4 July 1776
Record places as city (county) state:
Chicago (Cook) Illinois

8   **Albino DeBARTOLO**   cont. chart (8)
- b. 15 Sep 1866
- p.b. Terlizzi, Bari, Italy
- m. 19 Mar 1892
- p.m. Terlizzi, Bari, Italy
- d. 2 Oct 1946
- p.d. San Francisco, CA

4   **Giuseppe DeBARTOLO**
- b. 1 Aug 1901
- p.b. Terlizzi, Bari, Italy
- m. 5 Sep 1926
- p.m. Rye, Westchester Co., NY
- d. 31 Jul 1934
- p.d. White Plains, Westchester Co., NY

9   **Lucia VALLARELLI**   cont. chart (9)
- b. 15 May 1871
- p.b. Terlizzi, Bari, Italy
- d. 22 Jun 1940
- p.d. San Francisco, CA

2   **Salvatore DeBARTOLO**
- b. 7 Mar 1931
- p.b. Brooklyn, Kings Co., NY
- m. 16 Aug 1953
- p.m. Harrison, Westchester Co., NY
- d.
- p.d.

10   **Salvatore EBETINO**   cont. chart (10)
- b. 27 Mar 1875
- p.b. Naples, Italy
- m. 27 Dec 1899
- p.m. Terlizzi, Bari, Italy
- d. 3 Oct 1957
- p.d. Rye, Westchester Co., NY

5   **Stella EBETINO**
- b. 27 May 1905
- p.b. Terlizzi, Bari, Italy
- d. 5 Aug 1981
- p.d. La Habra, CA

11   **Angelina VALLARELLI**   cont. chart (11)
- b. 22 Oct 1877
- p.b. Terlizzi, Bari, Italy
- d. 19 Jul 1937
- p.d. Rye, Westchester Co., NY

1   **Sharon Ann DeBARTOLO**
- b. 17 Oct 1956
- p.b. Port Chester, Westchester Co., NY
- m. 19 Aug 1977
- p.m. Las Vegas, Clark Co., NV
- d.
- p.d.

12   **Sidney Wallace FITZHUGH**   cont. chart (12)
- b. 2 Apr 1870
- p.b. Green Co., VA
- m. 23 Nov 1893
- p.m. Yalaha, Lake Co., FL
- d. 29 Oct 1926
- p.d. Green Springs, Louisa Co., VA

6   **Pressley Medlin FITZHUGH**
- b. 10 Jan 1903
- p.b. Rockville, Hanover, VA
- m. 19 Mar 1926
- p.m. Greenwich, Fairfield, CT
- d. 7 Sept 1955
- p.d. Port Chester, Westchester Co., NY

13   **Kathryn Jane RHODES**   cont. chart (13)
- b. 29 Aug 1875
- p.b. Edgefield Co., SC
- d. 26 Jun 1960
- p.d. Gordonsville, Orange Co., VA

3   **Mary Louise FITZHUGH**
- b. 21 Jan 1933
- p.b. Harrison, Westchester Co., NY
- d.
- p.d.

14   **David NORRIS**   cont. chart (14)
- b. 6 Jun 1860
- p.b. Tyrone, Ireland
- m. ca. 1886
- p.m. prob. Greenwich, CT
- d. 22 Aug 1902
- p.d. Greenwich, Fairfield Co., CT

7   **Rose Mary NORRIS**
- b. 30 Oct 1896
- p.b. Greenwich, Fairfield Co., CT
- d. 2 Apr 1957
- p.d. Port Chester, Westchester Co., NY

15   **Delia GORDON**   cont. chart (15)
- b. 29 Apr 1867
- p.b. Co. Cork, Ireland
- d. 19 Apr 1925
- p.d. Greenwich, Fairfield Co., CT

Stephen Harold CARMACK
- b. 13 Dec 1952
- p.b. Watsonville, Santa Cruz Co., CA
- d.
- p.d.

Source: National Genealogical Society

uncles, or siblings; that will come next. You may have seen charts similar to the one in Figure 1.1. This one is printed by the National Genealogical Society. In the Appendix of Addresses, I've listed other companies that sell pedigree charts. Each company has a slightly different format, but the charts all contain the same basic information: a person's name, date and place of birth, date and place of marriage, and date and place of death. Some charts allow you to record four generations, some five, some six. There are also wall charts that can accommodate up to fifteen generations and decorative charts suitable for gifts. Personally, I like to take a four- or five-generation pedigree chart with me on research trips.

Number the pedigree chart as shown in the example, where my name appears as number 1. Continue to number the chart accordingly. This pedigree chart allows you to insert numbers, using the standard *Ahnentafel* numbering system; other charts are prenumbered and force you to start all charts with number 1.

The German word *Ahnentafel* means ancestor table. In the *Ahnentafel* numbering system, you are number 1, your father is number 2, your mother is number 3. Men are assigned even numbers, women odd. Men appear on the top line, women on the bottom. For every person on the chart, if you double that person's number, you will have the number of the father; double the number and add one and you get the mother's number. For example, in the chart shown:

> Pressley Medlin Fitzhugh is number 6.
> Double his number, making 12, and you get his father, Sidney Wallace Fitzhugh.
> Double Pressley's number and add one, making 13, and you get his mother, Katherine Jane Rhodes.

If you are working with a prenumbered chart, the next chart will begin with number 1 again. But because we're working with a chart without numbers, we can continue to use the *Ahnentafel* system. Let's look at Albino DeBartolo, number 8. He will be continued on chart number 8, but in the number 1 position we'll place a number 8, as in the example in Figure 1.2. There will be no charts numbered 2 through 7. Albino is number 8 on chart 1, and number 8 on chart 8. He will always be number 8. Doubling his number, then, his parents will be numbers 16 and 17. The chart continues to be numbered in the same fashion.

The same will hold true if you want to start a chart for Sidney Wallace Fitzhugh, number 12. He will be continued on chart 12, placing him in the number 1 slot; he will be given the number 12. His parents will be 24 and 25. It may be confusing at first, but once you get the hang of it, it is quite simple.

RECORDING INFORMATION

Before you begin to fill out any of the charts, you need to know some standards in the way information is recorded.

NAMES

- Write all names as spoken: first, middle, and last name: Sharon Ann DeBartolo.

- Write last names in capital letters: Sharon Ann DEBARTOLO. This helps to distinguish a surname, especially if you run across a man named John GEORGE or a woman named Rose LESLIE. We want to know that this is the last name.

- Record women by their **maiden** names.

- Record the name given at the time of birth. Place nicknames in quotes: Joseph "Joe" DEBARTOLO.

- Record spelling variations, name changes, or translations with a slash: Francesco/Frank, Ebetino/Abatino, Smith/Smythe, DeBartolo/Bart.

DATES

- Record dates as the day, the three-letter abbreviation for the month, and the full year: 5 Feb 1996. This avoids any confusion that numbered dates can entail. For instance, is 2-5-96 February 5, 1996, or May 2, 1896? Leave nothing to chance when it comes to dates.

PLACES

- Record the place by the smallest geographical locality first. Town/city, county, state: Simla, Elbert Co., Colorado. Or in the case of non-United States localities: town/village/hamlet/city, province, country: Terlizzi, Bari, Italy.

- Use two-letter standard postal abbreviations for the state: Virginia = VA.

FIGURE 1.2   PEDIGREE CHART

Compiler _S.D. Carmack_

Address _P.O. Box 338,_

Simla, CO 80835

Date _5 Feb 1996_

CHART NO. (8)

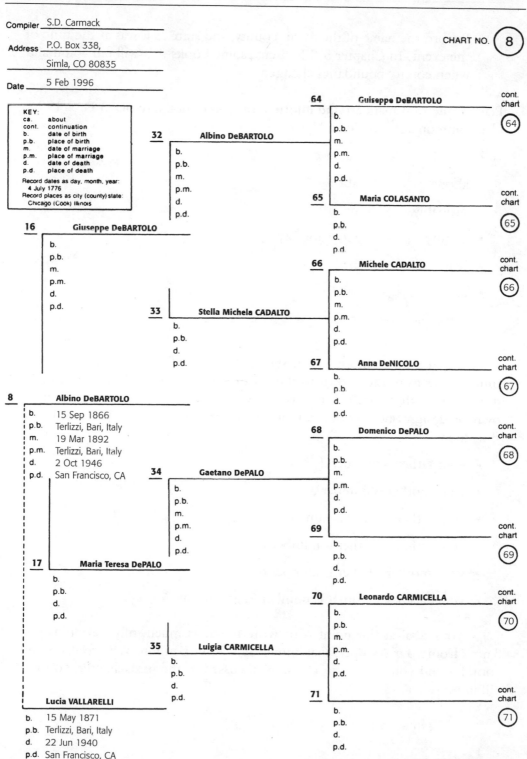

KEY:
ca.   about
cont. continuation
b.   date of birth
p.b.   place of birth
m.   date of marriage
p.m.   place of marriage
d.   date of death
p.d.   place of death
Record dates as day, month, year:
   4 July 1776
Record places as city (county) state:
   Chicago (Cook) Illinois

32   Albino DeBARTOLO
b.
p.b.
m.
p.m.
d.
p.d.

16   Giuseppe DeBARTOLO
b.
p.b.
m.
p.m.
d.
p.d.

33   Stella Michela CADALTO
b.
p.b.
d.
p.d.

8   Albino DeBARTOLO
b.   15 Sep 1866
p.b.   Terlizzi, Bari, Italy
m.   19 Mar 1892
p.m.   Terlizzi, Bari, Italy
d.   2 Oct 1946
p.d.   San Francisco, CA

34   Gaetano DePALO
b.
p.b.
m.
p.m.
d.
p.d.

17   Maria Teresa DePALO
b.
p.b.
d.
p.d.

35   Luigia CARMICELLA
b.
p.b.
d.
p.d.

Lucia VALLARELLI
b.   15 May 1871
p.b.   Terlizzi, Bari, Italy
d.   22 Jun 1940
p.d.   San Francisco, CA

64   Guiseppe DeBARTOLO
b.
p.b.
m.
p.m.
d.
p.d.
cont. chart (64)

65   Maria COLASANTO
b.
p.b.
d.
p.d.
cont. chart (65)

66   Michele CADALTO
b.
p.b.
m.
p.m.
d.
p.d.
cont. chart (66)

67   Anna DeNICOLO
b.
p.b.
d.
p.d.
cont. chart (67)

68   Domenico DePALO
b.
p.b.
m.
p.m.
d.
p.d.
cont. chart (68)

69
b.
p.b.
d.
p.d.
cont. chart (69)

70   Leonardo CARMICELLA
b.
p.b.
m.
p.m.
d.
p.d.
cont. chart (70)

71
b.
p.b.
d.
p.d.
cont. chart (71)

Source: National Genealogical Society

- Record the name of the town, county, and state as it was at the time of the event. In Chapter 5, I'll discuss some books that will tell you if and when county boundaries changed.

Place a question mark around information you're not sure of: ?5 Feb? 1996. Use common abbreviations:

- circa   —   ca. or c.
- about   —   abt.
- probably   —   prob.
- county   —   Co. (not Cty.)
- before   —   bef.
- after   —   aft.
- township   —   twp.

In genealogy, the rule is to start with yourself and work backward in time, going from the known to the unknown, so you will begin your pedigree chart with yourself. When you have a chart (you can even draw your own or design one on your computer), place your name in the number 1 slot, then:

- your father is number 2
- your mother is number 3
- your father's father is number 4
- your father's mother is number 5
- your mother's father is number 6
- your mother's mother is number 7, and so on.

Your goal at this point is to write down as much information as you know from your own personal knowledge. After you interview relatives and look around your house for clues, as discussed in the next chapter, you will fill in more blanks.

FAMILY GROUP SHEET

The next commonly used chart is the *family group sheet*. This is where you will record all the children of a couple. Take a look at the example in Figure 1.3. If you were filling out a family group sheet on one of your maternal grandparents as I've done, you would record all the information you know about your grandfather and grandmother in the husband and wife sections. Then you would list all their children in birth order, your mother included. If you are aware of any children who did not survive, you would also list them. Place an X or check mark by your mother's name to indicate your lineage.

Ideally, you would want to begin by having a family group sheet for every couple listed on your pedigree chart. From there, you might want family group sheets for aunts, uncles, or cousins. If someone has been married more than once, begin a new family group sheet for each marriage. If John Atkins married Sarah Johnson first, then she died (or they divorced), and he married Mary Paulson second, you would have two family group sheets, one for each marriage. Record the children that belong to each couple. For example, if John and Sarah had three children, they all go on the sheet with John and Sarah; these children don't belong on the family sheet of John and Mary. Only John and Mary's children, if they had any, go on that sheet. If Mary had children from a marriage prior to John, her children by that marriage would go on the sheet listing her and her other husband. In other words, no stepchildren are listed; only biological or adopted children of a couple.

Family group sheets may be purchased from companies that sell pedigree charts. The one shown here is from Genealogical Books in Print (see Appendix of Addresses). Here, too, the format of family group sheets varies from publisher to publisher. Some allow you to record up to fifteen children, others only eight or ten. You may try out several, as I did, before you settle on one that you like best.

COMPUTER SOFTWARE PROGRAMS

A genealogical computer software program is another option for recording information. The software program generally assigns a numbering system and will connect people and group them into families for you. You need only enter the information once; the program will link individuals to families and arrange the data into whichever chart or form you choose.

There are several genealogy software programs on the market: *The Master Genealogist, Brother's Keeper, Roots V, Family Tree Maker, Family*

FIGURE 1.3   FAMILY GROUP SHEET

Husband's Code . . . .
Wife's Code . . . .

HUSBAND'S NAME _Pressley Medlin FITZHUGH_

Date of Birth _10 Jan 1903_ (3) Place _Rockville, Hanover Co., VA_ (3)

Date of Death _7 Sep 1955_ (2) Place _Port Chester, Westchester Co., NY_ (2)

Present Address (or) Place of Burial _Greenwood Union Cemetery, Rye, Westchester Co., NY_

His Father _Sidney Wallace Fitzhugh_ (3) His Mother's Maiden Name _Kathryn Jane RHODES_ (3)

Date of Marriage of HUSBAND and WIFE on this sheet _18 Mar 1926_ (3) Place _Greenwich, Fairfield Co., CT_ (3)

Check here if there was another marriage: By husband ☐ By Wife ☒   Was this couple divorced? Yes ☐   No ☒   When? ___

WIFE'S MAIDEN NAME _Rose Mary Norris_ (Use separate sheet for each marriage)

Date of Birth _30 Oct 1896_ (4) Place _Greenwich, Fairfield Co., CT_ (4)

Date of Death _2 Apr 1957_ (5) Place _Port Chester, Westchester Co., NY_ (5)

Present Address (or) Place of Burial _Greenwood Union Cemetery, Rye, Westchester Co., NY_

Her Father _David NORRIS_ (4) Her Mother's Maiden Name _Delia GORDON_ (4)

Items of interest about the above couple (occupations, hobbies, achievements; social, civil, and political activities; physical descriptions—include photos if possible; military service; cause of death):

Use reverse side for additional information

Have family sheet		CHILDREN (Arrange in order of birth)	Code	Birth Information		Death Information		Marriage Information	
	1	James Pressley	(5)	ON 24 Oct 1928 (7) / AT NYC, NY (7)		ON 4 Sep 1977 (7) / AT Oceanside, CA (7)		ON 18 Aug 1952 (7) / TO Barbara SLATER (7)	
	2	Kathryn Jane	(5)	ON 20 Feb 1930 (7) / AT Harrison, NY (7)		ON / AT		UN 2 Sep 1951 (7) / TO Anthony ADAMCZYK (7)	
	3	Mary Louise	(5)	ON 21 Jan 1933 (8) / AT Harrison, NY (8)		ON / AT		ON 16 Aug 1953 (8) / TO Salvatore DeBARTOLO (8)	
	4			ON / AT		ON / AT		ON / TO	
	5			ON / AT		ON / AT		ON / TO	

Check here if there are additional children ☐

Footnoting. To substantiate the information recorded on this page, please use the footnotes listed below. One of these numbers should be placed in the circle provided next to each answer on the questionnaire. If you got the information from a source not listed, place that source on a vacant line and use the number next to which it has been placed as your footnote number.

Use ① only if you have filled in the blank from personal knowledge (such as the name of your brother). If you must look up his marriage date, give as the source wherever you looked it up. If you asked him, give his name as the source.

① Name and address of person filling in this sheet.   Date _5 Feb 1996_

Sharon DeBartolo Carmack, P.O. Box 338, Simla, CO 80835

② Death cert., Bureau of Vital Statistics, ESP Tower Bldg., Albany, NY

③ Family Bible in possession of Lillian & Louise Fitzhugh, Gordonsville, VA

④ Birth Cert., Public Health Statistics, 79 Elm St., Hartford, CT

⑤ Obituary, _Port Chester Daily Item,_ Port Chester, NY; 3 Apr 1957, p. 18

⑥ Obituary, ibid, 8 Sept 1955, p. 19

⑦ Personal knowledge, Kathryn Adamczyk

⑧ Personal knowledge, Mary DeBartolo

Source: © 1969 Netti Schreiner-Yantis, 6818 Lois Drive, Springfield, Virginia 22150

Gathering, Reunion, Personal Ancestral File, to name a few. I've listed the most popular ones in the Appendix and where you can purchase them by mail. Prices, of course, are subject to change, and you may be able to purchase these software packages at computer discount stores for less.

Like the charts and forms discussed earlier, preference for software is an individual thing. What suits one person may not suit another. Of course, it is a lot more expensive to try out different software than it is to try out different preprinted forms, but there are two ways to find out about the software before you purchase it.

1. Join a local genealogy computer interest group or find one on the Internet. Chapter 3 will discuss how to find organizations like these. The groups usually have sample software packages for you to try, or the members can tell you what they like or dislike about a program, showing you sample printouts of charts and forms.

2. Read reviews of software in national genealogical publications and national genealogical computer-interest newsletters. Chapters 3 and 5 go into more depth on the availability of journals and magazines and how to find product and book reviews.

The biggest complaint I have heard about genealogical software is its limitations. For instance, some programs allow you to type in only a certain number of characters for a name. If you have an ancestor with a particularly long name, you'll have problems. Another limitation is the field for documentation. Once again, some software programs allow you to type in only a limited amount of information for your sources. Some programs don't allow for unspecified dating, such as "born about 1906–08" or "died between 24 Nov 1852 and 7 Jan 1853."

Students are always asking me which genealogy software I use. The answer is I don't. I have four programs that were given to me, but I don't use any of them; in fact, I have never broken the cellophane wrapper on one program. At this stage in my genealogical life it would take me months to enter into the computer all the research I've done. It took long enough to record the names and dates the first time around! I prefer to spend my time doing more research. Had the programs been available when I started many years ago, I might have decided differently. The other reason I don't use genealogy software is the limitations I've mentioned. Between the old-fashioned paper method and my word-processing software, I can do just about whatever I want.

Many people get involved in genealogy because they have acquired a personal computer and decided to purchase a genealogy software program or they received a program as a gift. How you get into genealogy makes no difference. But remember, just entering names into the computer does not classify you as a genealogist. Conducting the research to properly connect one generation to the next and placing your family into historical perspective is what makes you a genealogist.

DOCUMENTATION

The importance of documentation in genealogical research cannot be stressed enough. *It is not optional.* Documentation is also known as citing your sources of information with footnotes or endnotes. Remember those annoying blurbs of information we used to dread when writing research papers for English and history classes? It's easier now, though, thanks to word-processor and genealogy computer programs that let us insert a footnote or endnote with the stroke of a key.

Simply put, for each and every piece of information you record on your family group sheets, you also need to record where the data came from. Notice I said the family group sheets, not the pedigree chart. Because at least sixteen people with many different surnames appear on the pedigree chart, it's easier to cite your sources on the family group sheet.

There are many reasons for documentation.

CONFLICTING INFORMATION FROM DIFFERENT SOURCES

Suppose you have consulted three different sources, and each one gives a different birth date for your ancestor. Which one is the most likely to be correct? If you haven't written down the source for each date, you can't begin to evaluate which one is most accurate.

FINDING PEOPLE WITH THE SAME NAMES

Suppose you have discovered two people by the same name, who are approximately the same age, living in the same town and county. How will you keep each person straight and figure out which one is your ancestor? Or how will you even realize that there *may be* two people by the same name, approximately the same age, who live in the same town? By keeping track of your research, documenting, and evaluating each source of information as you gather it.

SUPPORTING EVIDENCE

Suppose you find someone who has already done quite a bit of research on your family, and you share information. You've been searching for years for the maiden name of your great-great-grandma, and your genealogy cousin provides it. "Where did you get this name from?" you ask. "I can't remember," your cousin replies. How reliable is it? How do you know this is truly Great-Great-Grandma's maiden name without something to support it? If you accept this new piece of information on faith alone, how do you know that you won't be tracing the wrong ancestors and family line?

HIRING A PROFESSIONAL

Suppose you are at a brick wall on one of your lines, and you decide to hire a professional genealogist to help solve your research problem. The pro wants to know what you've searched and what you haven't so that your research efforts aren't duplicated and your bill run up. The only problem is that you neglected to write down where you found each piece of information. The professional has no choice but to start from scratch.

GIVING YOUR GENEALOGY AUTHORITY

"But I'm just doing this for my family. They want me to do a little book for the family reunion next June, and my relatives aren't going to look at the endnotes or even care." Well, trust me, somewhere along the way, some generous family member will donate a copy of your "little book" to one of the genealogical libraries. Then it will get microfilmed so that others can get it through interlibrary loan. Remember the old adage about once something's in print, it practically becomes gospel? It's true. Correcting lineage errors can be a formidable task. As Elizabeth Shown Mills stated in an article on the subject of documentation, "If your family history is to be a useful tool for others and is to possess any 'note of authority,' then footnotes and bibliography are very necessary."

SHARING SOURCES WITH OTHERS

Suppose you find a rare, published family history on your ancestors, and the author gives information from a will that you would absolutely love to have a copy of to show at the next family reunion. The only problem is the author doesn't tell you where the will came from. What courthouse? Archive? Basement? Or worse, the author gives scanty information, like this: Will of

Joshua Jenkins, Orange County Courthouse. In what state? Which will book? What page? Do you want other researchers to feel the same frustration when they stumble upon your genealogy one hundred years from now?

Are you convinced yet? One of the best reasons I've found for documenting my sources is that my research knowledge constantly changes, so I find myself restudying sources that I've looked at once, twice, a dozen times. And I'm forgetful. When I was a baby genealogist, I thought I'd remember where each piece of information came from. I hate to admit this, but I don't. So . . .

IN CASE YOU FORGET WHERE YOU FOUND INFORMATION

Suppose you found a source ten years ago that gave you lots of information, which you dutifully recorded on your charts. Now you realize you may have overlooked something. Or you have another family to work on that may be mentioned in that source. Or, because your knowledge has changed and grown, you want to recheck that source for clues you may have missed ten years ago. But when you go back to the library you realize—horror of horrors—that they've rearranged books and moved that fat, green volume with the gold lettering that was sitting on the third shelf from the top. Now what?

There are still other reasons for citing sources:

1. Editors demand it if you want to get an article published.

2. The Board for Certification demands it if you want to become certified.

3. When you publish your family history, you will want it to be respected and useful to others.

HOW TO CITE YOUR SOURCES

Sources should be cited on your family group sheets. There may be a place for them on the front, such as in Figure 1.3, or you can make your own citation table on the back. For each piece of information you record, assign a foot/endnote number to it and list the note either on the front or on the back. A citation table format can look like this:

TABLE 1.1   REFERENCE

Number	Source Pertains to Whom	Citation
1.	Sal Bart/DeBartolo	Personal knowledge, Sal Bart/DeBartolo.
2.	DeBartolo and Ebetino family	Oral history interview with Stella Ebetino DeBartolo, 1981, La Habra, CA.
3.	Salvatore Ebetino	1910 federal census, population schedule, Westchester Co., NY, Rye Town, Rye Village, district 123, sheet 6A, dwelling 102, family 128, Maple Ave., National Archives Microcopy T624, roll 1092.

When writing a narrative family history for publication, the citation should look more like a true foot/endnote:

1. Passenger arrival record listing Salvatore Ebetino, ship *Italia*, sailing from Naples, Italy, on 25 April 1906, arriving at New York on 10 May 1906, group 7, list 23, National Archives Microcopy T715, roll 706, vol. 1564.

Essentially, a citation needs to contain all the information necessary for you or anyone else to be able to find that source again. For example: [type of record] deed of sale; [people involved] from Catherine Thompson to Salvatore Ebetino and wife, Angelina; [date of event] 29 May 1926; [date recorded] 1 June 1926; [where recorded] Liber 2674, pp. 211–13, Westchester County Clerk's Office, White Plains, NY.

The citation needs to be very specific. Some unacceptable forms of citing your sources would be:

- "History of the Smith Family" (Is this a book or an article? Who wrote it? When was it written? When and where was it published?)

- Information collected by my best friend during her trip to Salt Lake (What information? What kind of record?)

- A Bible in South Carolina (Where is the Bible in South Carolina? To which family does it pertain?)

- The National Archives (There are millions of records in the National Archives!)

- The 1880 census (What state? County? Page number?)

- My cousin's book (Did your cousin write it? What's the title? Where and when was it published?)

- Ohio Deed Book, p. 13 (What county? What time period?)

- The yellow book on Virginia in the public library (What book? What was the title, author, publication information? What library?)

- "I think someone told me."

In the Bibliography I've listed documentation guidebooks that will show you how to cite a source for almost every possible type of circumstance. Remember, citing sources is a vital part of your research.

RESEARCH AND CORRESPONDENCE LOGS

Another form you will want to use is a research and/or correspondence log, such as the ones in Table 1.2. These, too, may be purchased from one of the suppliers listed in the Appendix, or you can create your own using a computer. The basic information you will need is shown on the next page.

The point is to keep track of all your research and correspondence. Some genealogists have a research and correspondence log for each family group sheet; others have logs for each surname on their pedigree chart. Personally, I like to have one for each family group sheet. This is the first step in organizing and keeping track of your research.

SETTING UP A WORK SPACE

When I became a "serious" genealogist several years ago, I read everything I could about research methods and sources. I visited the library at least once a week to work on my family history. I wrote so many letters that the postal carrier had to get a bigger truck. At that time, we lived in a small, three-bed

TABLE 1.2

RESEARCH LOG
Salvatore and Angelina Ebetino

Date of Search	Repository	Type of Record	Source Citation or Remarks
3 Sep 1996	National Archives Washington, DC	1910 census	Westchester Co., NY, Rye Town, Rye Village, district 123, sheet 6A, dwelling 102, family 128, Maple Ave., National Archives Microcopy T624, roll 1092.
3 Sep 1996	National Archives Washington, DC	1900 census	could not locate in Soundex for state of New York

CORRESPONDENCE LOG
David and Delia (Gordon) Norris

Date	Type of Record Requested	Address	Response
3 Sep 1996	birth certificate on daughter, Rose Mary Norris	Public Health Statistics 79 Elm St. Hartford, CT	rec'd copy
26 Oct 1996	obituary on Delia Norris	Greenwich Public Library Greenwich, CT	none found

room house with no attic or basement. All the bedrooms were in use: one for my husband and me, one for my daughter, and one that served as a combination guest room, exercise room, and storage room. My genealogy "office" began on the dining room table. Every morning after my husband went to work, I plugged in my portable Smith-Corona electric typewriter and spread my papers and books out on the table. Every evening when he came home, I put away my typewriter in the closet, found a spot on my nightstand for my books, and put my files and charts in an ugly green metal file box.

Today we live in a five-bedroom house. Our family hasn't grown—my genealogy has. I still have that green metal file box, plus two four-drawer file cabinets, a half-dozen or so plastic filing crates, a computer desk and computer, a used secretarial desk with a used IBM Selectric typewriter, a six-foot sturdy folding table, a microfilm reader, a microfiche reader, a fax machine, a photocopy machine, and six huge bookcases. My genealogy takes up two rooms. This wasn't a cheap hobby.

If you're going to get involved in genealogy and you don't have a computer, you may want to consider purchasing one. As I mentioned earlier, I don't use a genealogy software program because of the time involved to input twelve years of research, but I do use my computer for writing letters, articles, and books, and I use its modem to connect with libraries across the country. When you decide to write your family history, a computer is a must, along with a laser printer so that you can print out camera-ready pages.

As a genealogist, whether hobbyist or professional, you will need to have a work space that can remain undisturbed. You will also need, at a minimum, file crates or a cabinet for your surname files, binders for your charts and forms, and shelves for your books.

ORGANIZING YOUR GENEALOGY

Genealogists, of all people, need to be organized so that they will know what research they've done and what they haven't. When one client hired me to research her family lines, it took me twenty-five hours to organize the material she had gathered over a number of years—just so I could *begin* research and not duplicate what she had already done.

One of the problems I had with arranging my client's research was that her husband had entered all her data into a genealogy software program. Every time she came across a new date, place, or other piece of information, he would enter it into the program and print out a new set of charts. The old charts never got thrown away, nor were the dates of the updates noted. I spent many of those twenty-five hours combining all the information onto one set of charts.

I knew I was crowned the "Queen of Organization" when I was invited to give a lecture on organizing genealogical materials for the National Association of Professional Organizers (NAPO). This condition (being well-organized) used to embarrass me since there seems to be so many people who are organizationally challenged. But because I have now spoken to professional organizers, I am more confident and can accept my condition.

As a beginner, you probably don't have much to organize yet, so this is the perfect time to start. Most people think that being organized means putting all of your genealogy stuff in several shoe boxes under the bed. While this organizational method may work well for you, I have some other suggestions.

While computer organization is a good method for some people, you will still have to deal with paper: printouts, photocopies of documents, letters you've received. So you need some sort of system that will manage all this paper, be easy to use and maintain, and allow you to retrieve a needed document within minutes. Enter the "Queen of Organization."

Of course, if you are already satisfied with your organizational system—shoe boxes under the bed—don't change just because the "Queen" said so. As a beginner you need to devise a system that will work for you, one that allows you to keep track of your research, notes, and documents at every stage. If you're spending more than a few moments rummaging through stacks of paper to find something, then your system isn't working. In that case, you've come to the right place.

You will need some supplies:

- A box of letter-size file folders. I don't recommend you use legal-size file folders since a legal-size file cabinet and folders cost more.

- A plastic crate to house your file folders, or a two- or four-drawer filing cabinet.

- Color-coded labels for the folder tabs. I use one color for my maternal lines, another for the paternal, another for my husband's maternal lines, and another for his paternal lines.

FILING SYSTEMS

There are as many ways to organize and file your genealogical documents as there are genealogists. I have found the following five methods of filing to be most common. Choose the one that suits you best.

1. *By surname.* Make a file folder for every surname that appears on your ancestor/pedigree charts. Every document pertaining to that surname gets filed in that file. The drawback here is that your files will get fairly thick, and you'll be sifting through a lot of paper to find what you need.

2. *By surname and locality.* Everything that pertains to the Johnson family while they were in Licking County, Ohio, goes in that file. Everything that pertains to this family while they lived in Dade County, Missouri, goes in that one. This is a better system than the previous one, but it still didn't suit me. I was sifting through files because I couldn't always remember in which locality an event had taken place.

3. *By individual.* Make a folder on every person listed on your charts. The obvious problem here is that you'll need a zillion file folders and cabinets. Remember that you double the number of ancestors every generation, so that by the tenth generation you have about 1,024 people to keep track of, not to mention cousins, aunts, uncles.

4. *By couple.* Make a folder on every couple listed on your charts. While better than the previous system, this is still a space-consuming method.

5. *By surname and type of record.* This is the method I use and recommend to my students and clients. My files are labeled "DeBartolo— Census Records," "DeBartolo—Immigration Records," "DeBartolo —Obituary and Cemetery Records," and so on. This way, if I'm looking for an obituary on Joseph DeBartolo, I can go straight to the file for that surname and record type and easily put my hands on that document. This system also grows with your research: you make a file folder only when you have documents of a certain record type to put in it.

As you begin your filing system, documents that refer to more than one surname—for example, wills, deeds, and marriage records—may be handled in one of two ways: either make a photocopy and put one in one file and the other in the other surname's file, or make a cross-reference note to the other file.

File women's records according to the surname that appears on the document. Everything that pertains to a female ancestor with her maiden name goes in the maiden-name file. Records carrying her married name go into her husband's surname file.

YOUR RESEARCH NOTEBOOK

Along with your files of notes and documents, you also need an organized research notebook to take with you on research trips. Because you don't want to risk losing any documents you've accumulated, your files will stay at home. I suggest purchasing a three-ring binder, no more than two inches thick. Granted, a three-inch binder holds more, but it is also heavier to lug around and more awkward to use.

In your notebook you should carry the following items at the minimum:

- Your pedigree/ancestor charts (you may want to keep backup copies of charts and family group sheets at home should these get lost).

- A family group sheet for every couple listed on your charts, including a list of sources from which the information contained on each sheet was obtained.

- A research and correspondence log for each family group sheet.

- A research plan for each family group sheet. One rainy Saturday, spend some time reviewing your family group sheets and making notes on what sources you still need to check for that family. This will save you lots of time later when you are ready to make your research trip. (See Chapter 6.)

- Abstracts of any lengthy records, likes deeds and wills, that you may want to refer to while you're at the research repository. (See Chapter 6.)

As your working notebook with papers expands (or explodes), you can divide it into two or more working notebooks.

Being organized is not a basic instinct everyone is born with. For most people, it's a trait that must be learned and practiced. It is especially important for genealogists to get organized early in the game in order to make research time more efficient.

But don't get the wrong impression. Although I am the "Queen of Organization," I confess that I have one or two piles of papers in my office (well, five, to be exact)—but they are *organized* piles.

Chapter 2

Searching at Home and Talking with Relatives

HOME SOURCES

After you have recorded what you know from personal knowledge, it's time to start looking for things around your home that may fill in some blanks. In your house, look for items and documents that may help you in tracing your ancestry, then move on to your relatives' homes. Of course, ask for permission before you start rummaging around in someone's house.

Remember, the rule of genealogical research is to start with the known (information on yourself) and work toward the unknown (your parents, grandparents, etc.). Although you know your own birth date, can you prove it? You were there, but do you have personal memory of it? Look for your birth certificate, then study it. Many people have been surprised to find that they were recorded as "baby" Smith or as a girl when they are in reality male. Do the date and place match what you've recorded on your charts? Does the document list your mother's maiden name? Your father's occupation? The number of babies your mother had and the number living at the time of your birth? Cite your birth record as your source of information for your birth date and place and the names of your parents. If there are discrepancies, note them in your source citation. This document connects one generation to the next; it connects you to your parents.

Look for other records that will give you genealogical information as well as telling you about someone's life:

- birth certificates, baby books
- baptism and confirmation certificates
- marriage certificates, wedding albums
- death records, prayer or funeral cards
- school report cards, yearbooks, scrapbooks
- deeds to houses, photographs of houses
- checkbooks, bank statements
- citizenship papers, passports
- military discharges, medals of honor
- family Bible
- letters, postcards, telegrams
- diaries, journals
- wills
- medical records
- newspaper clippings
- recipe books
- photographs (discussed in more detail below)

Also look around for items and artifacts that may give you genealogical clues or tell you about a person's life:

- needlework, quilts, sewing
- dishes, china, silverware
- weapons (knifes, guns, swords)
- clothing, shoes, hats
- jewelry

- books, magazines

- knickknacks, souvenirs

- toys, games

- furniture

- collectibles (coins, stamps, bottle tops, baseball cards)

- musical instruments

- tools

FAMILY PHOTOGRAPHS

In a perfect world, all photographs would list on the back the full names of all the people in the picture, the place where the picture was taken, and the date it was taken. Alas, none of us live in a perfect world. Few of us find photographs with this kind of information. My family photos said things like, "Edna and me at the beach." "I'm really not that fat." "The kids camping." "Me." "Guess who?" "Paul and the neighbor boy." (I guess I should consider myself lucky that there was anything written at all!) While I try to do better for my descendants and label my photos more descriptively, I'm sure I've missed a few.

Sometimes you can identify Cousin Mary in a photo from looking at other photos that you know are of Cousin Mary. Sometimes you can pinpoint the time period a photo was taken by the clothing the people are wearing. If the photo was taken outside, you can guess an approximate time of year based on the seasonal appearance of the trees and shrubs. Photograph analysis is an interesting aspect of genealogy. Books listed in the Bibliography will help you to identify and analyze family photos. Bringing the pictures with you when you conduct an oral history interview with relatives will help in identifying the people.

There are several different types of historic photographs: daguerreotypes, tintypes, ambrotypes, *cartes de visite,* cabinet cards, glass-plate negatives, and cyanotypes. Their use and times of popularity will also help you to date the photo. For example, daguerreotypes were popular from 1839 to 1857; tintypes from 1856 to 1938. A book such as Thomas L. Davies's *Shoots: A Guide to Your Family's Photographic Heritage* will help you date and analyze old photographs.

PRESERVING HISTORIC DOCUMENTS
AND PHOTOGRAPHS

When you find historic photographs, handle them with great care. Do not write on the photograph, front or back. It is best to put it in an acid-free sheet protector and label the sheet protector. *Never* put photographs or newspaper clippings, historic or otherwise, in albums with "magnetic" sheets covered with plastic, and never use tape, glue, or other non-archival-quality adhesive products. These and various laminating methods will do permanent damage to the photo or clipping. In the Appendix, I've listed companies that sell photo albums and other archival preservation products.

If you do not have a negative of a historic photo, check with commercial photographers and see how much they charge to make a "copy neg." Many photographers also do photo refinishing on damaged pictures. You can also copy the photograph and create a negative yourself. If you have a focusable 35mm camera, you can take a picture of the picture. It's not the greatest copy in the world, but if you have a lot of old photos, this may be the most economical way to create negatives. Black-and-white film will last longer, both the negatives and prints, than color film.

You could also take your photos to a quick-print copy shop that has a color photocopy machine and make copies that way. A word of caution, however: You don't want to expose old photographs or documents to repeated doses of the bright light that is used in making photocopies. In the long run, it will harm your photograph. If you do copy pictures this way, do it only once and make other copies from the first one.

For newspaper clippings, make photocopies instead of laminating the original. The paper used in newspapers is highly acidic. The higher the acid content in a paper, the lower its life. Newspapers weren't meant to last; that's why they're microfilmed. Again, in a perfect world all the news clippings you find would give the name of the newspaper, where it was published, the date, and the page number. None of my clippings ever had this information, but you may be able to deduce clues from the content in the clipping. If you run across the source citation, treat it like your photographs: Put the original in an acid-free sheet protector, then label the sheet protector. Or photocopy the clipping and write the pertinent details on the copy.

Similarly, if you come across other historic documents as you rummage through your or your relatives' possessions, make one photocopy, then handle and work with the copy. Put the original in an acid-free sheet protector. Never mark on the original, even in pencil.

Keep all historic documents and artifacts in a safe, dry, cool place away from vermin. If you live in a humid environment, pay particular attention to preservation. When we lived in Florida, my husband's and my high school yearbooks were packed away in a cardboard box in a spare bedroom. When we unpacked them upon moving to Colorado, we discovered mold and mildew had eaten away many of the pages. If you want something to last for generations, don't leave it to chance. Make sure you take precautions to preserve your precious items now.

ORAL HISTORY INTERVIEWING

Another beginning step in the search for your ancestry is to talk with relatives—the older the better. While your first inclination may be to ask questions to fill in the blanks of your charts—questions such as "When and where were you born?" "When did you get married?" "What were your parents' names?"—understand that there is more to an oral history interview than names, dates, and places. It is also important to learn the family stories, traditions, legends, and customs.

Ideally, all names, dates, and locations you obtain from talking with your relatives should be supported with documentation from original records such as birth, marriage, and death certificates. After all, memories do fail, and the statistical information you receive may have some inaccuracies. Even people in their twenties may have problems remembering or even knowing exactly when their parents were married.

The details of names, dates, and places are only the framework for your research. The really interesting part is the stories and traditions. As you become more involved in genealogy, you will find that preserving the family stories has received the least amount of attention from the genealogical community. That's because as a story is passed down from one generation to the next, details can get distorted, elaborated, or omitted. It's similar to playing the childhood game of "gossip" or "telephone," where everyone sat in a large circle, one person whispered something to the next, and by the time the story completed the circle, it was completely different from the original.

I'm afraid most family stories suffer the same fate. Uncle John adds his version; Aunt Cindy decides to make the story more interesting and embellishes "just a little"; Grandpa leaves out the dull parts; and Cousin Paul wasn't there, but he likes to tell it as if he were. But as you will also learn as you get more involved in genealogy, no source—printed or oral—is totally reliable.

Census enumerations are inconsistent from decade to decade; death certificates contain errors; even tombstones have mistakes carved in stone.

Oral history is no less reliable. Yes, people's memories are prone to lapses, distortions, and errors. But, again, it depends on the information you seek. If you ask Great-Uncle Mortimer the dates of when all twelve of his brothers and sisters were born, or when they all got married, then you're asking for trouble. If you ask Great-Uncle Mortimer to recount memories of his teen years and to tell you about the first car he owned—how did it smell? what did it feel like to get behind the wheel? what color and make was it? where did he first drive it?—then you're on pretty stable ground. When you ask Aunt Mildred to tell you stories about her own life, chances are the stories are reasonably accurate. When you ask her about people's lives before she was born—such as "Why did our family come to America in the 1600s?" or "Why did our family move to Ohio in 1840?"—then you need to support the story with research.

Common family legends include descent from Native Americans (usually a Cherokee Indian princess), the "three brothers" saga ("Our branch of the family began when three brothers decided to leave the Old Country . . ."), the family name being changed at Ellis Island (an "Ellis Island baptism"), and royal or famous ancestry (generally, relation to a famous person just because the surname's the same. By the way, if someone in your family claims you're descended from certain presidents, like James Buchanan, Warren Harding, Andrew Jackson, James K. Polk, or George Washington, remember, none of these men had children!). All of these tales add color to the family history, and it's interesting to trace the origins of such stories. By all means, these legends should be recorded and added to your notebook with your charts and forms. But they should be noted as "legends" until proved or disproved.

Genealogists learn to use the information from these stories as clues. The general theory is that there is usually a grain of truth somewhere in the story. What comes as a shock is when the budding genealogist, either purposely or inadvertently, proves through documented research that the family story is wrong. For some reason, older relatives, who have taken great care to pass the story along to the "younguns," don't take kindly to being told that Great-Great-Grandma was not a Cherokee Indian princess after all. This is where you will need to use some diplomacy and tact.

INTERVIEW GOALS

The first question you need to ask *yourself* is, "What is the purpose of conducting an oral history interview with this relative?" Is your goal to "get the facts, ma'am, nothing but the facts"? Or is it to learn about what life was like for that person? Yes, you will have to start with the facts—the who, where, and when—but keep in mind there's a good chance you'll find all that information in some record anyway.

When I was a baby genealogist, I dutifully interviewed my grandmother, asking her questions like the names of her parents, when she was born, when they were born, when they came to America. Then, as the genealogy how-to books told me, I verified everything she told me in one record or another. I hated doing oral history interviews. My grandmother hated being interviewed.

My next interviewing experience was with my grandmother's cousins. I followed the same procedure, asking about names, dates, and places. Tired of my constant harassing, they finally told me, "Please don't ask us any more questions. We've told you everything we know." Then they stopped answering my letters, and they pretended I had the wrong number when I called.

It didn't take me long to realize that interviewing relatives for genealogical information was not a pleasant experience for anyone. So I stopped interviewing people. What was the point? Why bother asking questions if I could find the information in a record anyway?

Grandma's gone now, and I'm afraid I missed the point. It wasn't until I became friends with a social historian that I realized I was doing it all wrong. The main goal of interviewing was not to ask questions about information I could find in a record; it was to ask questions about things I could not and would not ever find in a record.

What you generally won't find in the records are people's experiences, thoughts, feelings, and motivations. And I discovered that people love to talk about themselves and tell you these things. Unless you have letters or diaries, you won't find any record of how your grandparents met and courted. You won't find a document telling how they felt about suddenly being poor during the Depression. These are the things that go to the grave with a person. These are the things that make a person "a person." The census record enumerating Great-Uncle Mortimer's family will still be around long after we're all dead and gone, but Great-Uncle Mortimer's days are numbered.

WHEN TO CONDUCT INTERVIEWS

Most genealogy how-to books, which give little attention to oral history interviewing, tell you that the proper time to conduct an interview is at the beginning of a research project. Actually, I believe talking to relatives should be done at least twice: once when you first begin climbing your family tree, then again after you have gathered quite a bit of research.

The first interview should be short, and the goal is to gather the essentials—names, (approximate) dates, places, stories about the origins of the family—in order to begin your research. But don't belabor this interview.

Once you are familiar with the first few generations from the interviews and your research, focus the second and succeeding interviews on augmenting the records and getting historical content *based on that person's life and experiences.* Anything Great-Aunt Esmeralda tells you about her ancestors is just hearsay anyway. I'm talking about getting stories about Great-Aunt Esmeralda's lifetime—asking her to recall her childhood, her adolescence, and what she remembers about the oldest people in her life: her grandparents or great-grandparents if they were alive when she was a child. Have her tell you stories about her fondest memories of her grandfather or grandmother. Ask her what these people looked like. How did they dress?

The second interview is the time to ask questions on events, emotions, and what you found in historical records, asking *why* did this happen or why do they think it happened, *how* did they feel about it, and *what* was it like? This is information you won't find in genealogical records.

You may formulate questions around a national historical event:

- What do you remember most about the Depression?

- How did your family support itself during the Depression?

- Was your daily life affected much?

Or you can ask questions about general topics of everyday life:

- How did you meet your spouse?

- Did you give birth to your babies at home?

- Who attended the births?

- Which child's birth is most memorable and why?

- How soon after a baby was born did you return to regular household duties?

- What did the house you grew up in look like?

- Would you draw me a floor plan?

- Who's the oldest person in your family that you remember?

- Were you close to your [grandmother]?

- What did she look like?

- What did you like/dislike about her? Why?

- What words of wisdom did she impart to you? In other words, what do you think was her guiding philosophy in life? What did you learn from her about life?

PEOPLE TO INTERVIEW

Don't limit yourself to relatives. If your goal is to learn what life was like during Grandpa's day, and he and his siblings and first cousins are gone, try to track down some of Grandpa's friends and neighbors. They would have had experiences similar to Grandpa's and may be able to tell you about him. Another helpful person might be the town or local historian where your grandparents grew up. Though this person may not have known your grandparents, he or she can probably tell you about the area during the time your grandparents' lived there.

PLACES TO CONDUCT INTERVIEWS

If you're conducting the interview in a relative's home, don't just sit at the kitchen table or in the living room. Have Uncle Sidney give you a tour of his home. Have him point out objects, souvenirs, and other special items that may trigger stories. Ask him to draw a floor plan of the house he grew up in. Have him draw in where the furniture went.

You might bring along videotapes or news releases about historic events from a particular time in Uncle Sidney's life. Or bring recordings of radio shows or music that he might have listened to. These are wonderful ways to trigger memories.

If this is the second interview after you've done some research in historical documents, bring along photocopies of those documents. When I interviewed my grandmother's cousin, I took along a copy of the ship's passenger list that recorded her coming to America. She was thrilled. She had never seen the passenger list.

Interviews don't have to be conducted in a relative's home. Here are some other places to talk to relatives that will bring about interesting stories:

- Cemeteries, around the family burial plot, having the relative reminisce about the deceased.

- The neighborhood where the relative spent his or her childhood or teen years.

- An antique shop. There are bound to be items that will bring back memories, even if the items did not belong to the person you're interviewing.

- A library. Order on interlibrary loan a newspaper from the town the person lived in. Get a newspaper from a significant date in that person's life, like the date he/she married or graduated from high school. Have your relative go page by page, reading the newspaper and talking about the events and how each affected him or her. Look through old magazines, like *Life,* that have lots of pictures that may jar memories. (Just remember, you are in a library and need to consider the other patrons.)

MECHANICS OF INTERVIEWS

There are many technical aspects to consider when conducting oral history interviews. Many guidebooks go into more detail (see the Bibliography). The following are a few things to think about:

1. *Length of an interview.* Oral historians agree that an interview should not last longer than one to two hours. It's tiring for the person being interviewed. If you don't get all the information you need, or if your goal is to write that person's memoirs, then schedule several interviews over a period of a few days or weeks.

2. *Behavior during an interview.* Do not correct the narrator. Even though you may have a historical document that you know is accurate, let your relative tell you the way he or she remembers the event. You can make a note of the discrepancy when you cite your sources. Show interest in the narrator and don't interrupt a story.

3. *Obtaining permission to make the interview "public."* Keep in mind that you do not own that person's memories; therefore, you may not use the information a relative tells you at your own discretion. Get written permission to use the material if you plan to

publish parts of the interview in a family history or donate your interview notes to a library.

4. *Taping the interview.* If the interviewee doesn't mind, it's a good idea to tape the interview so that you don't have to take notes. You will, however, want to take notes when you verify spellings of names, places, or unusual or archaic words. Audiotaping is the least interfering to the interview. While videotaping also captures the person's look, facial expressions, and personality, some people are more intimidated by a camera than a tape recorder and behave unnaturally. Ask the person being interviewed which method he or she prefers. Audio- and videotapes have a limited shelf life, so be sure to make backup copies and store the original in a dry place.

5. *To transcribe the tape or not to transcribe.* If the interview is left as an audio- or videotape, it will not be as useful to you or your descendants as a written account. Technology changes so fast. If you recorded an interview years ago using a Beta video camera, how will you play it back now? If you recorded an interview using a reel-to-reel tape, how will you play it back? The printed word is still the most widely used form of preserving history, but transcribing tapes is time-consuming. To transcribe, edit, and proof the transcript against the tape and make a final copy, you will spend about twenty-two to twenty-five hours for every hour of an interview. Personally, I never have transcribed an oral history tape. Instead, I take notes from the tape and pull particularly interesting quotes. In my notes, I also detail what topics were discussed in what order: childhood, food, school, teen years. . . .

USING ORAL HISTORY

What do you do with the life stories once you've gathered them? You combine them with the research you've done in historical documents and the general, relevant historical context, writing a narrative account as part of your family history. Here's an example:

> Meals were an important aspect of Italian-American life, and the Vallarelli family household was no different. Family life revolved around the dinner table for two reasons. First, food to the Italian was a symbol of life; it was the product of the father's labor prepared by the mother. To Italian Americans, "meals were a 'communion' of

the family." To waste food was a sin and to refuse food from an Italian hostess was an insult. Rosa Vallarelli always asked anyone who came to her home, "Did you eat?"; then she would offer them food. Another reason family life revolved around the Italian dinner table was because this was the one time during the day when the whole family was, and was expected to be, together. Isabel, Rosa's daughter, recalled that dinner time was practically the only time she saw her father.[1]

And don't forget to cite your sources:

1. All specific information pertaining to the Vallarelli family was obtained from an oral history interview between the author and Isabel Vallarelli on 27 April 1993. The interview was conducted in her home in Harrison, Westchester County, NY, when she was 76 years old. Isabel is the daughter of Felice and Rosa (Albanese) Vallarelli. General information on Italian Americans came from Richard Gambino, *Blood of My Blood: The Dilemma of the Italian Americans* (New York: Doubleday, 1974), p. 17; and Frances Malpezzi and William Clements, *Italian-American Folklore* (Little Rock: August House Publishers, 1992), p. 224; the "communion" quote came from Gambino, p. 17.

Before you start an oral history interview, think of this African proverb: "When an old person dies, a whole library disappears." Make the most of your interviews. Ask *who, when,* and *where*; but really emphasize *how, what,* and *why.*

Once you've explored your home for information and talked with some relatives, it's time to find other genealogists—some who may turn out to be distant cousins—who can help you with your genealogy.

Chapter 3

Finding Others Like You

The hobby of genealogy has been likened to a virus: the genealogy bug. Once you're bitten, it's incurable. Just as there are support groups for victims of cancer, lupus, AIDS, alcoholism, and drug addiction, there are also support groups for genealogists. We call them genealogical societies. Unless you live in a small, rural community—like Simla, Colorado, where I live—you can almost bet that there is a local genealogical society near you. Check with your local public library or historical society.

JOINING A LOCAL GENEALOGICAL SOCIETY

Why join a local society if no one there is likely to share your ancestry? While you just never know when you will find a "genealogy cousin," joining a local group is worthwhile for a number of reasons and will foster your search for your ancestors.

MONTHLY LECTURES

Many local societies sponsor monthly lectures or programs on different aspects of genealogy. While not every topic will benefit your own research, most of the monthly programs are general in nature, filling the needs of a majority of the society's members.

ANNUAL SEMINARS

Some local societies sponsor annual seminars where they engage a nationally known genealogical speaker. These seminars are usually one-day events, with the keynote speaker giving three or four lectures on a general theme so as to attract the largest number of people. Some groups do not charge members to attend these annual events; other societies charge a fee (usually around $15 to $35) to cover the expense of sponsoring a renowned genealogist.

GENEALOGICAL SUBGROUPS

Many local societies have subgroups for those interested in computer genealogy, ethnic genealogy, or regional genealogy. The Pikes Peak Genealogical Society in Colorado Springs, for instance, has a computer interest group, a Pennsylvania research group, and a Palatine/German ancestry group.

NEWSLETTERS

Most local societies publish a newsletter that will keep you informed of genealogical events in your area as well as activities sponsored by genealogical groups in surrounding areas and national events. These newsletters may print "queries," which I'll discuss later in this chapter.

VOLUNTEERING OPPORTUNITIES

Local societies sponsor numerous committee projects that need volunteers. Many societies index the local newspaper or record the tombstone inscriptions in a local cemetery, then publish the results of these projects. Volunteering for one of these committees gives you an opportunity to learn about the community in which you live, and offers research experience that may help you in your own family history research.

LIBRARY VOLUNTEERING

Members of the local genealogical society also volunteer time to work in the public library's genealogical section or the society's library. Here you will learn about a variety of original and published sources. Helping patrons is a great way to learn a library's collection. Most genealogical libraries and societies will do one to two hours of free research for a member who lives at a distance. Researching someone else's ancestry gives you experience that will benefit your own research. It can also give you an idea of whether you like genealogy enough to take it on as a profession.

BEGINNERS' CLASSES

Most local societies sponsor beginners' classes and workshops (see Chapter 4 for more on this aspect of education). Like any other addict, we want everyone to see how wonderful genealogy is and to share the great feeling we get from it. Providing beginner classes is one way a society attracts new members.

SOCIALIZING AND NETWORKING

Local societies are great places to socialize and network. Everyone there has the same affliction as you do. Just as it is therapeutic to hear another cancer survivor tell his or her story, it is also helpful to listen to other genealogists talk about their research endeavors. Another genealogist may teach you about a source you have yet to explore. Another may share with you the steps in solving a difficult research problem, steps that may also work for you. These are just a few reasons to talk to other people about genealogy.

Keep in mind that joining a local society doesn't mean you just join a society where you live. It also means joining a society in the area where your ancestors lived. If your great-great-grandfather lived in Dade County, Missouri, it would be beneficial for you to join a genealogical or historical society in Dade County for many of the same reasons you joined one in your area. There are additional reasons, too:

- The society newsletter may publish record abstracts or indexes for that locality, which will help you obtain records by mail on your ancestor.

- If the society maintains a surname file, you may find cousins who still live in the area.

- If the society offers distant members an hour or two of free research, you can have a local member check records for you that you could not access without visiting the repository personally.

- You'll learn about publications the society has compiled and offers for sale on the area where your ancestor lived—publications that may contain information on your ancestor.

Dues for most local genealogical societies are reasonably priced, ranging from $10 to $30 a year. Often I will join a distant organization for a year to see if it meets my needs, then base my decision to renew on that and whether I am still interested in researching that area.

JOINING A STATE GENEALOGICAL SOCIETY

Most states have a state genealogical society. Some of these oversee or govern the local societies; some operate independently. These groups are larger in membership since they encompass the whole state, and their dues may be higher. Because of the group's larger membership, a state society is more likely to sponsor an out-of-town, nationally known speaker for an all-day seminar. State societies offer many of the same benefits as local groups. You may have to travel a distance to a meeting in another part of the state, however. You can locate state societies either through your local organization or by consulting Elizabeth Petty Bentley's *The Genealogist's Address Book.*

JOINING AN ETHNIC GENEALOGICAL SOCIETY

We all have ethnic ancestry, regardless of whether the ancestors came from England, Scotland, Ireland, Italy, Germany, France, Africa, Norway, Japan, Mexico, or whether they were here to greet these colonists and immigrants. While not every ethnic group has an established national genealogical society, many do. Bentley's *The Genealogist's Address Book* will tell you if an ethnic society exists and where to write for membership information. Once you get your research past American shores, belonging to one of these societies will greatly aid your search. You may find members who can translate foreign documents for you. Some organizations sponsor genealogical research trips to other countries. Ethnic societies may also sponsor one- or two-day conferences with several speakers offering advice on researching ethnic ancestry.

There may also be genealogical societies in the foreign country from which your ancestors came. Be aware, however, that some of these organizations may not focus on the "common folk," but on those ancestors who were the nobility and descend from royalty. By joining an ethnic genealogical society in America, you can learn about foreign ones and what these have to offer.

Research in foreign countries differs from research in America in the types and availability of records, and every country is different. No single book can cover research methods and sources in every country. Guidebooks specific to foreign research (see the Bibliography) will be beneficial when you are ready to bridge the ocean. Even if your ancestry keeps you on the North or South American continent (Native American, Canadian, and South American, for example), there are guides that will help you seek the records for these groups. By joining an ethnic genealogical society, you will learn about new books and journals dedicated to researching foreign ancestry.

JOINING A NATIONAL GENEALOGICAL SOCIETY

While there is really only one national genealogical society in the United States, appropriately called the National Genealogical Society, two other groups are considered national organizations: the Federation of Genealogical Societies and the New England Historic Genealogical Society.

NATIONAL GENEALOGICAL SOCIETY

The National Genealogical Society (NGS) was established in 1903. Its goals are to collect and preserve genealogical, historical, biographical, and heraldic data; to promote interest in research; to foster and promote careful documentation and scholarly writing; to provide quality genealogical instruction; and to produce genealogical publications. NGS has more than 15,000 members.

NGS is headquartered in Arlington, Virginia (see Appendix of Addresses). Current annual membership dues are $40. Members receive the *National Genealogical Society Quarterly (NGSQ)*, the *NGS Newsletter,* and the *CIG* (Computer Interest Group) *Digest* (see Chapter 5). The society sponsors an annual national conference usually held in May or June, a home-study course (see Chapter 4), a library loan service (see Chapter 10), awards programs, writing contests, and other benefits. Joining NGS keeps you up-to-date on standards, events, resources, records access, and new publications in the field.

NGS also offers opportunities to volunteer. Few of the people involved in the NGS committees live in the Arlington area; volunteers are scattered across the nation. The indexer for the *NGSQ,* for example, lives in Dallas, Texas, while the editor lives in Tuscaloosa, Alabama. Once you join NGS and learn about all the committees, you may wish to volunteer some of your time. This is a great way to get to know the movers and shakers in the genealogical community. Some may be research specialists in areas where your research has taken you. Keep in mind, however, that many of the people involved at the national level are professional genealogists who make their living from research services. Do not expect to get unlimited free advice. Asking a question of a renowned Kentucky genealogist such as, "What source would you recommend for learning how to research in Kentucky?" is most appropriate; asking "Could you look up this record for me?" is not, unless you have also asked how much the researcher would charge.

FEDERATION OF GENEALOGICAL SOCIETIES

The Federation of Genealogical Societies (FGS) was founded in 1976. Made up of more than 400 genealogical and historical societies and libraries, the organization represents more than 100,000 individuals. According to its purpose as stated in its newsletter, the *Forum,* "The Federation actively represents and protects societies, coordinates and facilitates their activities, and monitors events that are critical to the future of genealogy. The Federation aims to serve the needs of member societies, provide products and services to improve organizational management, and marshal the resources and national efforts of historical and genealogical organizations."

When you join an organization such as NGS and most local or state societies, you are also becoming a member of FGS. Part of your dues to these other societies goes to FGS, so that the organization becomes a member-society of FGS. In order to get the newsletter, however, you must pay for the subscription. If you do not belong to a member society, the subscription price is currently $15; if you do, the rate is $9.

Like NGS, FGS sponsors an annual conference, usually held in August or September. FGS also has many committees that need volunteers, no matter in what part of the country you live. FGS is especially concerned with record access. Some states have started limiting availability of historical documents to the public, and FGS takes an active role when made aware of these problems.

NEW ENGLAND HISTORIC GENEALOGICAL SOCIETY

The New England Historic Genealogical Society (NEHGS) is the nation's oldest genealogical society, founded in 1845. Its headquarters and library are located in Boston, Massachusetts. Current membership dues are $50 a year. Members receive a subscription to *The New England Historical and Genealogical Register,* a quarterly journal, and *NEXUS,* a newsletter published five times a year.

In addition, NEHGS has a circulating library (see Chapter 10) and sponsors conferences and seminars throughout the country. These conferences are smaller versions (two-day seminars) of the ones sponsored by the Federation of Genealogical Societies and the National Genealogical Society.

The NEHGS library in Boston has nearly 150,000 volumes and more than 10,000 rolls of microfilm. It also subscribes to more than 400 periodicals. The manuscript collection contains items dating back to the 1500s: diaries and letters, account books and business papers, church and town records, maps, wills, deeds, unpublished New England town and family genealogies, and the papers of many renowned genealogists deposited at the society since the 1850s. Naturally, the library specializes in New England families and research, but there are also volumes on Mid-Atlantic, Southern, Canadian, English, and Scottish ancestries.

One of the NEHGS's latest projects, under the direction of Robert Charles Anderson, CG, FASG, is the Great Migration Study Project. Its purpose is to produce biographical and genealogical sketches of all those people known to have come to New England between 1620 and 1643, which make up the majority of seventeenth-century immigrants. The study has accumulated material scattered among many reference works and from original, contemporary records to provide a narrative description of the settlement process in the New England colonies.

The project has resulted in two publications. One is called the *Great Migration Newsletter,* which offers news of the project, a bibliography of relevant new articles and books, information on new source material, plus an in-depth article on one of the towns settled during the Great Migration (for example, Lynn, Charlestown, Roxbury, Salem, Piscataqua, Ipswich, and Hartford). The second publication contains biographical and genealogical sketches. This three-volume series was published in 1995 by NEHGS and is titled *The Great Migration Begins: Immigrants to New England 1620–1633.* An introductory essay precedes the sketches, explaining the methodology used in gathering and analyzing the evidence and the sources consulted. Future volumes will take the study through immigrants of 1643.

JOINING A LINEAGE/PATRIOTIC SOCIETY

According to the 1994 edition of the *Hereditary Society Blue Book,* there are 147 lineage and patriotic societies in America, with organizational chapters across the nation. Many genealogists can qualify for one or more of these organizations:

- National Society, Daughters of the American Revolution (DAR)

- The National Society of the Sons of the American Revolution

- The National Society of the Daughters of Founders and Patriots of America (DFPA)

- General Society of Mayflower Descendants

- The National Society of Colonial Dames of the XVII Century

- Flagon and Trencher—Descendants of Colonial Tavernkeepers

- Descendants of the Illegitimate Sons and Daughters of the Kings of Britain

- Sons and Daughters of the Victims of Colonial Witch Trials

In order to join any of these organizations, you must be able to document your lineage back to the qualifying time period or ancestor. For example, to be a member of the DAR you must have an ancestor who served the cause for American independence, either serving in the military as a recognized patriot or by rendering material aid. To be a member of the DFPA you must descend in the *direct male line* of either parent from an ancestor who settled in any of the colonies between 13 May 1607 and 13 May 1687. You would need to trace the line following your father or mother, grandfather, great-grandfather, great-great-grandfather, and so on, all of whom had the same surname. I joined this organization on my mother's Fitzhugh line, which is an unbroken male line back to the qualifying time period:

1. me

2. Mary Fitzhugh (my mother)

3. Pressley Fitzhugh (my grandfather)

4. Sidney Fitzhugh (my great-grandfather)

5. Catlett Conway Fitzhugh (my great-great-grandfather)

6. James Madison Fitzhugh (my great-great-great-grandfather), and so on.

My daughter, however, would not be able to join DFPA on this same line since she would have to go through two females (me and my mother) to get to the male line; but she could join on her father's Carmack lineage, which would also qualify.

Each organization provides you with forms to fill out on your lineage, to which you must attach proof: vital records (birth, marriage, death certificates), land deeds, wills—anything that proves that one generation connects to the next and that your great-great-grandpa was born when you say he was born.

Most societies don't let you attempt this alone; they assign a member, usually the chapter's volunteer genealogist, to help you compile "your papers." Some organizations encourage non-genealogists to hire a professional, like a Certified American Lineage Specialist, to do the research and complete the forms. Once the lineage application is complete, it is reviewed by the national organization's genealogists for accuracy. If everything is appropriate, you become a member; if not, you are given the chance to secure additional documentation.

One organization I joined, which shall remain nameless to protect the inexperienced, assigned me a genealogist who "corrected" my lineage form and who assured me that this in "no way affected my membership." By "correcting" my application, this genealogist, who thought he/she knew my lineage better than I, linked me to the wrong ancestor! One of my great-great-etc. grandmothers had married a Henry Fitzhugh. When he died she married his cousin, who had the same name, was born about the same time, and lived in the same area. I descend from the first husband Henry. The genealogist "corrected my mistake" and had me descending from the second husband Henry. It took many letters and additional proof before they would give me back my heritage. Although it doesn't happen often, I have heard others tell of similar experiences. If it happens to you, and you know you have the correct documentation, make sure you let the society know.

One of the many benefits of joining a hereditary/lineage society is that you are documenting your lineage for the future. Each society maintains the application forms; some publish books with members' genealogies. These sources help new members, who descend from ancestors who have already been documented, to join the organization, as well as preserving a part of history. Even if you quit the society or die, your lineage is still preserved with that organization. A lot of these societies maintain a library or archive that members may use free of charge.

When I first became involved in genealogy, I joined nine lineage societies and was eligible to join many more. But when I totaled how much I was paying in dues annually, I dropped my membership in all but two. My "papers," however, are still on file with all of these organizations; and it was a great way to meet people when I first moved to Colorado and knew no one.

Like genealogical societies, lineage/patriotic societies have goals and missions and committees that need volunteers. By either writing to the organizations (see Bentley's *The Genealogist's Address Book*) or consulting the *Hereditary Society Blue Book* or *The Source: A Guidebook of American Genealogy,* you can learn all the qualifications for membership in these organizations. In the Appendix, I've listed a few of the most popular lineage societies.

THE INTERNET AND WORLD WIDE WEB

Genealogy has found its way onto the Net and into the Web. As you will see from the Appendix of Addresses in this book, many of the major societies, book vendors, and magazines have Internet addresses and Web sites. You will have no trouble finding genealogists from all over the world from the comfort of your own home by using your computer.

America Online, for example, offers a Genealogy and History Forum, which has message boards, libraries, and chat sessions. The chats are usually informal exchanges of genealogical or historical information, but sometimes there are "speakers" or guest lecturers who chat for fifteen to twenty minutes on a topic or specialty. This is a great place to get advice if you plan to research in a locality you have never tried before. It is also a way to get to know specialists in the field, as well as another way of keeping informed of happenings in genealogy, such as learning about the PBS-TV series *Ancestors* that made its debut in January 1997.

Don't limit yourself to looking for genealogy sites. Other areas on the Internet and World Wide Web benefit researchers, such as the Vital Records Information State Index, which contains information about where to obtain vital records for each county of each state in the nation; its address is http://www.inlink.com/~nomi/vitalrec/staterec.html. There is also a Census Data for the United States 1790–1860 at http://icg.harvard.edu/census. The Civil War Center contains Civil War related information including some regimental lists and diaries at http://www.cwc.lsu.edu/.

One of the best ways to learn about various sites is to read magazines like the *NGS/CIG Digest* and *Genealogical Computing*. These journals publish up-to-date information on computer genealogy (see Chapter 5). Also see Thomas Kemp's *Virtual Roots: A Guide to Genealogy and Local History on the World Wide Web*.

PLACING QUERIES TO FIND "GENEALOGY COUSINS"

If Samuel Townsend, born in 1682, had twelve children who survived to adulthood; and if each of those children had about ten children; and if each of his grandchildren had an average of eight to ten children, how many descendants did Samuel have in just these two generations? If this question made you shiver and recall your high school algebra days, then think about how many descendants Samuel would have today! My point is that you are literally related to more people than you know. In fact, you could even be related to your spouse. How do you find a few of these thousands of descendants of your ancestors? By placing "queries" in genealogical magazines.

Queries are one-paragraph advertisements in society newsletters and genealogical magazines. They usually read something like this:

> Would like to exchange information on the family of Jonathan Sinclair, who married Ester Simmons in 1895. Lived in Orange County, Virginia, in 1910. Children: Jonathan Jr., Samuel, Daniel, Mary, and Sally.

> or

> Need information on Benjamin Lounden, born ca. 1801 in North Carolina, and died ca. 1865 in Virginia.

> or

> Need parents and grandparents of William Beesley, born 1868, Whitely Co., Kentucky, died 1902; married Jane Dunlap.

> or

> Seeking descendants of Anna Mayhew, born ca. 1732, Dutchess Co., NY, daughter of Austin and Mary Mayhew.

Many genealogical societies print a limited number of queries in their newsletters at no cost to their members. Magazines like *Everton's Genealogical Helper* and *Heritage Quest* charge a classified advertising fee. These rates are reasonable, running about 35 cents a word, so that a 40-word ad would cost $14. This is why it is important to make the most of your ad and be as specific about your needs as possible. The following example is a waste of money, yet you will find many such ads in magazines all the time:

> Doing research on the following surnames: Adams, Anderson, Bates, Cox, Ford, Hancock, Hoffman, Marshall, Phillips, Powell, Scott, Smith, Summers, Thompson, White, and Williams.

Those surnames are so common that it's not worth a 32-cent stamp to find out if you're related to the person who placed this ad. It screams "name gatherer," not researcher. To get the most out of your query dollar and responses, be specific.

You may also try placing queries in newspaper classified ads or writing letters to the editor of the local newspaper where your ancestor lived; there may still be descendants in the area. Some newspapers publish genealogical columns that also run queries. Consult Anita Cheek Milner's *Newspaper Genealogical Column Directory* for columnists and newspapers.

SURNAME ORGANIZATIONS AND FAMILY ASSOCIATIONS

Hundreds of organizations are dedicated to research on particular families or specific surnames. These groups often maintain genealogical files or a database of their members and the lines they are researching. Many of these groups are listed annually in *Everton's Genealogical Helper* March–April issue. Also check Elizabeth Petty Bentley's *Directory of Family Associations*.

Once you start joining societies and organizations, surfing the Net, and placing queries in genealogical magazines, you'll begin to wonder how stamp and coin collecting rank above genealogy as a pastime. While you may find only a handful of people researching your ancestry, you will find several handfuls of helpful researchers out there. When you join a society, get involved, whether it's at the local, state, or national level. You will be amazed at how much you will learn that will help you climb your family tree. Just by volunteering in the genealogical section of a library one afternoon a week, you will expand your research knowledge more quickly than by researching twenty of your own ancestors. There's no quicker or more economical way to educate yourself in genealogical research. If you desire a structured learning experience, however, read on.

Chapter 4

A Genealogical Education

I started climbing my family tree when I was about nine or ten. While my parents and I were visiting friends in New York one summer, our friends decided to take me to an old cemetery. They knew I liked *Dark Shadows*—that macabre TV soap opera of the 1960s—and thought I might like to look at some colonial headstones. During that field trip, I read many interesting tombstones, which piqued my curiosity about the past. While we were in the cemetery, we met a man—a live one—who was copying down tombstone inscriptions. He explained he was a genealogist. Our friends invited him home with us for cake and coffee and to learn more about genealogy. (These were in the days when you *could* invite a stranger you met in the cemetery to your home.) On that fateful night, I learned about pedigree charts and family group sheets.

When I returned home, I wrote to all my relatives and filled in as many blanks as I could. I was thrilled when my three unmarried aunts sent me my mother's Fitzhugh line that dated to the 1600s. I remember gazing down at my semicompleted pedigree charts with pride, then thinking, "So now what?" The charts were placed in a file folder and tucked away into a drawer.

After I married and decided that my husband should support me while I became a "domestic engineer," I took out the charts. They hadn't changed.

61

They were still just names and dates on a piece of paper. I decided to go to the bookstore and see if there were any books on how to "do" genealogy. I found one and eagerly purchased it. Ah, you could write away for birth, marriage, and death certificates that would help fill in some of the blanks on the pedigree chart. So I did. Though some of the certificates had interesting tidbits about cause of death, they were kind of dry, too. I knew there had to be more to this "ancestor thing."

Fate being what it is, in the newspaper I found a notice of a four-week class being offered on genealogy at a community college. I signed up. I learned only slightly more than I had from reading the guidebook. I did find out that there was a genealogy section in the local library. I went there, but I still had no clue what I was doing or what I was supposed to be looking at.

My pedigree charts found their way back into the drawer.

A few years later, with baby in tow, I read in the newspaper about a local genealogical society that met once a month. I decided I would try out one of their meetings. On that night in February 1985, I finally learned what genealogy was all about and what gems the library held for me. All of a sudden, it clicked. I can't even recall what turned on the light bulb over my head, but I found people willing to guide me in the right direction.

I learned how to research by trial and error, ordering the wrong microfilms and poring over books that didn't deal with my family. Then a society member told me about a weeklong institute dedicated to educating people on research methods and sources. For this young mother, a week away—anywhere—was most appealing. A group from the society piled into a van, and we were off for a week of genealogy. It was great. I spent a whole week with people who were just as crazy as I was about the past, in a library and classroom with no windows, and with no care to ever contact the outside world again. The United States could have declared war on Canada, and I would not have known it. I was in heaven. I learned so much in that one week.

While many people learn the ins and outs of genealogical research by reading self-help books, you might want to consider national institutes and conferences, home-study courses, and local classes offered by genealogical societies. Many of these classes offer hands-on research experience, either using your own family or a family in a given area, to give you the opportunity to try out what you're learning.

NATIONAL CONFERENCES

National conferences are the perfect places not only to get an education, but also to network and talk with people. As mentioned in the previous chapter, two national conferences are held each year. One is sponsored by the National Genealogical Society (NGS), the other by the Federation of Genealogical Societies (FGS). The conference locations change every year, and the registration fee is around $100 for the full conference. When you become an NGS member and subscribe to the FGS newsletter, you will automatically receive conference brochures and information. Otherwise, write to the addresses in the Appendix to get on the mailing lists. FGS and NGS conferences are similar in structure. They begin on a Wednesday afternoon and run through Saturday evening, usually with a beginners' workshop held on the first day of the conference. There are about six hour-long lecture sessions a day; each session offers about six different lectures, so you must choose which lecture to attend each hour. Here is a sample of the lectures offered in a one-hour session from the FGS's "A Conference for the Nation's Genealogists," which was held in August 1996 in Rochester, New York:

Saturday, 5:00–6:00 P.M.

- "CD-ROM Research Strategies: Slow Down and Discover Hidden Information," by Kathleen W. Hinckley

- "Love Letters, Diaries, and Autobiographies: Let's Leave 'em Somethin' to Talk About," by Sharon DeBartolo Carmack

- "First Fruits of the Great Migration Study Project," by Robert Charles Anderson

- "Using Nineteenth-Century Newspapers for Family History," by John Philip Colletta

- "But I Just Don't Love You Anymore! Divorce in Antebellum America," by Gale Williams Bamman

- "Preponderance of Evidence: When CAN It Be Used?" by Christine Rose

It can be tough to choose which lecture to attend; there may be two or more given at the same time that you want to hear. Most of the lectures are taped by a company called Repeat Performance, and you may purchase the tapes either before you leave the conference or by mail (see Appendix). Many people also buy tapes of the lectures they attended so that they can review the speaker's helpful tips and advice at home. If you cannot afford to attend a conference, you may want to purchase tapes. The only drawback is that you won't have the handout material and you'll miss seeing the visual aids; therefore, you won't get as much from the lecture as if you had been there in person.

A great variety of lectures are offered at conferences; rarely will there be an hour or when you won't find a session to attend. If by chance there is a free hour in between the lectures, you will want to visit the exhibit area where more than a hundred vendors sell everything from genealogical novelties such as T-shirts and mugs to software, books, and forms. Many of the national and local societies, the conference-sponsoring society, the Association of Professional Genealogists, and the New England Historic Genealogical Society, for example, also have booths where you can talk to members and get more information about the organizations.

In the exhibit hall you will learn about the latest genealogical software. Most computer vendors have several computers on site so that you may try out programs. The book vendors have copies of the most popular genealogical books so that you may look them over before purchasing. Sometimes I find that my time spent networking in the vendor area is just as valuable as attending the lectures.

An independent, educational, nonprofit corporation held its two-day national conference in January 1997. With a theme of "Technology Applied: The Genealogist's Craft," GENTECH offered a variety of topics presented by nationally known genealogists who use technology such as computers, modems, scanners, CD-ROMs, cameras, and microfilm. The exhibit area included product demonstrations, genealogy software publishers, representatives of genealogy/computing books and periodicals, online services, and hardware dealers. Sample lectures included "What Should I Look for in a Genealogical Program," "Finding the Needle in the Cyberstack: Practical Methods for Researching on the Internet," "The World Wide Web: Speeding Your Climb Up the Family Tree," "Taking Your Portable Computer on a Research Trip," and "The Future of Online Genealogy." The cost of attending this conference was $85, which included all events.

REGIONAL CONFERENCES AND SEMINARS

Organizations like the New England Historic Genealogical Society, the Utah Genealogical Association (UGA), and some other state societies sponsor regional conferences around the country. These are mini-versions of national conferences, having several speakers but for only one or two days.

For instance, NEHGS offered a regional conference in October 1997 in Seattle. The conference featured one principal speaker and several other presenters. More similar to the NGS and FGS conferences' format, the UGA's conference in Salt Lake City lasts two days and has several sessions per hour with a number of speakers. The St. Louis Genealogical Society is one of several that hosts an annual one-day genealogy fair featuring nationally known speakers. These smaller-scale conferences and seminars also have exhibits and vendors. The FGS *Forum* and *Everton's Genealogical Helper* have a fairly comprehensive calendar of events listing these mini-conferences and seminars as well as one-day seminars featuring a nationally known genealogist. Check these publications for offerings in your area or in localities you might be visiting.

NATIONAL INSTITUTES AND SCHOLARSHIPS

Currently, four national institutes offer weeklong courses in genealogy each year. Many offer "tracks," ranging from beginner, intermediate, and advanced to specialty topics. When you attend, you choose one "track" to follow for the week. Tuition runs from $195 to $325, depending on the institute. To get on the mailing lists for any of the following institutes, write to the addresses listed in the Appendix.

NATIONAL INSTITUTE ON GENEALOGICAL RESEARCH

The National Institute on Genealogical Research (NIGR) is held in mid-July at the National Archives in Washington, D.C. Begun in 1950, NIGR is an annual one-week seminar that focuses on federal records of genealogical value at the National Archives. NIGR is an independent, self-supporting, nonprofit corporation whose board of trustees consists of representatives of the American Society of Genealogists, the Association of Professional Genealogists, the Board for Certification of Genealogists, the Federation of Genealogical Societies, the National Genealogical Society, and the National Institute's Alumni Association. Class size is limited to forty. The program is geared for experienced researchers (genealogists, historians, librarians, archivists).

Tuition is approximately $200. The National Institute's Alumni Association members receive a 10 percent discount on tuition. The fee includes one luncheon on Monday afternoon; otherwise, students are responsible for all meals. Special lodging rates are available through a local hotel.

The National Institute on Genealogical Research Alumni Association offers the Richard S. Lackey Memorial Scholarship, which covers tuition to the institute. It is offered to an individual working with the public in the field of genealogy (such as an instructor, librarian, library volunteer). You may request an application from the President of the NIGR Alumni Association, P.O. Box 14274, Washington, DC 20044-4274. The application deadline is usually March 1.

The American Society of Genealogists also offers the ASG Scholar Award. The award is based on excellence in research as demonstrated by a manuscript or publication of 2,000 to 10,000 words. This award carries a $500 scholarship applicable toward institute tuition and expenses. Contact the ASG Scholarship Committee, 1732 Ridgedale Drive, Tuscaloosa, AL 35406-1942.

INSTITUTE ON GENEALOGY AND HISTORICAL RESEARCH

The Institute on Genealogy and Historical Research (IGHR) is held each mid-June at Samford University in Birmingham, Alabama. It was begun in 1964. Cosponsored by the Board for Certification of Genealogists and Samford University, each IGHR offers seven courses. There is also a special three-week overseas course held in London at the Samford University London Center. The 1997 research course/tour included a week in Ireland (Dublin and Belfast). The cost was $3,100, which included round-trip airfare from Atlanta, major ground transportation to and from Samford's London Center, lodging and continental breakfast, and all associated lectures and tours in England and Ireland.

The seven courses offered in a recent year in Birmingham, Alabama, were:

Course 1:   Fundamentals of Genealogy and Historical Research

Course 2:   Intermediate Genealogy and Historical Studies

Course 3:   The Trans-Appalachian South

Course 4:   Advanced Genealogical Methods

Course 5:   Genealogy as a Profession

Course 6A: U.S. Military Records

Course 6B: Scottish Genealogical Research at Home and Abroad

Students may choose one of these weeklong courses; however, a prerequisite to the Advanced Methodology track is either previous enrollment in the Intermediate Genealogical Studies course, completion of the National Genealogical Society's home-study course, or genealogical certification/accreditation.

Tuition is about $325, which includes the banquet dinner. Accommodations are available on the university's campus in dormitories, the price of which includes meals. Enrollment is limited in some of Samford's IGHR sessions.

The American Society of Genealogists offers the ASG Scholar Award for this institute. See the discussion earlier on the NIGR for complete information.

GENEALOGICAL INSTITUTE OF MID-AMERICA

The Genealogical Institute of Mid-America (GIM) began in 1994 and is sponsored by Sangamon State University and the Illinois State Genealogical Society. GIM is held in July at the Sangamon State University campus in Springfield. There are usually four levels:

1. Genealogical Family History Research Methods, Part I

2. Genealogical Family History Research Methods, Part II

3. Military Record Resources

4. British Isles Research Sources

A post-institute workshop was held on the "Internet for Genealogists." Students experience a hands-on approach with research visits to a courthouse, the state historical library, the state archives, and one of seven Illinois Regional Archives Depositories.

Tuition is about $310, which includes conference materials, three dinners, and one banquet. Hotel accommodations are at a special rate.

SALT LAKE INSTITUTE OF GENEALOGY

The Salt Lake Institute of Genealogy held its first sessions in 1996 in Salt Lake City. This institute is offered in late January. Similar to the other institutes, students take one course of instruction for the entire week, attending twenty classes (seventy-five minutes each). In addition to classroom instruction, teachers and course coordinators provide exercises and feedback to the students. Enrollment is limited to thirty students per course. Tuition is approximately $240. The eight courses offered recently were:

1. Intermediate United States Research: Beyond Vital and Census Records

2. United States Southern States Research

3. Computers and Family History

4. Researching Scandinavians

5. Researching Irish Ancestors

6. Genealogical Librarianship

7. Professional Genealogy

8. Producing a Quality Family History

HOME-STUDY COURSES

Home-study courses, also called independent study, offer you the freedom to work at your own pace in your own home. The most popular home-study course is the National Genealogical Society's American Genealogy: A Basic Course, which was recently accredited by the Accrediting Commission of the Distance Education and Training Council. NGS's objective in the course is to teach the basics of genealogical research in a more comprehensive, systematic, and hands-on manner than is available anywhere else.

Sixteen lessons cover what information can be found in various types of records, how to locate the records, and how to document and describe the information each record contains. The course covers the following subjects and records: family tradition and family records; interviews, correspondence, and queries; secondary sources; getting organized; census; vital records; probate; land and tax; military and veterans records; immigration and naturalization; church and cemetery; migration routes and maps; interpreting and evaluating evidence.

Along with learning how to record information on charts and forms, students also learn how to abstract essential information from wills and deeds, write citations for various sources, and compile, analyze, and evaluate genealogical evidence.

You work at your own pace in this course. Each lesson gives an overview of the topic, followed by a glossary of terms and a reading and reference list. A sample assignment:

> Having determined the approximate date and place of death of an ancestor, search the probate records of that county in person or on microfilm. If you cannot visit the courthouse, write to the probate court for a photocopy of the probate records for your ancestor.

You are assigned an instructor for the course, who reviews your assignments and makes comments. The cost to members is $295; to nonmembers, $375. There is a payment plan for both members and nonmembers.

BYU INDEPENDENT STUDY

Brigham Young University in Provo, Utah, offers independent (home) study courses in genealogy resulting in a Certificate in Family History–Genealogy. The certificate program, however, should not be confused with the certification offered by the Board for Certification of Genealogists (see Chapter 12). The BYU courses will help prepare you for certification or accreditation, should you desire to seek one of these credentials.

The independent study courses BYU offers include:

- Introduction to Family History

- American Family History

- The Family and the Law in American History

- Writing Family Histories

- Writing Personal History

- Oral History Interviewing and Processing

- Sources in Family and Community History

  — Northern States and Canada

  — Southern States

  — Midwestern States

  — England and Wales from 1700

  — Scotland and Ireland

— Germanic Sources: An Introduction

— Hispanic Family History

In order to earn a certificate, you must complete eighteen credit hours. Current tuition is $78 per semester hour. Textbooks are extra. For more information, write to the address given in the Appendix for a course catalog.

BYU also offers conferences each August in genealogy and family history. There are ten different tracks: U.S. Localities; U.S./Canada Records; Emigration and Immigration; Scotland/Ireland/Wales; England; Germany; Europe/Scandinavia; Computerized Genealogy; Family Histories; and Research in Libraries. Registration for the four-day conference costs about $145.

ONLINE GENEALOGY COURSES

There are also online genealogy courses available through Carl Sandburg College in Galesburg, Illinois. They offer beginning and intermediate courses and one called "Genealogy on the Internet." There are enrollment and completion deadlines, and you are assigned an instructor who posts a new lecture weekly for eight weeks. Assignments and instructor feedback are handled each week through e-mail. The assignments consist of about twenty questions to be answered. Information is available online at http://csc.tech-center.org/~mneill/csc.html.

EXTERNAL DEGREES

Some colleges and universities offer independent-study, off-campus degree programs known as external degrees. These are undergraduate and graduate programs that do not fall under the traditional degree plans such as history, English, or psychology. An alternative degree may be obtained in, say, "history with an emphasis on American genealogy and family history." The School for Professional Studies at Regis University in Denver, New College External Degree Program at The University of Alabama in Tuscaloosa, and the Adult Degree Program at Vermont College of Norwich University in Montpelier are three institutions that offer alternative education programs (see Appendix for addresses). You may also want to consult the following guidebooks if you are interested in pursing a degree with an emphasis on genealogy and family history: John and Mariah Bear's *College Degrees by*

Mail (Berkeley, Calif.: Ten Speed Press, 1997) and the Academic Research Institute's Best's *External Degree Directory* (Northridge, Calif.: ARI, 1989).

COMMUNITY CLASSES

Other places to check for genealogy classes are community colleges and community and/or senior centers. The Elderhostel travel program for senior citizens also offers genealogy research trips and classes. Check with these places to see if any adult education programs are available in your area. Usually, the library or genealogical society will know about them, too.

BEGINNERS' WORKSHOPS

As mentioned in Chapter 3, one of the benefits of joining a local genealogical society is that the organization may sponsor beginners' workshops or classes, or a member may teach classes privately in his or her home or at a public school. Sometimes these classes are open only to members, but some societies use the beginners' workshop as a means to draw in new members. Workshops may be offered free or for a nominal fee to cover the cost of handouts.

How do you determine whether a community class or workshop is taught by a seasoned genealogist and whether the class is credible? Ask for the instructor's credentials and a copy of the course syllabus. A course that teaches a systematic approach to research as well as an emphasis on documentation and evaluating sources is likely a good one.

SELF-STUDY WITH INSTRUCTIONAL MANUALS

You do not have to take classes to learn how to research. Many genealogists are self-taught, having studied several guidebooks and read major genealogical journals and magazines such as the ones discussed in the next chapter.

The widely accepted, general genealogical guidebooks are listed in the Bibliography; following is a short summary of some of the books that are available as of this writing and what each offers at different learning levels (see the Bibliography for publication information). It would be beneficial to read several of these, getting more than one genealogist's opinion and experience.

BEGINNING

Family History Made Easy: A Step-by-Step Guide to Discovering Your Heritage, by Sandra Hargreaves Luebking and Loretto Dennis Szucs (available in 1998). This guide tells what records are available, where the records can be found, and how to interpret and use them most efficiently. The authors use firsthand accounts and case studies to illustrate genealogical methods and sources.

The Genealogist's Companion and Sourcebook, by Emily Anne Croom. This popular and widely available beginners' book covers all the basic records and includes chapters on African American and Native American genealogy. As the title implies, this book offers more in the way of helping you find the records than methods for using the records.

How to Climb Your Family Tree, by Harriet Stryker-Rodda. This 144-page guide gives an overview of how to get started climbing your family tree. It is a quick and easy read and is a good "first" book. Don't stop here, though.

Searching for Your Ancestors: The How and Why of Genealogy, by Gilbert Doane and James B. Bell. Doane and Bell add some humor to the typical how-to guide. They cover the basics as well as devoting from a paragraph to a page or two each to research in twenty-two countries.

Shaking Your Family Tree, by Ralph Crandall. Although most of the examples in Crandall's book deal with New England research (Dr. Crandall is the director of the New England Historic Genealogical Society), this is an excellent beginners' book. It gives many case examples to accompany the information on where and how to find records.

Unpuzzling Your Past: A Basic Guide to Genealogy, by Emily Anne Croom. This is another good, basic guidebook. It goes into more depth on starting research using home sources and recording oral family history. Croom gives an overview of original and published sources, but she goes into more detail on this aspect in her *The Genealogist's Companion and Sourcebook.*

Voices in Your Blood: Discovering Identity Through Family History, by G. G. Vandagriff. Basic genealogical sources are covered in this book with an emphasis on the FamilySearch computer database available at the Family History Library in Salt Lake City. It offers good fundamentals on using genealogical records.

INTERMEDIATE

Pitfalls in Genealogical Research, by Milton Rubincam. This is a wonderful little book—only 74 pages—that really makes you think about the pitfalls in doing historical and genealogical research. Some of the pitfalls discussed are calendar changes; same name, same place, same time period; family traditions; and the printed word, to name a few.

The Researcher's Guide to American Genealogy, by Val D. Greenwood. Greenwood's book has been dubbed the bible of genealogy. This guide goes into more detail on records and methods of research than the beginners' guides. Everyone who's anyone in genealogy has read Greenwood.

The Source: A Guidebook of American Genealogy, edited by Loretto Dennis Szucs and Sandra Hargreaves Luebking. This is a revised edition of a popular book. Practically everything you ever wanted to know about a particular record is written in *The Source.* This is an intensive look at a multitude of records. It's not a book to sit down with and read cover to cover—it's far too heavy, for one thing. If, for example, you're ready to do research in court records, you'll find a pertinent chapter in this book.

ADVANCED

Genealogical Evidence, by Noel C. Stevenson. An attorney, Stevenson approaches genealogical evidence as a lawyer would. He puts records "on trial" and asks you to do the same, taking a critical look at each piece of information contained in a record. This is another book that is widely read by the genealogical community.

There are always plenty of books and journals about genealogy to read. Even the "experts" in genealogy must constantly stay on top of new developments and trends in research, methodology, and sources. Regardless of whether you attend conferences and institutes or take home-study classes (or both), you will continue to learn new things as you embark on your research. The learning never stops.

Chapter 5

Genealogy Books and Journals

Before you visit a research repository or write for records, you need to know what is available to help you discover your ancestors. If you are planning a research trip to the National Archives, for instance, you can save a lot of valuable time if you already know what records are there and how to access them. Reading a book such as *Guide to Genealogical Research in the National Archives* will help prepare you for that trip. You could also avoid countless hours searching a record group if you know that someone has created an index to that record.

Reading is as much a part of genealogy as doing the research. You can't successfully begin your research if you don't know what records exist, whether there's an index, what the pitfalls of the records are, what time periods the records cover, and how to access the records. Jim and Paula Warren, two professional genealogists from St. Paul, Minnesota, plan days just for reading. They subscribe to and read more than ten journals—not just genealogical ones, but historical, archival, and library publications. On research trips, they read the journals from the locality they are visiting. Along with the articles, they also read the letters to the editor, editorials, and president's columns. According to Jim, "That's where we often learn about good collections and events. . . . We don't only read periodicals from the areas we research, but from all over the United States and Canada. Our general genealogical knowledge has benefited dramatically."

Genealogical books are available at genealogical libraries (although no library has every book), for purchase through mail order or at some bookstores, or through loan via one of the genealogical lending libraries discussed in Chapter 10. Most genealogical libraries subscribe to the major journals (discussed below), but you may also subscribe to the periodicals yourself. Subscription information may be found in the Appendix.

Every year, more and more books are published dealing with different aspects of genealogy: record transcripts and abstracts, cemetery/tombstone transcriptions, guidebooks on record sources and research repositories, family histories and genealogies, county and local histories, and indexes to records. Added to the books, a number of genealogical publications publish in mini-version many of the items just mentioned, plus case studies on difficult research problems.

Whether you are a hobby genealogist, a budding professional, or a seasoned professional, staying current on books and publications in the field will enhance your research and may save you countless hours. Let's say you have an Italian ancestor who came through the Port of New York about 1889. You visit a repository that has microfilm copies of passenger arrival lists for that port. To your horror, you discover that indexes are available for 1820–1846 and 1897–1902. What happened to the years between 1846 and 1897? There's no index; and there are about eight to ten rolls of microfilm for each year during that gap. It would take weeks to go through all those rolls of names of passengers. You're not even sure it was 1889 when your ancestor came; it could have been the year before or the year after. Now what? If you are doing your reading and keeping current on what's been recently published, you would discover a series of books published by Scholarly Resources called *Italians to America: Lists of Passengers Arriving at U.S. Ports, 1880–1899,* covering the time period when your ancestor arrived. Although indexes are never perfect—omissions and misspellings occur—any index is better than none.

Let's look at the different types of books and journals that are available and how they will help your research, then I'll show you how to find these items. Chapter 7 will go into more detail on the research repositories that house many of these books and journals.

GENEALOGIES AND FAMILY HISTORIES

Before you begin your research, you should check to see if anyone has already written a genealogy and family history. One of your genealogy "cousins," who is related to you by a common ancestor in the tenth generation, may have compiled and published a genealogy. Though this book may not extend the descendants down to you or your parents' or grandparents' generations, it may help you make a connection with another generation. If a published genealogy exists, this may save you countless hours of research. Or it could *create* countless hours of research if you discover the genealogy has flaws or is not documented. The challenge is in finding whether a history of your family is out there and how to obtain or look at a copy. Three main finding aids exist to make this search easier:

1. When someone researches and compiles a genealogy, the most likely place to assure widespread availability is to donate a copy to the Family History Library in Salt Lake City, Utah (discussed in Chapter 7). The Family History Library catalogs by several different categories: one is by surname. The catalog is on computer CD-ROM, so it is as easy as typing in the last name of your ancestor. On the screen will appear a list of books that focus specifically on a surname as well as books that may contain your family as an "allied" branch. If the book is on microfilm, you may rent the film through your local Family History Center; if not, you will need to go to Salt Lake to look at the book or engage a researcher to look for you.

2. Another tool for determining if someone has written a genealogy on your family is a set of volumes called *Genealogy and Local History Books in Print,* which is now in its fifth edition and available at most libraries with genealogical collections or for purchase (see book dealers in the Appendix). Besides listing genealogies, *Books in Print* also lists general genealogical reference books and research sources by locality. A surname index makes it easy to check for your ancestors' names. Each listing gives a brief description of the publication, the price, and a vendor cross-reference number so that you may order a copy. Keep in mind that if the book is out of print, it won't be listed. So Great-Great Aunt Tilda could have written the family history, made a limited number of copies, and the only copy available is the one that was donated to

the Family History Library, or to another repository, or is in the trunk in a cousin's attic. Another problem with *Books in Print* is that the vendor or author must pay to have a work listed. When I wrote *The Ebetino and Vallarelli Family History,* I did not think it would be worth the publisher's fee to list it in *Books in Print,* so it's not listed.

3. Theoretically, once someone has written a genealogy book, the author should register it with the Library of Congress Copyright Office. To register, a writer must send two copies of the work with the application and fee. Once the copyright is approved, the book is donated to the Library's genealogical section. Marion J. Kaminkow's *Genealogies in the Library of Congress: A Bibliography* (two volumes, and two supplements) and *A Complement to Genealogies in the Library of Congress* help locate family histories that have secured a copyright, as well as copies that were donated to the Library of Congress. (Since I obtained a copyright on my Ebetino and Vallarelli book in 1990, it is listed in the latter volume.) These reference books are usually found among genealogical collections in libraries.

Just because you don't find a reference to your surname in any of the finding aids I've mentioned here does not mean that no written family history exists. A lot of books that are not in the Family History Library may be deposited in other genealogical libraries. If an author did not donate a copy to the Family History Library, did not pay the fee to be included in *Books in Print,* and did not file for a copyright, then the work won't appear in any of these sources. But many authors who go to the trouble of compiling and publishing a family history make it available through at least one of these avenues. Another way to check is to put a query in magazines like *Everton's Genealogical Helper* and *Heritage Quest* (see Chapter 3), asking if anyone is aware of a published family history on one of your surnames.

Once you find a copy of a compiled genealogy, you need to evaluate whether its information is reliable and accurate. Remember the old adage, "Just because it's in print doesn't make it true." Look for reviews of the genealogy in respected journals and newsletters (discussed in more detail below), like the *National Genealogical Society Quarterly, The American Genealogist,* and the Federation of Genealogical Societies' *Forum.* Reviews usually appear within a year or two of publication and give insights into the work's strengths and weaknesses.

Also, fact-check some of the author's sources. Are you able to find a document based on the footnotes or endnotes? Reputable genealogists always include references so other researchers can acquire the documents themselves. If you have trouble locating a document from a reference, the author was not careful and did not subscribe to the standards established by genealogical professionals and scholars.

When you do obtain a copy of a cited record, do you analyze it and come to the same conclusion as the author? Some records give what we call "direct evidence": John is the son of Samuel. Other records may be vague and difficult to decipher and may need interpretation. Historical documents that are handwritten may be especially prone to different interpretations. Do you read the handwriting and interpret the contents as the author did, or do you transcribe some words differently? (For more on the reading and interpreting of documents, see Chapter 9.)

Here are some other considerations when you locate a published genealogy and family history:

- Both good and bad genealogies exist.

- Evaluate what you find. A bad genealogy perpetuates errors.

- Try to locate all reviews written about the book.

- Look at the author's sources. Is there a heavy reliance on other published sources, or did the author do original research, citing historical documents such as wills, deeds, censuses, and vital records?

- Check the author's facts.

- Only you know where your genealogical research begins. Is it where the book leaves off?

- Does the published genealogy list information that conflicts with what you have learned about your family from other sources?

- Do the dates make sense? For example, a woman born in 1870 can't give birth in 1875. A man born in 1742 won't be getting married in 1753.

Finding published genealogies on your family is a starting point, not the end of your research. Even if the book is well documented and you are satisfied that the lineages covered are sound, no family history is all-comprehensive. There are always other surnames to pursue that are not covered in this particular book.

RECORD TRANSCRIPTS, ABSTRACTS, AND INDEXES

While another rule of genealogy is always to try to look at the original record, a book of published record transcripts (a word-for-word copy of a record) or abstracts (a summary of the essential facts in a document) can save you lots of research time, especially if you aren't sure in which county an ancestor settled. Let's say the genealogical library you're visiting has a good collection of Virginia books. According to family stories, your ancestor, Jacob Monroe, died in Tazewell County, Virginia, on 30 November 1890. There are published death records for that county, but you can't find him listed. You decide to check to see if neighboring Russell County has any published records since oral history has said that some family members lived in that county, too. Russell County's death records have been abstracted. Checking the index, you find a Jacob Monroe who died on the same day as your ancestor but in Russell County. His parents' names are included, and they match what you've been told. You hit pay dirt—and in just a few minutes.

Genealogical societies and individuals adopt projects to transcribe, abstract, or index a group of records found in a courthouse or other repository—such as land deeds, wills and probates, or vital records—giving reference information so that a copy of the original can be ordered by mail. Sometimes these are referred to as "compiled records." The society or individual generally privately publishes the results, then donates or sells copies to other genealogists and libraries. This saves researchers from personally visiting the repository. For example, the late George H. S. King abstracted many Virginia records, then privately published them. One of his books is *King George County, Virginia, Will Book A-I, 1721–1752*. Here is an example from it:

> UNDERWOOD, JOHN [SENIOR] (d.t., 1723). COB#1, p. 109:
> 5 April 1723=The last will and Testament of John Underwood, deceased, was presented into court by Elizabeth Underwood, his widow and executrix, and she gave bond as his executrix with William Underwood and Francis Jett, her securities. She promptly returned his inventory to court and it remains of record in I#1, pages 28–30.

Turning to the beginning of the book, you can learn what all of the abbreviations mean:

d.t.	died testate (leaving a will)
COB#	Court Order Books by number
I#	Inventory Books by number

Thus, if you wanted to obtain a copy of this document, either by mail or in person, you would look in Court Order Book #1 on page 109 for John Underwood's will being presented into court, and in Inventory Book #1 on pages 28–30 for the inventory of his estate.

Cemeteries are a popular transcribing project for many genealogical societies and for some individuals, and one you may want to consider in the future. A few years ago, I transcribed five rural eastern Colorado cemeteries. After I completed my project, I privately published 100 copies (meaning I took the original manuscript to a quick-print shop and had them photocopy and bind it). Most of the books I sold to local people who had relatives buried in one or several of the cemeteries; the rest I donated to libraries across the country. It feels good to know that now someone living in or visiting the Washington, D.C., area, who has roots in Elbert or El Paso County, Colorado, can visit the Daughters of the American Revolution Library and find out what an ancestor's tombstone has carved on it.

Be cautious of published transcripts or abstracts, however. As I mentioned earlier, errors and omissions may occur, especially if the person doing the transcribing or abstracting of a historical document has trouble reading the handwriting. What looks like an *R* could really be a fancy *P* with an extra flourish of the pen. Just because you don't find your ancestor in one of these published aids doesn't mean the person was not really in the records. Even the most reputable genealogists make mistakes. This is one reason to check the original document yourself. Another reason is that you may interpret the record differently since you have family knowledge on your side. A transcriber may record a name found in a document as "Henry," but you know that it's "Harry."

Another problem with compiled records, which is not as common in the last few years as it once was, is the tendency for the compiler to alphabetize the records, supposedly for convenience and to avoid making an index. At first glance this would seem to make the transcripts or abstracts easier to search, but you end up losing a sense of what was happening at the time your ancestor's will was recorded or when she was buried. Many of the tombstones around your ancestor's may be those of relatives. If the compiler arranged all the tombstone inscriptions in alphabetical order, then you will miss that an in-law with a different surname was buried right next to your ancestor. People don't live, die, or create records in alphabetical order; they shouldn't be listed in a published abstract that way either.

Indexes to published and original records may be found in book form. Many early genealogies and county histories did not originally include an index, so individuals, societies, and indexing firms take on the project of indexing these works as well as original record groups, such as censuses. Always use indexes with caution. Errors and omissions happen. If the indexer is working with an original handwritten document, there is also the likelihood of misreading someone's handwriting. In script, a *T* could be mistaken for an *F*, sometimes a *P* will look like an *R*, or an *L* like an *S*. Other commonly confused letters are *J*, *G*, and *Y*; *K* and *R*; *U* and *W*; *I* and *J*; *O* and *Q*. Inks also fade, making handwriting difficult to read. Sometimes, as is the case with census indexes, two or more companies may have indexed the same group of records. Make sure you check both.

Most compiled records—transcripts, abstracts, and indexes—are donated to the Family History Library in Salt Lake or other major repositories. Copies may also be found in the library or repository of the locality to which the records pertain since these are helpful to staff members who answer mail requests.

GUIDES TO RECORDS

Some groups of records are fairly comprehensive, so there are guidebooks that will tell you where the records may be located, what kind of information you can expect to get from the records, how to use the records, whether there is an index, any pitfalls of using the records, and usually examples of what the records look like. One such guidebook is to federal records stored in the National Archives in Washington. *Guide to Genealogical Research in the National Archives* details commonly used documents like censuses, passenger lists, naturalization records, military and pension records, and federal land and court records. Another popular work is *The Source: A Guidebook of American Genealogy*, revised edition. As mentioned in the previous chapter, this book covers many different types of records in great detail. Two other examples of record guidebooks are John Philip Colletta's *They Came in Ships*, which details passenger lists, and James C. Neagles's *U.S. Military Records*.

GUIDES TO LOCALITIES

Some professional researchers who live and specialize in certain localities have written guidebooks to help other genealogists. These authors have worked with the records and know their strengths and weaknesses. They also discuss types of records that may be unique to the area. Here are some examples of guides to localities: *Genealogical Resources in the New York Metropolitan Area,* edited by Estelle M. Guzik (New York: Jewish Genealogical Society, 1989); *Kentucky Ancestry: A Guide to Genealogical and Historical Research,* by Roseann Hogan (Salt Lake City: Ancestry Publishing, 1992); *Chicago and Cook County: A Guide to Research,* by Loretto Dennis Szucs (Salt Lake City: Ancestry Publishing, 1995); and *Research in Indiana,* by John D. Beatty (Arlington, Va.: National Genealogical Society Special Publication, 1992).

There are two guides to localities that give a genealogical account of counties and what records are held in which courts: the *Handy Book for Genealogists* and *Ancestry's Red Book*. The *Handy Book,* as it is called in the field, is arranged by state, along with a county map of each state. The entries are alphabetical by county, giving the date the county was created, the "parent" county from which it was formed, and the county seat. It also cites in which court records are held. Here's an abbreviated example:

> Ohio, Miami Co., created 1807 from Montgomery Co.
> County Seat: Troy.
> Clerk of Courts has divorce and civil court records from 1807;
> Probate Judge has marriage, death, and probate records, County
> Health has birth records.

The *Handy Book* also gives a historical overview of each state and briefly discusses major research repositories and their holdings.

The *Red Book* is similar in content, but the arrangement of county details is slightly different. The historical overview of the states is slightly more in-depth, as are the resources and repositories for each state. The same entry for Miami County, Ohio, lists everything the *Handy Book* does, plus more specific dates of records:

birth records from 1853	land records from 1807
marriage records from 1807	probate records from 1807
death records from 1867	court records from 1807

Both books also give the address of the county courthouse.

Why are these books so important to genealogists? As you will learn in Chapter 7, many of the records you will be looking for on an ancestor are held at a county courthouse or have been consolidated at a state archive. It is important for you to know not only what records they have and when those records began, but whether you are searching in the right county. Suppose your ancestor lived in Miami County, Ohio, since 1800. He married, supposedly, in that county in 1802. The problem is that Miami County didn't exist until 1807. Where do you go to find the marriage record of your ancestor prior to this creation date? You go to the "parent county" from which Miami was formed: Montgomery. That's where the marriage record is likely to be filed.

Sometimes a county was formed from more than one parent county, or it was originally part of another state or territory. This is the value of the *Handy Book* and the *Red Book*. Each will tell you exactly where you need to look for your ancestors' records at a given time period.

GUIDES TO RESEARCH REPOSITORIES

Quite a few research repositories have published guidebooks that tell you not only about their collection of historical records and books, but also the hours of operation and whether records may be accessed by mail or through interlibrary loan. Examples of these aids are *The Immigration History Research Center: A Guide to Collections*, by Suzanna Moody and Joel Wurl (New York: Greenwood Press, 1991); *The Archives: A Guide to the National Archives Field Branches*, and *The Library of Congress: A Guide to Genealogical and Historical Research* (both published by Ancestry Publishing). Before you embark on a research trip to a repository, check to see if a guidebook has been published. It will save you time when you get there.

GUIDES TO RESEARCHING FOREIGN ANCESTRY

When you are ready to bridge the ocean or cross the Canadian or Mexican borders, there are many guidebooks that will help you understand the records in a foreign country, as well as how accessible these documents are. If you are planning to visit the ancestral homeland to do research, these works will be invaluable to read and study. Some examples are Trafford Cole's *Italian Genealogical Records: How to Use Italian Civil, Ecclesiastical, and*

Other Records in Family History Research; Joy Wade Moulton's *Genealogical Resources in English Repositories;* and Maralyn A. Wellauer's *Tracing Your Czech and Slovak Roots.*

FINDING GUIDEBOOKS

How do you learn if one of these wonderful guidebooks exists for the area or topic of your research, and where can you find it? Along with checking library catalogs, you need to get on the mailing lists of genealogical book vendors. Their addresses are listed in the Appendix. Even if you don't plan to buy a book, you will know that one is out there, so you can check the library shelves.

LOCAL AND COUNTY HISTORIES

Around the time of our nation's centennial in 1876 and its bicentennial in 1976, many towns, cities, and counties published histories of their areas. These are excellent sources to get a feel for the life and times of an area during certain periods of history. Many local and county histories cover the geographic look and climate of the area, the first settlers, why the area was founded, who served in major wars and battles, how the area grew and changed, who its elected officials were, maps, names and founders of churches, names and locations of cemeteries, and historic photographs of buildings and people.

Some also contain biographical or genealogical sketches of the area's first settlers and/or contemporary residents. For a fee, descendants could submit a short narrative and, sometimes, photographs of themselves or their ancestors. This is one way the history book was funded for publication. This is also the reason genealogists have come to know local and county histories as "mug books." Little or no research went into these biographies and genealogies; they contained what the family knew about its ancestry from family traditions. Naturally, if you felt that Great-Great-Grandpa's being a chicken thief was a skeleton in your closet, you didn't mention that in his biography. Some people made themselves look as prosperous and virtuous as possible. There may be mistakes in parental names of early settlers as well.

The best use for local and county histories is for the historical context and setting in which your ancestors lived. Any personal information on your family should be used with caution and supported with historical documents.

To find if a county history exists, write to the county historical society. They may still have copies for sale. Along with checking catalogs and library holdings, look at P. William Filby's *A Bibliography of American County Histories.* This book is arranged by state, listing about 5,000 county histories.

ATLASES, MAPS, AND GAZETTEERS

Your ancestors may have originated from some tiny little town in America or another country that you have never even heard of. Checking atlases, maps, and gazetteers will help you locate the area. Many historical atlases and maps are available in libraries, archives, and county courthouses; some have been reproduced and are available for sale. There are many different kinds of maps. County road maps, for example, may mark all the cemeteries in the area. Plat maps in the county courthouse break down the area by sections and list who owns the property.

A gazetteer is a dictionary of places. The great advantage of a world gazetteer is that you don't even need to know the state or country to find even the smallest towns. Suppose you find a letter written by your Great-Uncle Murray, saying he is going to visit his sister in Fountain Green, but because he knows where Fountain Green is and so does the person to whom he's writing, he doesn't need to mention the state in his letter. A gazetteer is your next stop. More than likely, you'll find the *Columbia-Lippincott Gazetteer of the World* in your local library's reference section. It's alphabetically arranged, so you can quickly turn to Fountain Green. You discover that there is only one town in the world by that name—in Sanpete County in central Utah, twelve miles southeast of Nephi. The population when the gazetteer was published (1952) was 767 and the major industry was wool. For a town or city no longer in existence, you would want to check earlier editions, like the one published in 1905. Though not considered a gazetteer, *Bullinger's Postal and Shippers Guide for the United States and Canada,* first published in 1897, also lists towns in alphabetical order.

PERIODICALS AND INDEXES

Believe it or not, there are more than 5,000 genealogical journals and newsletters currently in publication. Naturally, I do not expect you to read them all, but you should be familiar with the major ones. These national periodicals will keep you informed on new books in the field, research methodology and standards, as well as newly published genealogies and family histories. Subscription addresses are included in the Appendix, or you can read these magazines at the library. Most libraries with genealogical sections subscribe to the major journals.

THE MAJOR GENEALOGICAL JOURNALS

The American Genealogist

This privately owned quarterly journal, known as *TAG,* was established in 1922 and has a readership of about 1,700. Its emphasis is mainly the colonial period in New England, the Mid-Atlantic, and the South. *TAG* publishes short compiled genealogies, careful discussions of difficult research problems, and book reviews.

Genealogical Journal

Published quarterly by the Utah Genealogical Association, this publication began in 1971 and has a circulation of approximately 900. It has a worldwide emphasis, publishing articles concerning research techniques and procedures, descriptions of genealogical collections and records, professionalism, and book reviews.

The Genealogist

The Genealogist was started in 1979 and is published by the American Society of Genealogists. It has a circulation of about 500 and is distributed twice a year. This journal publishes single-family studies and compiled genealogies, single-line descents, and articles that demonstrate a technique for solving common research problems. *The Genealogist* also publishes genealogies that are too long for other journals.

National Genealogical Society Quarterly

Published quarterly by the National Genealogical Society, *NGSQ* was established in 1912 and has a readership of about 15,000. This journal's primary emphasis is on essays that include methodological case studies, discussions of major resources, compiled genealogies, and guides to research in specific states. Secondarily, it publishes abstracts of unusual records that cover a broad geographical area. It also prints book reviews.

New England Historical and Genealogical Register

Known as *The Register* and published quarterly by the New England Historic Genealogical Society, this publication began in 1847. It has a circulation of about 14,000. The journal's emphasis is on English or European origins of New England immigrants, the first five generations of New England families, historical background essays, and source records for New England genealogy, and it includes book reviews and library acquisitions.

The New York Genealogical and Biographical Record

The Record is published quarterly by the New York Genealogical and Biographical Society and has a readership of about 2,000. It was established in 1870. This journal prints compiled genealogies and source records from New York State, primarily the sections settled before the American Revolution (Hudson Valley, New York City, Long Island), and material on northern New Jersey and western Connecticut. It also publishes book reviews, queries, and library acquisitions.

The Virginia Genealogist

Privately owned, *The Virginia Genealogist* was established in 1957, has a circulation of about 1,000, and is published quarterly. Emphasis is on Virginia and West Virginia, mostly pre-1850 subjects. The journal includes articles, compiled genealogies, abstracts of source material, and book reviews.

Western Maryland Genealogy

This quarterly journal began in 1985, is privately published, and has a circulation of about 700. It contains original source records, genealogies, book reviews, and queries relating to the Maryland counties of Frederick, Washington, Montgomery, Allegany, Garrett, and part of Carroll, and the District of Columbia.

THE MAJOR GENEALOGICAL NEWSLETTERS

Federation of Genealogical Societies Forum

This quarterly newsletter is published by the Federation of Genealogical Societies and has a circulation of about 5,000. It publishes a variety of material: articles on methods and sources, current record access information, news from society publications and announcements, ethnic news, an international calendar, and information on repositories and collections. Regular columns include book reviews, "The Editor's Craft," family associations, and ethnic/international news items.

National Genealogical Society Newsletter and the *NGS/CIG Digest*

The *NGS Newsletter* is published bimonthly by the National Genealogical Society and was established in 1975. It prints news of the society, news and articles of interest to a diverse national membership, queries, and library acquisitions. The *NGS/Computer Interest Group Digest* is a 16-page insert of the *NGS Newsletter.* Articles include all aspects of genealogical computing, from buying computers and peripherals to reviewing software, as well as information on the Internet and World Wide Web.

GENEALOGICAL MAGAZINES

Unlike genealogical journals that publish articles of a more scholarly nature, genealogical magazines offer the types of articles you would expect to find in a trade publication. The articles are more general in nature, dealing with topics like "how to research your Scandinavian ancestry in 10 easy steps," "here's a source and how to use it," and so on. Journals, as you read above, publish compiled genealogies, record abstracts, and case studies. There are several genealogical magazines on the market; the ones discussed here, however, are the most widely read.

Ancestry

Ancestry magazine is published bimonthly by Ancestry Incorporated and has a circulation of 11,000. It contains articles by many of the professionals in the field. The magazine has regular columns about ethnic origins, library sources, and computer technology. Other articles are more general in nature. Here's a sample of a few published in 1996: "Historic Photography: Identification and Preservation," "Living Histories," "Trail of Tombstones," and "Harvesting Rural Research."

Genealogical Computing

This quarterly magazine/newsletter is published by Ancestry Incorporated. It contains articles and news items pertinent to all aspects of genealogical computing, from software to online information sources to computer hardware. The July/August/September 1996 issue published an excellent resource called the "1996 Directory of Genealogy Software." It covered such software programs as lineage-linked databases, report/chart-making, biography and history writing, graphics, indexing, research tools, and add-on utilities, giving the ordering information, specification, data handling, output, utilities, and a reference as to when it was reviewed in *Genealogical Computing.*

Everton's Genealogical Helper

Everton's Genealogical Helper, more commonly known as *The Helper,* is published six times a year and is the most widely read genealogical magazine, with a circulation of about 46,000. It contains a few feature articles but is mostly comprised of advertisements: people looking for other people with the same ancestry (queries), professionals seeking clients, people announcing new books and publications, people seeking out-of-print books, and family association announcements. The magazine has many useful columns: "Question and Answer Box" is where subscribers may submit genealogical questions to be answered; in "Free Help" you may find someone who has picked up a family bible at a garage sale and is offering it to descendants; the "New Periodical Publications" will let you know if a genealogical society or family association is now printing a newsletter or journal; and there are genealogy book notices and software reviews. *The Helper* also publishes different directories each year. The January–February issue includes a directory of locality periodicals; the March–April directory is of family organizations and surname periodicals; the May–June issue publishes a directory of genealogical libraries; in July-August, the directory covers genealogical societies; and in September–October, the directory is of professional genealogical researchers.

Heritage Quest

Heritage Quest, published six times a year, is similar to *The Helper* in that it prints queries; the difference is that *HQ* publishes mostly articles. These articles deal with a wide range of topics. Issues contain feature articles, questions answered, records and resources, genealogy in foreign countries, adoption research, and a computer corner. These are some sample article titles: "Family Historians Must Have a Goal in Mind," "County Histories as a Resource," "A Passage in Time: The Ships That Brought Our Ancestors to America," "Research in the Former Austro-Hungarian Empire," "British Periodicals: An Often Untapped Source for Family History Help," and "Genealogically Valuable Records of the Cherokee Removal of 1838."

Reunions Magazine

Reunions Magazine has a readership of 18,000 and is published quarterly. Its format is different from the other genealogical magazines, since its main focus is not genealogy but reunions of all types: family, military, school, birth parents/adoptees, and anything else you can think of. They also publish articles on genealogical topics. Regular columns include "Branch Office" (a genealogical column), "RSVP" (about family reunions), "Alum and I" (about class reunions), "Origins" (covering adoption reunions), and "Searching?" (which deals with military reunions). Some sample articles from 1996 were "Reunion Technology," "Catering Reunions," "Holding a Cemetery Reunion," "Atlanta Rich in African-American History," and "One-Room School Reunions: Oak Grove School."

FINDING JOURNAL ARTICLES

All of these publications will be helpful to your research, but how do you find out if an article appeared—say, in the last year or twenty years ago—that pertains to your ancestry? How can you locate articles that include a discussion of a record type or research methodology in an area where your ancestors settled? How do you find reviews of books and software that you want to purchase? Thanks to the Allen County Public Library Foundation in Fort Wayne, Indiana, an index was developed to keep track of all the articles and book reviews published in more than 5,000 genealogical journals. The *Periodical Source Index,* known by genealogists as *PERSI,* covers genealogical periodicals from 1847 to present. Most genealogical libraries have *PERSI* in their collections.

There are five categories of topics in *PERSI,* so that you can search by a surname, a state, a county, or type of record (census, probate, land). The five categories are:

1. Places: United States

2. Places: Canadian

3. Places: Foreign

4. Families

5. Research Methodology

By checking all volumes of *PERSI* for a surname or locality, you can determine whether someone has already compiled a genealogy or information on your ancestry that was published in one of the many genealogical periodicals.

When you begin researching your genealogy, you will be inclined, as we all were, to read and look for articles about your own family only. While this is certainly beneficial, you will also find that reading case-study articles will enhance your research knowledge and skills. Though the family under discussion may hold no interest for you, the sources, methods, or way in which research was conducted could unlock a door in your own family history. For example, I was reading an article by Lloyd DeWitt Bockstruck in the October 1996 *The American Genealogist* titled "The Identity and English Origin of Elizabeth Felkin, Wife of Thomas Page of Saco, Maine." Neither my ancestry nor that of any of my clients contains a Felkin or Page surname, and none of my research interests deal with Maine. Within the article, however, Bockstruck discussed a record source he used dealing with tailors in London since Thomas Page was a tailor from London. Coincidentally, one of my client's ancestors was a tailor from London, too. I had no idea when I began reading the article that I would learn about a new source that would help with my client's research. You just never know. Read anything and everything you can. Even if it doesn't benefit you at this point in your research, later on you may think, "Hey, I remember reading an article about that a few years ago."

Some sample case-study articles published in the *National Genealogical Society Quarterly* are Elizabeth Shown Mills's "The Search for Margaret Ball: Building Steps over a Brick-wall Research Problem" and "In Search of 'Mr. Ball': An Exercise in Finding Fathers"; Marsha Hoffman Rising's "Problematic Parents and Potential Offspring: The Example of Nathan Brown"; and Richard Pence's "Which Jacob Pence? A Case Study Documenting Identity." All the major journals—*NGSQ, TAG, The Genealogist, The Register, The Record*—publish case studies. If the study was conducted in a geographic area where your ancestors lived, you can learn about the sources in that locality by reading the article and studying the source citations.

Another reason to use *PERSI* and to read these journals is for the book reviews. As mentioned at the beginning of this chapter, new books are made available in genealogy all the time. To learn about these books' strengths and weakness, read the reviews. Reviews are written by colleagues who have knowledge in the subject area. Review editors expect objective, critical reviews. Be aware, too, that there is a difference between book *reviews* and book *notices* or *summaries*. The major journals print book reviews; *Everton's Genealogical Helper* prints book notices and summaries, not critical essays.

As you can see, there's good reason genealogists like Jim and Paula Warren set aside days to read genealogical and other periodicals. There's a lot of information out there, and you never know what piece of data will open the door to your research problems.

STARTING A HOME GENEALOGICAL LIBRARY

I have yet to meet a genealogist who does not love books. Karen Green, owner of Frontier Press, became a book vendor because she loves books. When you attend a genealogical conference, the book-vending tables are always the most crowded. And some genealogy books are not inexpensive. While many are in the $10 to $25 range, most of the major guidebooks like *The Source: A Guidebook of American Genealogy* run about $40 to $50. The most expensive book I've bought was $75. Naturally, I did not run out and buy all of my books at once. My collection has been growing for several years. I put some titles on my Christmas wish lists, pilfered $5 a week from the grocery money, worked at odd jobs, and started doing research for paying clients to finance my book purchases. (I told you it was addicting.)

There are some basic books that line just about every genealogist's shelves. You may want to consider purchasing these. Granted, you can find almost all of these books at your local genealogical library or Family History Center; but like most genealogists, you'll find that it's far more convenient to have them in your home so that you can study them in your favorite chair, with your cat on your lap, while you sip hot chocolate.

The basic books you'll want to consider owning are listed in the Bibliography, so I'll only list the authors and titles here.

- One or two basic how-to books as discussed in Chapter 4

- Greenwood's *The Researcher's Guide to American Genealogy*

- Either Eichholz's *Ancestry's Red Book*, or Everton's *Handy Book for Genealogists*

- Szucs and Luebking's *The Source: A Guidebook of American Genealogy*

- Either Kemp's *International Vital Records Handbook* or the U.S. Government's *Where to Write for Vital Records*

- Rubincam's *Pitfalls in Genealogical Research*

- Stevenson's *Genealogical Evidence*

- Either Bentley's *The Genealogist's Address Book* or Smith's *Ancestry's Address Book*

- *Guide to Genealogical Research in the National Archives*

- Either Kirkham's *The Handwriting of American Records for a Period of 300 Years* or Stryker-Rodda's *Understanding Colonial Handwriting*

Don't expect your favorite bookstore to stock many of these titles. A few may be there, or you may be able to special-order some of them, but the best way to get these books is through a genealogical book vendor. In the Appendix under Genealogical Books and Supplies, I've listed several book dealers; others have smaller offerings. Drop each a postcard, fax, e-mail, or whatever, and get on their mailing lists. Then you can begin your genealogical book wish list. I tack mine up on the bulletin board in my office, along with the price and vendor's name, and cross off the books as I order them.

You'll also want to buy other books that pertain to your research specialty. For instance, if you have African American ancestry, you'll want to get a guidebook or two that focus on that ethnic group. If you have a lot of ancestors who lived in Ohio, you'll want to buy reference books covering this area.

When I began researching my family history, I was interested primarily in my mother's Fitzhugh line of Virginia. I acquired county histories, a general history book on Virginia, a few books that described researching and the availability of records in that state, a couple of compiled genealogies that included the Fitzhugh and allied lines, and some published record transcripts for the counties in which many of my ancestors settled.

Then my interest took a turn to my Italian families, and now my biggest collection of books reflects this. Not only do I have every guidebook written on Italian ancestry (there are only half a dozen), but I also have Italian American social histories, cookbooks, travel guidebooks on Italy, histories on other Italian families, as well as books on immigrants in general.

Now my interest is women's history: time to buy a new bookshelf.

If you decide to invest in books, you should consider some kind of cataloging for insurance purposes. Do this as your library begins to grow—not when your collection has reached one hundred books or more. Most of my books are cataloged on three-by-five-inch cards that are kept in a card-file box. But if my house burns down, the cards will go with it. It would be better to create a database or purchase a computer program that will help you make an inventory of your books and other office equipment. Keep a backup diskette of the data in a location other than your home. (This would be wise, too, for your genealogical computer files.)

An advantage of being on the mailing lists of book vendors is that you can see what source books and record transcripts are available for your ancestor's locality. Though you may not purchase these books, you can add them to your research plan and look for them on your next research trip. Before you buy any book, especially an expensive one, it's a good idea to read the reviews of it first. These will tell you the volume's strengths and weaknesses.

USED-BOOK STORES

On occasion you will find genealogy books in used-book stores. This is also a good place to look for the basic how-to guides. The problem is that genealogists tend to hold onto their books, so the chances may be slim that you'll find most of the books you're looking for in used-book stores. When genealogists die, their books may end up anywhere if they have not made provisions for them in their wills: at a yard sale, in a secondhand book store, or donated to a library.

The type of books I have found in these stores that are especially helpful to my research are social histories. Social histories tell about the everyday person in everyday life throughout history. You will be more apt to find books like Earle's *Home Life in Colonial Days,* Mintz and Kellogg's *Domestic Revolutions: A Social History of American Family Life,* and others that I've listed in the Bibliography. Used-book stores are also good places to find ethnic, religious, occupational, and other types of social histories.

Now that you know what kinds of books and journals are available, it's time to start planning your research trip.

Chapter 6

Preparing for a Research Trip

Once you've learned as much as you can from oral interviews, home sources, and books that are available about your area of research, then you are ready to prepare for a research trip. Whether the research repository is across the street, across town, or across the country, you need to do some preparation before you walk in the door. Along with learning about the repositories' record holdings, there are other aspects to consider. For instance, there's nothing more frustrating than driving many miles to discover the courthouse is closed for three weeks to remove the asbestos in the ceiling, or the town clerk takes a two-hour lunch, or it's a state holiday. There's nothing more upsetting than driving many miles to discover you forgot your file folder on the one ancestor you had planned to research. And there is nothing more agonizing than driving many miles and then getting a headache right before you begin a day's worth of research.

The Boy Scouts' motto of always being prepared is also the genealogist's maxim. And, as my mother says, "It's better to have it and not need it, than to need it and not have it," which accounts for why I feel inclined to take two suitcases for a weekend trip, while my husband takes an overnight bag.

Before you plan any research trip, even if it's just to the local county courthouse, call to see what the hours are or if it will be closed for any special reason, like a holiday. Other questions to ask if you haven't been to that repository before are:

- Is there a photocopy machine for public use?

- How much do photocopies cost?

- Can I make change there, or should I bring dimes, quarters, and nickels?

- How much does it cost to obtain a copy of a [birth, death, marriage] record?

- Where is the nearest place to eat? to park?

- Is there access for the handicapped?

- Can researchers take in briefcases or must these be locked up?

- Are laptop computers allowed?

- Is there a particular person I need to see about looking at certain records?

- Does the office close for lunch?

- Are any records stored elsewhere, and how can I get access to them?

- Is there a pamphlet I can obtain outlining the repository's holdings?

WHAT TO TAKE WITH YOU

Although I try to keep my tote bag or briefcase stocked with necessities and ready to go, inevitably I take things out of it when at home and forget to put them back. So I have created, on an index card, a checklist of things to take with me. You may decide you don't need some of these items, and you will think of others to include. Obviously, you will need a tote bag or briefcase in which to carry these things:

- Research notebook with your pedigree charts, family group sheets, and research plan (discussed later).

- Abstract forms (discussed later).

- Research and/or correspondence logs.

- Sheet of pastel-colored (blue preferred) plain paper. When you are using microfilm readers that project down onto a white screen, placing a sheet of blue or other light-colored paper on the screen may cut the glare and make the image easier to read.

- Pens, pencils, and highlighters. A word of caution about highlighters: on certain types of photocopies, the highlighted portion will darken over time, becoming difficult to read and impossible to photocopy. It's better to use a red pencil or pen to underline important information.

- Note paper. Even if you plan to take notes using a laptop computer, you'll still need note paper on which to copy film numbers and make other notations.

- Magnifying glass.

- Change for the photocopier, unless there is a change machine or cashier.

- Pocket calculator. Unless you're a math whiz, it's quicker to use a calculator to figure when Grandma was born if she was thirteen in the 1910 census.

- A map of the local area.

- Tissues. There's nothing like getting musty paper dust in your sinuses and not having any tissues.

- Medications. Carry painkillers should you get a headache; bring sinus medicine if you're prone to dust allergies; take antacids in case you eat something at lunch that disagrees with you.

- Snacks. I don't know of a single library, courthouse, or research repository that will allow you to bring in food; however, you should take along a snack to eat outside. Researching requires a lot of mental activity, and you need to feed your brain.

THE RESEARCH PLAN

As I mentioned earlier, you need to know what kinds of records the repository contains so you'll know what to look for. You don't want to walk into a courthouse and ask for birth records when they are housed in the vital records office ten blocks away.

Another part of the planning is analyzing your family group sheets for the types of records you need. If you are a raw beginner, then you need everything and anything. If you have already begun doing some research, then make a research plan for each family group. Here's a sample from my workbook:

Research Plan for
James and Mollie (Montgomery) McMasters

- Look for them in 1910 and 1920 Dade County, Missouri, federal censuses.

- Write to the Dade County recorder's office for their marriage record.

- Order death certificates on both from Missouri Bureau of Vital Records.

- Look for Mollie with her parents in the 1900 Dade County, Missouri, federal census.

- Write to the probate clerk in Dade County to see if James left a will.

- Check for land records in the recorder's office.

By doing this analysis of what I've done and what records I still need to seek, I can pick up my notebook and know where I left off. This saves me time when I get to the research center: I know what records are housed there and what records I need. If I'm making a weeklong trip to the Family History Library in Salt Lake City, for example, and I run into a brick wall on one family, I know where to pick up research on another family by looking at my plan.

Between the documentation that accompanies your family group sheet and this research plan, you don't need to take along any extraneous material. It amazes me to see genealogists bringing several file boxes and binders, carried on a luggage dolly, to the library. What would happen if there was a fire? Do you think these people would put a higher priority on saving a life or on making sure those files got out safely?

There should be no reason for you to take along your file folders containing copies of records you've acquired. If you think you will need to refresh your memory about what was in a particular will, then make an abstract and put that in your workbook.

ABSTRACTING RECORDS

There are several different methods to obtain a record: photocopy it, copy it word-for-word either by hand or on your laptop computer, or abstract it. Photocopying is by far the quickest and best way to obtain a copy of a record, but it can get costly. There may be a dozen or more two-to-three-page land deeds recorded on your ancestor in the deed books. (Sometimes you'll wonder if your forebears did anything except buy and sell land and have babies—of course, there were no natural birth control devices then, such as TV and the Internet.) In some repositories, photocopying historical documents is prohibited. Rather than photocopying or typing verbatim, you may decide it's best to abstract the record. Abstracting means to leave out all the legal mumbo-jumbo and record only the important information about your ancestor and the event. Deeds and wills are the two most commonly abstracted documents.

In abstracting a deed, get these facts:

- the type of record (warranty deed, quitclaim deed, gift deed, etc.)

- the citation (book, page numbers)

- the name and location of the repository

- name of grantor/s (who's selling the land) and grantee/s (who's buying it)

- date of the deed and the date it was recorded

- the consideration (was it a gift, was it sold for $1, was it traded?)

- signatures or marks

- names of witnesses

- legal description of the property

- release of dower (where the wife relinquishes her rights to the property)

- date, place, and by whom the deed was acknowledged

- other pertinent information such as residences, occupations, relationships of all parties mentioned

In abstracting a will or probate, get these facts:

- type of record (will, inventory, intestate proceedings, etc.)

- the citation (book, page, or file numbers)

- the name and location of the repository

- name of the testator (person making the will)

- personal information ("of sound mind and weak body," desired burial, etc.)

- names and relationships (if given) of executors

- date the will was signed and when it was admitted for probate (which can narrow down a date of death)

- signature or mark of the testator

- names and residences of witnesses

- bequests (names and relationships, if given, and any other identifying information about the heirs, as well as what each person is to receive, including any land descriptions)

Some vendors and societies, such as the National Genealogical Society, sell abstracting forms that will prompt you on what information should be recorded. Many genealogists find the forms limiting, however, and prefer to do abstracting on their laptop or in their notebooks.

There are also extraction forms for censuses and passenger lists. These forms have essentially the same headings as the original records, so all you need to do is fill in the blanks with your ancestors' data. The Family History Library in Salt Lake, as well as many of the vendors listed in the Appendix, sell these forms.

PREPARING FOR A TRIP TO THE CEMETERY

Up to this point, I've discussed preparing for a trip to the conventional research repository—a building that houses historical documents. Now it's time to take a field trip to the cemetery, because that's where most of your ancestors are (unless they were cremated and had their ashes spread across the Himalayas).

There are many aspects to consider when researching in a cemetery. Don't just rush to find your ancestor's grave, photograph the tombstone, then leave. Look around you. This is your ancestor's final resting place. What does it look like? Take some pictures of the overall cemetery, of the gateway into the graveyard. What kind of cemetery is it? I bet you didn't know that there are at least eight different categories of cemeteries:

1. Church graveyards. These were our country's first cemeteries. In Europe, the elite were buried inside the church under the stone floor. In America, this wasn't feasible because the churches were so much smaller, so everyone was buried outside.

2. Family burial plots. These were on private property and may be difficult to locate today if the cemetery has not been maintained and is not well known among the community.

3. Country cemeteries. These are the ones you see as you drive down the highways of America. They often contain homemade or mail-order markers.

4. Elite garden cemeteries. The garden-type cemetery began in the early nineteenth century; Mount Auburn Cemetery in Cambridge, Massachusetts, was the first of its kind in 1831. These cemeteries are parklike, containing pathways, ponds, trees, foliage, and benches. Before we had public parks, this is where people went on Sunday afternoons to picnic, contemplate, make love, and take leisurely strolls.

5. Ordinary urban cemeteries. These might look like a "stone yard." They are just rows and rows of tombstones with straight paths and little foliage.

6. Veterans' cemeteries. These are for the honorably discharged and their families. In 1989 there were 110 around the country; Arlington Cemetery in Virginia is the most well known.

7. Memorial parks. These are flat, grassy lawns with barely any visible evidence that people are buried there. The tombstones are flat and flush with the ground, listing the name of the deceased and usually just a birth and death year. There's nothing to tell family relationships or to show personalities.

8. Potter's fields. This is where the county or city buries the poor, the unknown, or the unwanted.

Now let's look at the tombstone. What kind of stone is it? Though parts of the inscription may be weathered and unreadable (usually the dates, naturally), or it may have sunk into the ground so that you cannot read the death date, you can still get an idea of when the marker was placed by the composition of the stone.

- Before the 1650s, grave markers were uncarved, rough-cut boulders.

- From the 1660s to 1850s, tombstones were made from sedimentary rock such as sandstone or limestone.

- In the late 1700s through 1880s, marble became popular, but it is especially prone to weathering and dissolves easily in acid (acid rain is a real enemy to marble tombstones). In the 1930s the Works Progress Administration revived the use of marble for veterans' markers.

- From the 1880s to 1910s, soft, gray granite and cast-metal markers began to be used.

- From the 1920s to the present, granite is the most popular.

As on your trip to the library or courthouse, you need to be prepared and to bring along your "cemetery tools." I have a separate tote bag for such excursions; in case I need to make an emergency trip to the graveyard, I'm ready to go. Here are the items you'll want to take along:

GENERAL ITEMS

- notebook and pens or pencils

- carpenter's apron (these have multiple pockets in which to put your equipment as you move from tombstone to tombstone)

- gardener's knee pads (you'll be getting down and dirty to clear away overgrown weeds and grass that hamper reading the inscription)

- garden shears (to trim away the weeds and grass)

- whisk broom (to remove the trimmed weeds and grass and some of the dirt from the base of the stone)

- sunscreen

- bug repellent

- wet wipes

- lunch

TO MAKE PHOTOGRAPHS

- camera and film

- sprayer with water

- plastic or nylon brush (never wire)

- rags

- jumbo sidewalk chalk

Before you take a photograph of the stone, it may need some light cleaning. Lichen and moss love to attach themselves to tombstones and birds find them irresistible to poop on, making the inscription harder to read and photograph. Spray the stone with water only, lightly use a nylon or plastic brush to loosen the debris, then gently rub with a rag. Keep in mind that tombstones are historical artifacts; some have been around since the 1600s. Just because it is made from stone doesn't mean it's durable. Some stones may already be crumbling, in which case, *do not do anything to the stone.* Acid-based compounds, like vinegar, can eat away marble. Many genealogists, myself included, used to use shaving cream to clean the stone and to bring out the image, but gravestone preservationists caution that shaving cream has a low pH, which means it is acidic. It's better not to use anything but water to clean the stone.

Photographs turn out better if you take them in early morning light. In many cemeteries, graves lie on an east-west axis with some inscriptions on the west side of the stone. If you wait until late afternoon to take a picture, you'll cast a shadow over the stone. Although I've yet to try it, I'm told a mirror's reflection will help light up the stone for a better photograph. Simply wetting the stone with water may bring out the inscription. Chalk is another method; either white or colored sidewalk chalk from your local department or toy store works well. Rub the chalk over the stone and then smear it in with your hands. It will fill in the crevices and sometimes make an unreadable, weathered stone readable enough for you to photograph it and copy the inscription in your notes.

Even if you are photographing the tombstones, it's a wise idea to also make a written record of the inscription. Sometimes the photo doesn't turn out, or worse, as a friend of mine discovered after getting home, there was no film in the camera!

TO MAKE TOMBSTONE RUBBINGS

- rubbing wax (see Appendix under Genealogical Books and Supplies for places to order)
- jumbo crayons
- scissors
- masking tape or a partner.
- nonfusible interfacing (Pellon is one brand name)

Remember when you were in kindergarten and you put a leaf or penny under a piece of paper, then rubbed a crayon on top of the paper? An image of the leaf or penny magically appeared on the sheet. A tombstone rubbing uses the same idea. Many people use large sheets of butcher paper to make rubbings. Kathleen Hinckley, a colleague in Denver, told me she uses interfacing fabric, and I think it works better than paper. If you're traveling, paper is harder to manage, and it tears and creases. Interfacing can be folded in your suitcase, it doesn't tear, and you can iron it when you get home.

Interfacing is inexpensive (about $1.25 a yard) and may be purchased at any fabric store (it's the stuff seamstresses use to make collars stiff). I use the medium to heavy weight type that is nonfusible. (Fusible interfacing has little glue pellets that melt when you iron the interfacing to a piece of fabric instead of sewing it in.) I buy interfacing in bulk, about ten yards at a time, to keep in my cemetery tote bag. If you take anyone with you to the cemetery, especially kids, they'll want to try making a rubbing, too, because it's so much fun.

Here's how it's done. Cut off a piece of interfacing a bit larger than the stone you want to rub. Either use masking tape to attach the interfacing to the stone or have a companion hold the fabric tightly around the stone. Using either jumbo crayons with the paper peeled off (give that job to a toddler, and it'll be done in half the time it'll take you) or special rubbing wax, rub the side of the crayon (not the tip) over the fabric and watch the image appear. If the fabric shifts, the image will be distorted, so it's important to keep the material taut.

When you get the rubbing home, put an old towel over it on an iron-ing board. With a hot iron, press down on the towel rather than using a back-and-forth motion. This will heat the rubbing beneath it and set the crayon or wax into the fabric. Always put a towel between the rubbing and your iron. And never put the rubbing face down on the ironing board cover and melt it with the iron that way. (My husband did not appreciate having the image of a winged death head on the back of his Air Force regulation blue shirt.)

Tombstone rubbings make great gifts for family members and can be displayed in your home. They become as much a family artifact to hand down as needlework and silver. Though she is not our ancestor, we have Lizzie Borden's tombstone rubbing framed and hanging in our living room. It's quite a conversation piece.

A WORD OF GRAVE CAUTION

Most graveyard preservationists today do not advocate cleaning, chalking, or making rubbings of any tombstones. They say that chalk (used to bring out the image as described earlier) can stain some stones. You *must* be able to distinguish between a stable and unstable grave marker before you attempt to chalk, make a rubbing, or gently clean away any debris. When in doubt, *don't*. I realize I'm sending you mixed messages here, but if you decide to undertake any of the methods I've described, you must take great care. As with historical documents, tombstones are artifacts that must be treated with respect and care. We do not want to do anything that will damage the stone or deprive future generations from enjoying and appreciating a cemetery as much as we do.

TIPS FOR CEMETERY RESEARCH

The best time of year to make a field trip to the cemetery is early spring. The weeds shouldn't be overgrown yet, and the snow and winter rain may have cleaned off the tombstones. And the snakes probably haven't come out of hibernation yet. Cemeteries are wonderful places to get chiggers, ticks, bug bites, and poison ivy rashes, so wear protective clothing and boots, and bring some bug repellent.

Watch for uneven ground; graves tend to sink. When my daughter was three or four, we went cemetery-hopping. Laurie was walking behind me, when all of a sudden I heard her call out for me. She had fallen into a sunken grave. She was okay, and her therapist says she still has a good chance of leading a normal life.

Along with copying the inscription on the tombstone, here are some other items you need to note:

- Who are the people buried around your ancestor? They could be relatives.

- What is the location of the grave from the entrance?

- Is there a map of the cemetery, giving sections and plot numbers?

- What kind of artwork is carved on the stone? These symbols have different meanings and were not chosen randomly. (See the Bibliography for books on tombstone artwork.)

- What is the tombstone made of? marble? granite? limestone? If the stone is granite and the death date is 1789, then this is not the original stone. Granite wasn't used until the 1880s.

Also be aware that stonecutters do make mistakes. Just because it's carved in stone, doesn't always mean it's accurate.

After making all these preparations, you're probably anxious to get started. Now let's see where all those historical records are stored.

Chapter 7

Research
Repositories

Where do you go to find more information on your ancestors, and what can you expect when you get to a research repository? There are places to conduct research in almost every locality. Even Simla—my small, rural community of about 500 souls in eastern Colorado—has one. If I had ancestry in Simla, I could just walk across the street to the town record hall and start looking in records (with Avelyn's permission, of course—she's the town clerk). Or I could stroll up the block and look for my ancestors' tombstones in the town cemetery. I could also venture thirty miles away to the county courthouse and look for land and marriage records, tax lists, and court cases. The only problem is, like me, most of you probably do not live where your ancestors lived, so we must make research trips to repositories that contain records either specific to a certain locality or pertaining to the whole country.

If you decide to make the journey to your ancestors' area, there are several places you'll want to check for possible historical documents. As you saw from the previous chapter on preparing for a research trip, always, always, always check with the repository before you make the trip. Find out the days and hours of operation, ask whether you can look at the records personally, whether they have a photocopy machine, and so forth. Never, never, never take the clerk by surprise.

TOWN HALL

In many New England states, the town hall may be the place you will go to find certain records on your ancestors, like marriages. This is why it is important to consult books such as Eichholz's *Ancestry's Red Book, The Handy Book for Genealogists,* and Thomas Kemp's *International Vital Records Handbook.* These will tell you whether you need to be searching in a town office, county courthouse, or state vital records office and which records are in which repository.

LOCAL LIBRARY

Local libraries usually have a local history collection that will contain items about the area: city directories, telephone books, maps, history books, manuscript collections, newspapers, and photographs. If there is no local history collection, ask if there is a town historical society that may have these items.

LOCAL HISTORICAL SOCIETY AND MUSEUMS

The local historical society may have many of the same items found in the local library, or it may supplement the library's collection. It may maintain a museum with historical artifacts from early settlers. The society may also have records of fraternal and civic organizations from the area.

COUNTY COURTHOUSE

This is *the* place to be. If you have never set foot in a county courthouse, you aren't a true genealogist. There's nothing like the smell of musty records, the feel of heavy deed books, the irritated look on the clerk's face when you say you're a genealogist. Many of the records you will seek on your ancestors are kept at the county level: land deeds, wills and probate, sometimes birth, marriage, and death records, civil and criminal court records, tax rolls, plat maps, and military discharges. In some courthouses you are allowed to search the indexes and records yourself; in others a clerk will do it for you. Some will only let you view the records on microfilm. Sometimes, the repository has off-site storage, which means you may have to wait a day or two for the records to be brought to the courthouse for research.

STATE HISTORICAL SOCIETY OR ARCHIVES

Many county courthouses have had their records microfilmed for patron use; the original records have been transferred for safekeeping to the state historical society or state archive. Even at these repositories, you may be allowed to look only at the microfilmed copies, but the advantage is that you may search several counties in one stop. This is a good place to find state and county histories, as well. Sometimes these institutions will allow you to use only a pencil, and they have lockers in which to store your personal belongings: only paper, pencil, and laptop computers are allowed.

NATIONAL RECORD REPOSITORIES

There are five major genealogical research centers in the nation. While there are substantial collections in major city libraries such as Chicago, New York, Boston, Denver, and San Francisco, and in society libraries like the National Genealogical Society in Arlington, Virginia, and Boston's New England Historic Genealogical Society, the ones discussed below have some of the largest and broadest collections that cover the United States. Three of these are located in our nation's capital: the Library of Congress, the National Archives, and the Daughters of the American Revolution Library. You may want to look at Christina K. Schaefer's *The Center: A Guide to Genealogical Research in the National Capital Area* for more details.

LIBRARY OF CONGRESS

This is the nation's library. As mentioned in the previous chapter, when someone writes a family history and the copyright is registered with the Library of Congress Copyright Office, a copy of the work becomes part of the library's genealogical collection. If you plan a trip to do research in the Library of Congress, you will want to look at these books: *Genealogies in the Library of Congress: A Bibliography* (two volumes and two supplements), *A Complement to Genealogies in the Library of Congress Since 1986,* and *The Library of Congress: A Guide to Genealogical and Historical Research* by James C. Neagles. The Library of Congress has closed stacks. In other words, you cannot browse titles on book shelves. At the reference desk you fill out a request slip, then wait until someone fetches the books for you. The most commonly used books are in open stacks, however. Along with its assortment of family histories, the Library also has one of the largest collections of city directories (see Chapter 8 for more information on city directories).

DAUGHTERS OF THE AMERICAN REVOLUTION LIBRARY

This is another repository that maintains a large book collection. Chapters of the DAR get "credit" for donating books to its society library, and this is how its collection has grown. You must be a member of the DAR to use the library without charge; otherwise, there is a nominal fee of a few dollars. The emphasis in this library, of course, is on helping members and those eligible to become members document their Revolutionary War ancestors. When a woman becomes a member of the DAR, as discussed in Chapter 3, she must fill out an application form (known as her "papers") that documents her lineage. These papers and "proofs" (the documents used to prove the lineage) are microfilmed and available to view.

NATIONAL ARCHIVES AND RECORDS ADMINISTRATION

Most of the records created by the federal government since its inception are housed in the National Archives. Now, that's a lot of paper. Obviously, it would take quite a building to store more than two hundred years of paperwork. Because it would be physically impossible to keep all that paper, some records are microfilmed and then—sad but true—destroyed. The National Archives research room contains rows of microfilm cabinet drawers and microfilm readers. There are also many original records and files that may be searched. (In other parts of the building open to the public you can view Old Glory and historical documents behind glass like the Declaration of Independence. They didn't microfilm and then destroy those.)

Before visiting this repository, you need to read and study the *Guide to Genealogical Research in the National Archives*. There is a more comprehensive, three-volume work called the *Guide to Federal Records in the National Archives of the United States*. This series covers all the records in the National Archives and is overwhelming for a beginning genealogist. The National Archives also publishes microfilm catalogs on the different censuses, passenger lists, and military records. By writing to them at the address in the Appendix, you can get a catalog of their publications, some of which are listed in the Bibliography.

There are twelve regional branches of the National Archives in the following cities: Atlanta, Boston, Chicago, Denver, Fort Worth, Kansas City, Los Angeles, New York, Philadelphia, San Francisco, Seattle, and Fairbanks.

These branches do not contain microfilms of every record housed in the National Archives in Washington. While all of the regional branches have complete sets of the population census schedules for the whole country, Revolutionary War pensions, and some other commonly researched records, each branch was established to maintain records from its region. Thus, the Atlanta branch covers the federal records produced in the southeastern United States: Alabama, Florida, Georgia, Kentucky, Mississippi, North Carolina, South Carolina, and Tennessee. A helpful guide to the Archives branches is Sandra Luebking and Loretto Szucs's *The Archives: A Guide to the National Archives Field Branches.*

ALLEN COUNTY PUBLIC LIBRARY IN FORT WAYNE, INDIANA

The Historical Genealogy Department of the Allen County Public Library is one of the largest genealogical collections in North America. It contains more than 171,000 volumes and nearly 200,000 items in microform. The library has a complete collection of federal population censuses; thousands of family histories; guides to genealogical research; state, county, and town histories; an expansive collection of city directories; vital record indexes; abstracts of court records; and the most complete collection of genealogical periodicals in the United States. This is the library that developed and compiles *PERSI*, the *Periodical Source Index* discussed in Chapter 5. On microfilm, the library has military records from the Revolutionary War to the Philippine Insurrection, and passenger lists for seventy-seven ports in America, Canada, and Germany.

FAMILY HISTORY LIBRARY AND ITS FAMILY HISTORY CENTERS

The Family History Library was established in 1894 by The Church of Jesus Christ of Latter-day Saints (Mormons) in Salt Lake City. The goal was to gather records that would help members of the church and nonmembers trace their heritage. This library is the world's largest collection of genealogical information. It has been affectionately referred to as the "Genealogists' Mecca."

The library has records on microfilm and in book form from throughout the world. There are more than two million rolls of microfilm at the Family History Library! On these rolls are documents from more than 2,500 archives, county courthouses, and other United States repositories. There are many more thousands of rolls from Canada, the British Isles, Germany, France, the Netherlands, Austria, Belgium, Hungary, Italy, Poland, Spain,

Switzerland, South America, Asia, and Australia. The book collection contains more than 258,000 volumes of local histories, published genealogies and family histories, periodicals, and other research aids. Sounds overwhelming? It can be. Read J. Carlyle Parker's *Going to Salt Lake City to Do Family History Research* or start small: visit one of the library's Family History Centers first.

In 1964 the library established Family History Centers to provide greater access to the records. Currently more than 2,650 centers operate in sixty-four countries. To find out if there is a center near you, check with your local genealogical society or in the phone book under "LDS churches" in the Yellow Pages. Or you can write directly to the library in Salt Lake City (see the Appendix) for a list of center locations.

Through the center, you can access the collection's catalog on CD-ROM or microfiche. Anything available on microfilm or microfiche may be rented from Salt Lake for a small fee. The film remains at the center, where you may rent it for a five-week period with extensions. You or anyone else may view these rented films whenever the center is open.

AN OVERVIEW OF THE FAMILY HISTORY LIBRARY'S UNIQUE COLLECTION

FamilySearch is an easy-to-use, computerized database of genealogical information that contains the following catalog file, databases, and indexes:

Family History Library Catalog is the computerized "card" catalog of the library's entire holdings—books, microfilms, and microfiche. The catalog does not contain the actual records, only descriptions of them. The CD-ROM version may be searched by locality or surname. The catalog is also available on microfiche. Although this version is not updated as frequently as the computerized version, it is sometimes easier to find things. The advantage of the microfiche is that you may also search by author, title, and subject (you can't on CD-ROM), as well as under the locality and surname.

International Genealogical Index (IGI) is a worldwide index of almost 200 million names of deceased persons. It is arranged by locality, then surname, and lists births, baptisms/christenings, and marriages, many dating from the early 1500s. It is updated continually and is not limited to LDS church members or their ancestors. This index provides a reference number for more information about the document that supplied the data contained in the IGI. A common problem, however, is that many beginning genealogists use the IGI as a *source*. Remember, this is an *index* only; you still need to go the extra step and get at the original document. You may print or download a single entry or up to two hundred entries onto a floppy diskette.

Ancestral File links individuals into families and pedigrees. Anyone may submit family information. Data are submitted on floppy diskettes converted from genealogy software programs like Personal Ancestral File to a GED-COM utility program. At the library in Salt Lake or at one of the Family History Centers, ask for a copy of "Contributing Information to Ancestral File." The information in this database, as in many of the others discussed herein, may be printed or downloaded to your own floppy diskette. Ancestral File also contains the names and addresses of the people who contributed the information, so you may contact contributors directly.

U.S. Social Security Death Index lists deaths reported to the Social Security Administration (of persons who had Social Security numbers), approximately 42 million people. It covers deaths from 1962 to the present, although there may be some records from as early as 1937. The files may also contain date of birth, the state of residence when the person applied for a Social Security number, and (usually) the place from where the death was reported. You do not need to know a person's Social Security number to access the information. Data may be printed or downloaded as an ASCII or GEDCOM file.

U.S. Military Index lists almost 100,000 U.S. servicemen and women who died or were declared dead in the Korean and Vietnam wars. The Korean index covers deaths, 1950–57, and the Vietnam one covers deaths, 1957–75. The index provides birth and death dates, the person's last residence, the place of death, rank and service number; for Vietnam only, it also provides religious affiliation, marital status, race, and the Vietnam War Memorial plaque number.

For more information on these collections and other details about the library, write to the address in the Appendix and ask for a free copy of "A Guide to Research."

The Family History Library consists of four research floors, and it will seem overwhelming at first. After a day, though, you'll probably feel right at home. There are short guided tours, and an informational overview of the collection is given by the library's staff on the main floor.

The main level contains American and Canadian published family histories, periodicals, and published sources, and looks pretty much like any other library when you walk in. The second floor is where you will find United States and Canadian records on microfilm. This area will probably look strange to you at first. As you walk in you'll see a reference station. To your left are banks of computers. As you look around, you will see nothing but row upon row of microfilm readers and people busily buried in them. The outer areas contain row upon row of microfilm filing cabinets. In order to get started researching, you need to know what film numbers the records are on. That's where you check either the microfiche or the computer version of the Family History Library Catalog.

The bottom two floors contain the British Isles Department and the European Collection. These floors have not only films, readers, and computers, but also books and periodicals pertaining to the appropriate collection.

OTHER IDEAS ABOUT RESEARCH

Sometimes beginning and seasoned genealogists alike get stuck in the genealogical section of libraries. They have blinders on that will only allow them to go for sources that contain their ancestors' names. Sadly, these researchers are missing much background material. Putting your ancestors into historical perspective, adding meat to the bones, is what makes your ancestors "people," not just names on a chart. You need to go beyond your ancestors' names and classify them into broader groups to help you with your historical background research: What ethnic group did they belong to? Asian, South American, African American? In what time period did they live in America? Colonial, National, Revolutionary, Civil War, twentieth century? What were their occupations? Farmers, factory workers, politicians, blacksmiths, teachers? What were their religions? Quaker, Mormon, Catholic, Jewish, Methodist? In order to gain historical context—learning what everyday life was like for an ordinary person in a given time and place—you need to venture into other sections of the library and into university libraries.

THE PUBLIC LIBRARY

In the reference section you will find books of a general nature that may not only help your research on a specific person, but may give you some background material. Encyclopedias are always a good place to begin for overviews of practically any topic: the Civil War, homesteading, a famous person who may be related to you through a cousin's marriage. There are also directories galore, different varieties of "who's who," and obituary indexes. Browse the shelves of the reference section and see what you find.

The children's section is a wonderful place to find background historical perspective information. Children's history books are unlike adult versions that focus on famous people and events. Kids want to know what life was like for the Pilgrims and the Indians and the frontier farmers, so their books contain this kind of information. Often there is a bibliography leading to adult histories of this type.

The circulating section is where you will find the histories that will talk more about everyday life. In the computerized catalog, type in the locality of interest—say, Pennsylvania—then the key words "social life and customs." Quite a few entries will pop up. To narrow your search, add "Quakers," or "Colonial Catholics," or whatever group your ancestor belonged to.

THE UNIVERSITY LIBRARY

If the college or university nearest you has a graduate program in history, then you really have a ton of resources at your fingertips. History majors need to write theses and dissertations, and they need lots of material for their studies. Even if there is only an undergraduate program in history, you should still find quite a few history books on most areas of interest. Check the university's computerized catalog using the same key words as above.

Keep in mind that you will not find *genealogical* sources in a college or university library. You won't find record collections, genealogical books and journals, and computer databases with surname indexes. Here you're looking for *history* sources that will help put your ancestors into historical perspective. For example, you are more likely to find Civil War regimental histories at the college library than in the public or genealogical library. Once you know the military unit in which your ancestor served, you can visit the university library to learn all sorts of details on the unit or the war itself.

College and university libraries, as well as many public libraries, may also have special collections containing manuscript files with people's papers—letters, diaries, or other loose documents. Maybe your ancestor left a diary, and it was donated by a descendant to a public or college library or to a historical society. A useful tool to find these hidden treasures is the *National Union Catalog of Manuscript Collections,* also known as *NUCMC.* These volumes may be found in the library's reference section. *NUCMC* has been published annually since 1959 by the Library of Congress. The Library of Congress requests repositories all over the country to report to them their manuscript holdings, then they publish this information in *NUCMC.*

TRICKS OF THE TRADE

MICROFILM, MICROFICHE:
WHAT THE HECK ARE YOU TALKING ABOUT?

As I mentioned earlier, many records are preserved in some sort of micro-form and then destroyed. There just is not enough space to store all that paper. Microfilm comes on a roll, usually in 16mm or 35mm format. Indexes are usually on 16mm rolls—skinny reels—whereas the records are usually on 35mm film. There are machines called microfilm readers so that you don't have to hold the film up to the light and then faint when you see how tiny the print is. Many readers have different zoom lenses and magnifications. Most readers have instructions permanently affixed on how to thread the film, but basically the full reel is on the left and an empty take-up reel is on the right. If you've never used a microfilm reader before, have a librarian or volunteer show you how.

You aren't a true genealogist until you've dropped a roll of microfilm and hopelessly watched it unrolling down the aisle. (We've all done it, so don't get too flustered.) If, for some reason, the film breaks as you are using it or rewinding it, don't panic. Report it immediately to the librarian or attendant. It's happened before, and the film does get brittle in dry climates. Although it's embarrassing, I promise they won't announce your name over the intercom ("Mary Seymore just broke a roll of microfilm on row 10") or revoke your privileges to use the repository.

Microfiche (pronounced either micro-fish or micro-feesh, depending on what part of the country you come from) is a flat piece of film that is viewed, appropriately, on a microfiche reader. There's no danger here of breaking the film or having it escape from you, unless you're particularly klutzy. The film is placed between two pieces of glass and is magnified for viewing.

There are also microfilm and microfiche printers so that you can make photocopies of what you find. Once again, ask the attendant for help; it seems like every machine is slightly different. At the Family History Library in Salt Lake, where there are a half-dozen microprinters on every floor, I find one I like that makes good copies and use that one the entire time I'm there, even if I have to wait to use it.

ETHICS FOR THE GENEALOGIST

Genealogists, whether by vocation or avocation, must abide by certain ethics. One of the most important is in the care and handling of historical documents and published records. It is not acceptable under any circumstance to tear, erase, mark, or remove any document, book, or microfilm. If you find an error in a record or published genealogy, it is your responsibility to correct it in *your own* article, book, or charts. Likewise, under no circumstance may you mutilate, deface, or destroy a document or book. We are a community of researchers who must respect each other, the people who assist us in our search, and the historical records that help us learn about our heritage

GENEALOGIST'S ETIQUETTE

Most genealogical how-to books don't even address this topic. It's generally only discussed in hushed tones among close friends. Although librarians in genealogical libraries usually share your interest and enthusiasm for researching dead relatives, clerks and other types of librarians are sometimes, shall we say, unsociable. They don't like to hear the "A" word or the "G" word (ancestor or genealogy). So it's best not to bring up these topics. If you are in a county courthouse or a university library and need help or information, just say you are doing historical research on a particular person or time period. You don't need to go into detail and say "my ancestor," or explain how you're related to this person, or how interesting your genealogy is. The clerks don't care. Even genealogical librarians want you to get to the point. While every genealogist finds his or her own ancestry fascinating, others usually don't.

As already mentioned in Chapter 3, it's important to find and socialize with other genealogists. This is a good way to learn and to get another researcher's opinion on a stumbling block. This kind of sharing and brainstorming is what genealogy is all about. But clerks and librarians are busy people. Along with helping patrons, they have other duties. Be as pleasant and friendly as possible, even though the person behind the counter may not be. Remember, they have what you want—the records. And you don't know what happened just before you came in, or how the last genealogist treated that person. Some researchers go the extra mile when they have a particularly helpful clerk and send a thank-you note, candy, even flowers. They refer to their visit in some way so that the clerk will remember them; then the next time they need help, the clerk is likely to be even more helpful.

When I became a researcher for hire, I was instructed by my colleagues to always dress professionally when I entered a courthouse or place of business. This adds an air of professionalism and shows the clerk that I'm serious about my line of work. Personally, I've dressed in a business suit on one occasion and casual slacks on another and didn't see a difference in the way I was treated. The type of clothing you wear does make a certain impression on people, however, so try to dress nicely. Frankly, it's been my experience that the mom with the crying baby—no matter how she's dressed—always gets better and faster service than anyone else.

Chapter 8

Researching in Historical Documents: Case Study #1

I n order to introduce you to the various records you'll consult in the course of researching your ancestry, let's look at some real ancestors, using examples from several time periods and localities. Keep in mind that some of these steps may be taken in a different order, depending on the information you have or have acquired from other sources. There are no set rules of order, although generally you start with oral history interviews and home sources. But suppose you're at the point where you're ready to research a seventeenth-century ancestor? There's no one to talk to—unless you have a really good Ouija board—and you may not have any artifacts that will give you clues. So your starting place would be in published records, abstracts, and indexes (see Chapter 5).

There are also many ways to obtain records:

- Looking through family papers

- Writing to the custodians of various record repositories

- Visiting a repository such as a courthouse where your ancestors' records are located

- Viewing records on microfilm at a research repository, such as the

Family History Library or one of its branches, or through a lending library

One researcher may find a marriage record while on a research trip to the courthouse; another may get the same record by mail; a third may get a copy by using microfilm at the Family History Library; yet another may have the actual record among family papers. In the following examples, then, I may have written for a record such as a passenger list, while you may choose to look at passenger lists on microfilm from a lending library.

No researcher consults just one source before compiling a family history. Genealogists look at every possible record that could contain information on the ancestors they seek—even if the ancestor is not found or they learn "nothing new" from a particular record. (See Marsha Hoffman Rising's "Accumulating Negative Evidence" in the *Association of Professional Genealogists Quarterly* cited in the Bibliography.) You will find that one record may conveniently lead you to another and that much of the information is interconnected in some way. You will also discover that several records may be used to verify one piece of data. For example, an exact birth date or an approximate birth year may come from a birth certificate, a death certificate, a marriage license, a census enumeration, a pension file, a passenger list, a tombstone inscription, a Social Security record, a family Bible, a letter, school records, a published genealogy, a passport, a baptism certificate, a funeral prayer card, or a newspaper obituary. And all of these may give you different dates! At the end of the next chapter you'll find a brief discussion on evaluating records for accuracy; however, to do research justice, you need a thorough knowledge of each type of record and its idiosyncrasies.

HANDWRITING PROBLEMS

Another part of researching in historical documents that you will have to deal with is handwriting. I'm afraid you won't find many typed records much before the 1900s, although a typewriting machine was invented in 1843. As mentioned in Chapter 5 under Record Transcripts, Abstracts, and Indexes, many script letters can be misread. Loretto Dennis Szucs in her chapter "Research in Census Records," in *The Source: A Guidebook of American Genealogy,* suggests making an alphabet of the person's handwriting if you are working with a microfilm copy of a record such as censuses. Placing a piece of plain white paper on the microfilm reader screen, trace the letters, making an alphabet with upper and lower cases. You may also want to study such books as E. Kay Kirkham's *The Handwriting of American Records for a Period of 300 Years* or Harriet Stryker-Rodda's *Understanding Colonial Handwriting*.

RESEARCHING ETHNIC ORIGINS

America is considered the "melting pot" of different nationalities, which becomes apparent when you begin to trace your family history. Few Americans can claim "pure-bred" ancestry of any nationality. Most of us are a mixture of different ethnic origins rich in traditions and customs. Although your research may ultimately lead you to another country, your search still begins in American records. Some people are overly anxious to find immigrant ancestors to make the connection to foreign lands. This is particularly true for those descending from immigrants who arrived during the nineteenth and twentieth centuries.

In researching ethnic origins, however, it is equally important to study the American generations. It is essential to learn some specific details to successfully research overseas, such as the name of the immigrant's native village. Knowing that Antonio Veneto came from Italy simply isn't enough. By working backward, thoroughly researching all available American records, you should be able to find or narrow down some origin possibilities.

Another important aspect is to learn your immigrant ancestors so well that you can identify them in foreign records. Conrad Bredlinger may be an unusual name in America, but it may be the John Smith of Germany. You won't be able to identify the right ancestor if you don't know his birth date, village of origin, his parents' names, his wife's name, and approximately when he emigrated. Ironically, this may be exactly the information you're seeking. If you have uncovered all the records Conrad created during his life in America, you should have a good idea of whether the Conrad in Germany is the same as the one in America.

Native American and African Americans also have unique research considerations. For example, if your ancestry includes slaves, you will need to research the white family or families who owned your ancestors. For Native Americans, a lot of your research will be in federal records, such as Indian censuses. Because of the special circumstances in researching these two groups, there are detailed guides you should consult. A good starting place is the chapters specific to Native American and African American research in

The Source: A Guidebook of American Genealogy (this book also contains chapters on Hispanic and Jewish American research). *The Source* will lead you to other guidebooks, and some are listed in this book's Bibliography as well.

Remember, if you are following the rule of genealogy by starting with yourself and working backward, the beginning of your research will be the same no matter from what ethnic group you descend.

Through the following case studies, I will touch upon many of the basic records you would consult in the course of beginning your research in America. Regardless of your ethnic background, many of the same basic records will be ones that you will explore when you begin tracing your heritage. But you should not stop with the information in this book. To get the raw, nitty-gritty details on records, there are plenty of guidebooks, such as *The Source: A Guidebook of American Genealogy,* that will give you in-depth information on how to find, use, and evaluate historical documents. This chapter and the next are meant simply as an overview to whet your appetite for research.

CASE STUDY #1:
EUROPEAN IMMIGRANTS TO AMERICA IN THE EARLY TWENTIETH CENTURY

Between 1880 and 1920 this country saw a big influx of southern and eastern Europeans. As a case example of researching ancestors who arrived during this time, I'll retrace my research on Salvatore and Angelina (Vallarelli) Ebetino, who arrived in the early 1900s from Italy.

PERSONAL KNOWLEDGE

Salvatore and Angelina were my great-grandparents, so I had no firsthand knowledge of them; in other words, I didn't personally know them.

INTERVIEWS WITH RELATIVES

My next step was to talk with a relative who did know them: my grandmother, who was their daughter. With pedigree charts and family group sheets in tow, she helped me fill in the blanks, giving me a starting point to my research. We looked over some of her home sources, such as funeral prayer cards, letters, and photographs. After our visit, my family group sheet looked something like this:

Salvatore EBETINO

    b. 26 Mar 1875, Terlizzi, Bari, Italy

    m. about 1899, Terlizzi, Bari, Italy

    d. 3 Oct 1957, Port Chester, Westchester County, NY

    father: Frank Ebetino

    mother: Stella ———

    other: immigrated to America around 1906

Angelina VALLARELLI

    b. 27 Sep 1877, Terlizzi, Bari, Italy

    d. 19 Jul 1937, Rye, Westchester County, NY

    father: Fortunato Vallarelli

    mother: Isabella Vendola

    other: immigrated a few years after Salvatore

Children:

1.	Frank	b. 21 Nov 1900, Terlizzi, Bari, Italy
2.	Fred	b. 25 Feb 1904, Terlizzi, Bari, Italy
3.	Stella	b. 27 May 1905, Terlizzi, Bari, Italy
4.	Isabella	b. 17 Dec 1911, Rye, Westchester, NY
		d. 1 Sep 1918
5.	Philip	b. 8 Apr 1912, Rye, Westchester, NY
6.	Michael	b. 12 Apr 1915, Rye, Westchester, NY
7.	Salvatore	b. 4 Apr 1917, Rye, Westchester, NY
		d. 25 Feb 1920

PUBLISHED SOURCES

One of the problems with working on early twentieth-century families, and an ethnic one in particular, is that it is unlikely you will find evidence of these people in published record abstracts or among printed genealogies. Most record transcriptions and abstracting projects cover the pre-1900s. Although the trend is changing and more family histories are being published about recent immigrants, more than likely you will be the one to write the book.

VITAL RECORDS

My next step was to send for birth, marriage, and death records to confirm the dates and names my grandmother had given me. Because Salvatore and Angelina were born and married in Italy, and I didn't know how to go about getting those records at the time, I skipped this part. Instead, I sent for their death certificates. Through my genealogical guidebooks I learned about a nifty government publication called "Where to Write for Vital Records" (see Bibliography). Another place you can check is the *International Vital Records Handbook,* compiled by Thomas Kemp.

Going to Kemp's book, I discovered that for the state of New York, births, marriages, and deaths are on file from 1880 to the present. I can write to either the New York State Department of Health or to the Registrar of Vital Statistics in the town where the event occurred. This book also gives the forms necessary to request records and lists the fee to send. Be aware, however, that fees change; it might be best to call or write first and find out the current cost.

Vital records are available for different time periods in different states. Statewide vital registration was not uniformly kept until the early 1900s; by 1933 all states had vital registration. So the chances of finding a birth certificate for someone born before the twentieth century are low in many states. From Kemp's book, you will learn for what time periods vital records exist and where to write for them.

Depending on the year and state, birth records will normally give the name of the baby (although sometimes it's just "Baby"), the names of the parents with the mother's maiden name, sometimes the parents' occupations, birthplaces, ages, and residences, and sometimes the number of births the mother has had.

Death records, also depending on the year, state, and person who supplied the information, will give varied information: the name of the deceased, date of birth (and/or age) and death, place of birth (sometimes just the state or county) and death, parents' names and sometimes their birthplaces, name of spouse, cause of death, place and date of burial, and the name and location of the funeral home or mortician handling the arrangements. This is what I call a "chain reaction" record. The information on the death certificate may lead you to an obituary, the cemetery and burial record, the funeral home record, probate record, and possibly a birth record.

The information I learned from Salvatore and Angelina's death certificates included their parents' names, their dates and places of births, how long each had resided in the community, Salvatore's Social Security number, their dates and places of death, causes of death, where they were buried, and the name of the funeral home. My next step was to write for their obituaries.

NEWSPAPER OBITUARIES

In order to find out what newspapers were published in the town where my great-grandparents had died, I went to the reference department of the library and found the *Gale Directory of Publications and Broadcast Media*. This directory is published annually and is arranged by state, then by cities and towns. The *Gale Directory* noted the newspapers published in Port Chester and Rye for the appropriate time periods: *Port Chester Daily Item* and the *Rye Chronicle*. I wrote to the addresses listed but received a response that all the back issues were on microfilm at the public library, giving me the address. I sent the librarians the names and death dates for my great-grandparents, and they found obituaries, made copies, and sent them to me. In return, they requested a nominal fee of a few dollars.

To find newspapers, go to the *Gale Directory* first. This will tell you when the newspaper was established and the address where to write. If the newspaper is out of print, try Clarence Brigham's *A History and Bibliography of American Newspapers, 1690–1820,* and Winifred Gregory's *American Newspapers, 1821–1936*. Another resource to check is the Library of Congress's *Newspapers in Microform*.

Many "newspaper morgues" are now microfilmed and kept at the local public library. The nice part of having the newspapers in the library is that volunteers from the genealogical society often index obituaries and birth and marriage announcements. Sometimes the library will make interlibrary loans of the microfilmed copies so that you can view the newspaper at your own library.

Along with obituaries, you may find marriage and engagement announcements, anniversary celebrations, family reunions, 100th birthdays, birth announcements, military press releases, legal notices, ships' arrivals, newcomers seeking lost relatives, local news items, and personal columns. I love this one:

> Local cowboys missed real rodeo action Sunday morning by not being at our corral. By virtue of a large knot on his forehead, Jim found out why Roberta refused to show one of his heifers in 4-H last year. After a wild scurry out of her path, then his meeting up with a panel she relocated, he roped her and the fun began.

Did he rope Roberta or the heifer, do you suppose?

Newspapers can also contain errors:

> Mrs. Viola Jones celebrated her 48th birthday on Sunday. She has
> been a resident of the area for 57 years.

Newspapers are a lot of fun. They're an excellent source to get a feeling of the times, allowing you to watch as history was being made. You can read about World War II as it was happening. From newspapers you can get a lot of that historical background I was talking about in Chapter 7. You can learn about:

- the cost of items your ancestor probably purchased

- what fashions were popular and how your ancestor may have dressed

- the economic condition of the area where your ancestor lived

- the political climate as reflected in the editorials

- the culture, lifestyles, and leisure activities of the period

If you get a roll of microfilm with a newspaper from the turn of the century, whether your ancestors are named in it or not, you'll be fascinated by the articles, advertisements, and editorials. It's hard to stay focused and just look for your ancestors. You'll be nudging the person at the neighboring microfilm reader and saying, "Look how much it cost to buy a whole dining room set in 1925."

The obituaries I obtained on Salvatore and Angelina gave me wonderful biographical material on their lives. But while I was waiting for the obituaries to arrive, I wasn't idle. I visited the cemetery where they were buried.

CEMETERY RESEARCH

In Chapter 6 I discussed how to prepare to search a cemetery, take photographs, and make tombstone rubbings. When I visited my great-grandparents' graves, I got an added bonus: their portraits had been made into tile photographs that had been embedded into the granite tombstone. You may find this type of memorial for some of your own ancestors. In this instance, I not only took photographs of the tombstone, I also took close-up pictures of my great-grandparents. At the time, these were the only photos I knew existed, and I wanted copies. Since the tombstone itself was too heavy to take home with me so that I could have the photos to display in my living room, I took pictures of the pictures. This is another good reason to come prepared: take along magnifying lenses to attach to your 35mm camera. I now have their photographs framed on my mantel. You would never know that these pictures were copied from a tombstone.

Along with transcribing and photographing the tombstone, you'll want to check with the cemetery caretaker to see what records there may be on your ancestors' burials. Some cemeteries are no longer in use—which sounds strange. They are in use by the people buried there, of course, but no new burials occur. Anyway, if the cemetery is an overgrown country cemetery, and no one has set foot on it since 1942, then you may have a tough time finding the burial records—if they still exist. Try local libraries, historical societies, and funeral directors in the area.

The burial record will likely give you the location of the plot, who paid for it, who's buried in it, and when the person was buried (and perhaps when they died). Don't think that everyone who is buried in a plot is listed on the tombstone. Many people have been surprised when they obtained the burial record and found that another relative or close friend was buried with an ancestor.

FEDERAL CENSUS RESEARCH

I love census research—as do most genealogists. It's one of those records that gives you lots of details on your ancestors and the community in which they lived. I was able to find Salvatore and Angelina on censuses for 1910 and 1920, which gave me information on when they came to America, when and where they became United States citizens, who lived with them in their household, where they lived, and the same information on their neighbors, many of whom I discovered later were relatives or came from the same village in Italy as Salvatore and Angelina.

A census (also known as the federal population schedule) is a count or enumeration of our country's population. It has had many uses for the federal government: to determine population, to see how many males might be eligible to serve in the military, to determine federal funding for an area, to evaluate the ethnic population and distribution.

The United States government began taking an enumeration of the population in 1790 and has done so ever since in ten-year increments. In the early days, census takers went door-to-door to each household to gather information. In the past few decades, census forms have been mailed to households. Perhaps you remember filling out the 1990 census—and, if you were thinking like a genealogist at the time, you made a photocopy of it and put it with your genealogy files for your descendants. If you didn't complete the form and return it, someone was supposed to visit your house.

According to the census takers' guidelines, when they went door-to-door collecting data they were supposed to talk with the head of the household or someone in the family whom they deemed credible. Rather than making a trip back to the household if Pa and Ma were gone but twelve-year-old Tommy was there, the census taker may have asked him the questions. "How old is your Ma?" "Oh, she's old. Probably about forty," (when in reality she was thirty-two). Do you see how the information recorded may not be quite accurate? Unlike death certificates that tell the name of the person who supplied the information, we don't know this for census records. Another stipulation in the guidelines was that if no one was home who was competent to answer the questions, the enumerator could get the information from the family or person living nearest to the family in question. Yikes! A neighbor ten miles away could have been the closest person to give information on your ancestors!

You can view population schedules from 1790 to 1920. The 1890 schedules, however, were destroyed in a fire. Small portions remain, and there is an alphabetical index to everyone listed on the extant portions on two rolls of microfilm. This index is available wherever population censuses are available. Census records fall under our country's Privacy Laws, which means that a census enumeration must be seventy-two years old before it is opened for the public to look at it. The 1930 census won't be released until 2002. You can get pieces of information from the 1930 through 1990 censuses by writing to the Personal Service Branch, Bureau of the Census, P.O. Box 1545, Jeffersonville, IN 47131. Write for Form BC-600. This will also tell you the cost. Be prepared; it's expensive. The cost a few years ago was about $25 for the enumeration of just one person in a household.

The kind of data you'll find in censuses will vary from one census year to another. The 1790 through 1840 schedules name only the head of the household; everyone else is tallied by tick marks in categories such as "Free white males under 10," "Free white females age 26–45," "Slaves," "Free colored." The 1840 census had a special column for listing the names of Revolutionary War pensioners or their widows receiving pensions. This information is found on the second page of the enumeration along with the number of slaves in the household.

The 1850 census was the first to list everyone in the family by name, giving their ages, occupations, and state, territory, or country of birth. A new question in the 1870 schedule was whether a person's parents were foreign born. In 1880, for the first time, the census asked the relationship of each person to the head of the household. So a family's listing may look like this:

Matheson, Paul
              Susan   wife
              Tom   stepson
              Cindy   daughter
              William   son
Shumway, Mildred   mother-in-law

Whose mother is Mildred? More than likely Susan's. Remember, it is supposed to tell you the relationship to *the head of the household*. Mildred is Paul's mother-in-law. Tom is Paul's stepson. He may be Susan's son—we don't know for sure; all we know for certain is his relationship to Paul.

The 1880 schedules also asked for each individual's marital status—single, married, widowed, divorced—and the place of birth for each individual's father and mother. Keep in mind that the enumerator was instructed to record the name of the birth *state*, not towns or counties. Sometimes you'll find a census taker who recorded the town, too. Alycon Trubey Pierce wrote two articles for the *National Genealogical Society Quarterly* identifying schedules that give this kind of unauthorized data (see Bibliography).

Everyone loves the 1900 census. It's the only one to ask people not only their age, but also the month and year of their birth. It also contains information on the number of years a person had been married; for women, how many children they had and how many are living; the year of immigration to the United States; the number of years in America; whether a naturalized citizen; if the home was owned or rented; and whether English was spoken. The 1910 enumeration is similar, only it no longer had the column for month and year of birth. Finally, the 1920 census asked much of the same information as 1900 and 1910, but also asked whether a person was an alien or naturalized and the year of naturalization.

Most genealogists agree that you start with the most recent census for your ancestors and work your way backward. With Salvatore and Angelina I began with the 1920 census, then looked at 1910. If they had been in this country prior to 1900, then I would have searched that census.

CENSUS INDEXES AND THE SOUNDEX

Almost all the censuses now have indexes that will help your search go more quickly. But, as with anything else, errors and omissions occur. Just because you don't find your ancestor listed in the index doesn't necessarily mean he's not on the actual enumeration. I couldn't find Salvatore in the index for 1920, but I knew he was living in Rye, New York. So I searched the microfilm for that town and looked page-by-page for him and found him. His surname had been misspelled on the census, and that was why I couldn't find him in the index.

The 1790 census is published in book form with an index at the back. Some of the 1800 schedules have also been published (e.g., Vermont and New Hampshire). The schedules for 1800 through 1850 have book indexes; the actual census is on microfilm. The 1860 and 1870 censuses are in the process of being indexed by independent firms, with many states already completed. Many census indexes through 1880 are available on CD-ROM from Broderbund Software (see the Appendix). For the 1880 through 1920 enumerations, the index is arranged by the Soundex system and it, too, is on microfilm.

The Soundex is a code based on the way a name *sounds* rather than how it is spelled. So for a name like Carmack that could also be spelled Cormack, Carmac, and Cormac, or a name like Smith that could also be spelled Smythe, all variations will have the same code and be arranged together. This is how the Soundex code looks and works:

The Number	Represents the following letters:
1	B P F V
2	C S K G J Q X Z
3	D T
4	L
5	M N
6	R

All vowels and *W, Y,* and *H* are disregarded, and the first letter of a surname is not coded; it is used as the first part of the code. You only code the first three consonants (after the initial) in a name.

For example, let's code Carmack. The *C* will be our first part of the code. Now we cross out all the vowels, *W, Y,* and *H*:

C a r m a c k

We're left with *C r m c k*. The *C* is not given a numerical code, but the next three consonants are. Looking at the coding system, the *r* is a 6; the *m* is a 5, and the *c* is a 2. So our code becomes C652.

Suppose the name was misspelled as Cormac? By dropping the vowels and using only the first three consonants, we'll still end up with C652. Try it.

The only glitch to this would be if the name was spelled with a *K* (Karmack) instead of a *C* for the first letter. Then we would have to begin our code with *K* followed by the numbers.

Let's try another one: Teffertiller. First rule is that the *T* will not be given a number. Now let's drop the vowels, *W, Y,* and *H*: T f f r t l l r. Now we assign numbers to the first three consonants. But we're dealing with double consonants. According to the Soundex rules, if there is a double consonant, drop one of them. So now we have these letters to work with: T f r t l r. The *f* is a 1, the *r* becomes 6, and the *t* is now a 3. We only need three numbers, so the rest of the consonants can be eliminated. So the code for Teffertiller is T163.

Here are a few more surnames I've coded as examples:

Smith	= S m t	= S530	(Remember, we don't code the *h*, and when there aren't enough consonants, just add zeros.)	
Smythe	= S m t	= S530		
Lee	= L - - -	= L000		
DeBartolo	= D b r t l	= D163	(For surnames with prefixes such as Di, De, Van, Von, Mc, Mac, etc., code with the prefix and without. The name could be listed either way in the Soundex.)	

This may seem confusing at first. In fact, I had one student who refused to learn the Soundex. She felt it was too hard to comprehend; she would rather just look for her ancestors page-by-page on the census—that is, until she needed to find someone in Brooklyn, New York, in 1900. That city alone encompasses twenty-seven very full rolls of microfilm. She quickly learned how to use Soundex.

Once you have the codes for your ancestors' surnames, now what? Four guidebooks published by the National Archives will tell you what roll of microfilm contains the code you are interested in:

1790–1890 Federal Population Census: A Catalog of Microfilm Copies of the Schedules

1900 Federal Population Census: A Catalog of Microfilm Copies of the Schedules

1910 Federal Population Census: A Catalog of Microfilm Copies of the Schedules

1920 Federal Population Census: A Catalog of Microfilm Copies of the Schedules (rev. ed.)

Let's go back to Salvatore and Angelina Ebetino and see how we find them in the 1920 census. Their surname code is E135. They lived in Rye, Westchester County, New York. I went to the *1920 Federal Population Census: A Catalog of Microfilm Copies of the Schedules*. The back section of this guide has the listing of microfilm for the Soundex, arranged by state, and it looks like this:

New York M1578
(roll number)

217.	D-653	Jack	thru	E-123	Otto
218.	E-123	Paul	thru	E-152	Voorhess
219.	E-152	W. Albert	thru	E-212	Bridget
220.	E-212	L.	thru	E-236	Zalek

The roll of microfilm we want based on the code E135 will be M1578, roll 218, since that roll covers the code numbers E123 (starting with the first name of Paul) through E152 (ending with the first name of Voorhess).

As you wind through the roll, you will see that there is a Soundex card for each household enumeration from the census. Because all the surnames are similar in sound and usually in spelling, the cards have been arranged alphabetically by first name. I've already told you that I couldn't find Salvatore and Angelina in the 1920 Soundex because their name had been misspelled on the census from which the Soundex card was made (on the census, his name was recorded as "Betenio"). But let's say I had found a Soundex card for them. The upper right corner of the Soundex card will give the census volume number, E.D. (enumeration district), sheet and line number. You don't really need the volume number unless the film is too dark to read the enumeration district numbers, but the other information is crucial, along with the county name. Salvatore Ebetino was in Westchester County, Rye Town, enumeration district 166, sheet 12, line 67. (It's important to copy everything on the Soundex card in case the actual census page is difficult, if not impossible, to read. If you are working with a difficult-to-read census microfilm, make a note of it, and check another repository's copy. I was working with one at the archives branch in Denver that was overexposed. When I viewed the same census in Salt Lake City, that copy was perfectly legible.)

Going back to the *1920 Federal Population Census: A Catalog of Microfilm Copies of the Schedules,* look under the census schedules section for New York. There are seven rolls of microfilm for Westchester County, but I know that Salvatore was in enumeration district 166. With that information I learn that E.D. 166 in Westchester County is on roll 1278:

> 1278. Westchester Co. (Eds 108–114, 124–134, 136–143,
>   and 163–177).

In the microfilm filing cabinet, I located roll 1278, then put it on the microfilm reader. The enumeration district is found in the upper right corner of the census page for 1920. I wound the film until I found E.D. 166, sheet 12. The line numbers are the preprinted, far-left numbers. Sure enough, on line 67, there is Salvatore. His wife and family follow on lines 68–74.

Sounds easy enough, right? Now let me throw some glitches into the picture, because every historical document you'll research will present some idiosyncrasies and problems. This is one of the challenges of genealogical research. Unfortunately, records were not created or kept with genealogists in mind. The records and indexes were created to suit the needs of the government or organization needing the information.

Soundex idiosyncrasies: Not all censuses are completely Soundexed. Here's a breakdown of those that are:

- 1920: all of the 1920 census is Soundexed.

- 1910: only twenty-one states were Soundexed for the 1910 schedules (it is also referred to as a "Miracode," but it's the same thing). The states that have indexes are Alabama, Arkansas, California, Florida, Georgia, Illinois, Kansas, Kentucky, Louisiana, Michigan, Mississippi, Missouri, North Carolina, Ohio, Oklahoma, Pennsylvania, South Carolina, Tennessee, Texas, Virginia, and West Virginia.

- 1900: all of 1900 is Soundexed.

- 1880: the 1880 schedules are Soundexed only for households with at least one child age ten or under, although commercial indexing firms are slowly indexing the entire 1880 census in book form and on CD-ROM.

Why all the differences? It boils down to the people who originally needed to find people in these censuses: the Social Security Administration. When Social Security came into existence in 1935, people had to be able to prove their age to get benefits. Since most states did not have mandatory birth registration, many people did not have birth certificates. The government allowed use of the census as proof of a person's age.

You will find federal census records on microfilm at the National Archives and its regional branches, and at the Family History Library in Salt Lake City and by microfilm rental through its Family History Centers. You may also rent microfilm of censuses from lending libraries and view them in your home if you own a microfilm reader, or you may take the films to your local library. Two companies offer this service: American Genealogical Lending Library and the National Archives Microfilm Rental Program (addresses are in the Appendix and Chapter 10). Many local libraries have censuses for their state only; for instance, Penrose Library in Colorado Springs has all of the Colorado censuses.

SPECIAL FEDERAL POPULATION SCHEDULES

In addition to the federal population schedules, other censuses were taken by the government and individual states. A federal act of 1879 encouraged any state to conduct its own interdecennial census of 1885 to report to the government. Five states and territories took advantage of this act: Colorado, Florida, Nebraska, the territories of the Dakotas, and the territory of New Mexico. There were four parts to this census:

1. Schedule 1 was a population enumeration similar to the federal census. It listed all inhabitants in a household by name, race, sex, age, relationship to the head of the household, marital status, occupation, place of birth, parents' places of birth, literacy, and whether sick or disabled.

2. The second part was an agricultural schedule (for more information on federal agricultural schedules, see Chapter 9). It gave the

name of the farm owner, acreage, farm value, expenses, estimated value of the farm products, number and kind of livestock, and the amount and kind of produce.

3. Schedule 3 was for industries. It listed the name of the industry owner, the name of the business or products, amount of money invested, number of employees, wages and hours, number of months in operation during the year, value of materials used, values of products, and the amount and type of power used. (Federal industry schedules are discussed in Chapter 9.)

4. There does not appear to be a Schedule 4; however, the Dakotas used a veterans' schedule as part of their state census, and this could have been the fourth part. Technically, the fourth part was called Schedule 5 and was a mortality schedule (federal mortality schedules are discussed in Chapter 9). Schedule 5 gave the name of the deceased, age, sex, race, marital status, place of birth, parents' places of birth, occupation, and the cause of death.

All four schedules are microfilmed together and are arranged by the county within the state or territory; however, Cherry County, Nebraska, was missed in the filming.

STATE CENSUS RECORDS

Many states took their own censuses at different times throughout their territorial or statehood history. Ann Lainhart's *State Census Records* lists all of these enumerations and notes whether indexes exist. Here is a sample of how varied these records are:

Arkansas	1865
Illinois	1810, 1812 (territorial), 1820, 1825, 1830, 1835, 1840, 1845, 1855, 1865
Massachusetts	1855, 1865
Nevada	1862–63 (territorial), 1875
New Jersey	1855, 1865, 1875, 1885, 1895, 1905, 1915

In my search for Salvatore Ebetino, I was able to locate him and his family in the 1915 and 1925 New York State censuses. State censuses sometimes asked people different questions than did the federal census, and there can also be discrepancies in information between state and federal censuses.

For instance, the 1920 federal population schedule stated that Salvatore immigrated in 1909 and was naturalized about 1916. His wife and children arrived in 1911. The 1925 New York State census listed him as arriving in 1905, his wife and children in 1910, and stated that he was naturalized in 1908 in White Plains (note that the federal census gave a naturalization date, but not a place). It was now time to look for naturalization records and ships' passenger lists to determine the correct dates.

NATURALIZATION RECORDS

Before you begin to look for naturalization records, it would be beneficial to look for a book about this subject. For instance, *The Source: A Guidebook of American Genealogy,* edited by Loretto Szucs and Sandra Luebking, has a chapter about naturalization records. Then you might go to a more detailed guidebook (if one exists on a particular record group), such as *Naturalization Records of the United States,* by Christina Schaefer.

First Papers

When someone wanted to become a citizen of the United States, the person had to fulfill residency requirements and make an application (before 1922, wives automatically became citizens when their husbands did). Prior to 1906 an alien could apply for citizenship at any court of law. An immigrant could file "first papers," or a declaration of intent, at one court and "final papers," or a naturalization petition, at a different court. After 1906, records were forwarded to the Immigration and Naturalization Service, and inquiries should be directed to the appropriate district office (see Appendix). Some naturalization records (declarations and petitions) have been microfilmed and are available through the Family History Library. In its catalog holdings, check under the state and county (and sometimes the city) in which the naturalization took place. You may also check directly with the county court in which you believe your ancestor was naturalized.

In the declaration of intention, or "first papers," an alien renounced any allegiance to the foreign homeland and declared he wanted to become an American citizen. Proof of United States residency was not required. The records created before 1906 primarily contain the applicant's name, (sometimes) country of birth, date of application, signature, and sometimes the age, occupation, and date and port of arrival. After 1906 the intention includes the applicant's name, age, occupation, and personal description; date and place of birth; citizenship; present address and last foreign address;

vessel and port of embarkation; United States port and date of arrival; date of application; and signature.

Second, or Final, Papers

In the naturalization petition, or "second or final papers," an adult immigrant who had already filed the intention papers and had met the residency requirements now made a formal application for citizenship. Information on post-1906 petitions includes name, residence, occupation, date and place of birth, citizenship, and personal description of applicant; date of emigration; ports of embarkation and arrival; marital status and name of spouse; names, dates, places of birth, and residence of applicant's children; date at which United States residence commenced; time of residence in state; name changes; and signature. After 1930 photographs may also be included. In the deposition that accompanies the petition, witnesses signed in support of the applicant.

As of July 17, 1862, an alien twenty-one years or older could acquire citizenship by enlisting in the military and receiving an honorable discharge. The alien did not have to make a declaration of intention or prove residency. He simply petitioned the United States government. The county courthouse may have the veteran's military discharge and petition. Also look for the individual's military records. See James C. Neagles's *U.S. Military Records: A Guide to Federal and State Sources.*

If you don't know exactly when or where your ancestor arrived, seek the naturalization record first; depending on the year, it may give you the immigration information, or at least narrow the possible time of arrival.

Somehow, I ended up writing to the Westchester County Archives for Salvatore Ebetino's naturalization records. They sent me his declaration of intention and his petition for naturalization. From these documents I learned that he arrived on the ship *Italia* "on or about" 10 May 1906 and that his wife came on the ship *Verona* "on or about" 18 February 1910. Isn't it nice how one record can lead to another?

PASSENGER ARRIVAL LISTS

Before you can begin to search passenger arrival lists, you must know your ancestor's original birth name, approximate age at immigration, the port of arrival, and at least the year of immigration. The more specific the date, of course, the better.

Original passenger arrival lists, 1820–1957, have been microfilmed and are available through the National Archives. Most of these are also available through the Family History Library in Salt Lake City and its branches, and through loan from American Genealogical Lending Library and the National Archives (see Appendix). A guide published by the National Archives, *Immigrant and Passenger Arrivals: A Select Catalog of National Archives Microfilm Publications,* details the availability of records and indexes for the major ports of arrival (Baltimore, Boston, New Orleans, New York, and Philadelphia) and some minor ports.

Official immigration records begin in 1820, although records for some individual ports may predate this. Created at the port of departure, the early records, known as Customs Passenger Lists, from 1820 to about 1891, were kept primarily for statistical purposes, so they contain relatively limited information for genealogists: name of ship and its master, port of embarkation, date and port of arrival, each passenger's name, sex, age, occupation, and nationality.

The records created after 1891 are referred to as Immigration Passenger Lists and span to the present. The United States Privacy Laws for passenger information restrict access to those records created after 1957. Information has varied over the decades, and as the influx of immigrants became greater, more details were recorded on the arrival lists: last residence; final destination in the United States; if going to join a relative, the relative's name and address; personal description; place of birth; and name and address of closest living relative in native country.

After 1906 the lists included a physical description of all passengers, giving their height, complexion, color of hair and eyes, and identifying marks. It was on such a list that I discovered that my sixty-two-year-old great-great-grandmother was only four feet tall! Another extremely important column on the post-1906 lists is "place of birth," which gives names of villages.

After 1907 the newly added column "Name and address of closest living relative in native country" is important for identifying those who were left behind: sometimes a wife, often a parent. The "address," however, may simply be the name of the town or village.

Several published sources will assist you with the use of passenger arrival lists. For a general overview of the subject, see John Philip Colletta's *They Came in Ships,* and for a more comprehensive discussion, see Michael Tepper's *American Passenger Arrival Records: A Guide to the Records of Immigrants Arriving at American Ports by Sail and Steam.* If you know the name of a ship but only an approximate date of arrival at the United States port, consult the *Morton Allan Directory of European Passenger Steamship*

Arrivals, which covers the Port of New York, 1890–1930, and the ports of New York, Philadelphia, Boston, and Baltimore, 1904–1926. This book is arranged by year, giving names of ships and their ports and dates of arrival. For example, on Salvatore's declaration of intention, if he had stated that he came through the Port of New York and arrived on the ship *Italia* in 1906, with no specific date, I would look in the *Morton Allan Directory* to determine the exact dates that ship docked in New York in 1906 and narrow the time frame. Or sometimes an immigrant gave an exact date, but it may be off by several days, months, or years. It may save you time in the long run to check the *Morton Allan Directory* first when you have a date of arrival, just to confirm that a ship docked on a particular date at a particular port.

Passenger lists were filed at the port where the ship first landed in the United States. Your ancestor may have landed at the Port of Boston, then taken a train to a final destination in New York. Or the ship may have stopped at other ports after docking first in Boston. Be sure to check other ports if your ancestor is not found where you think he or she should be.

When you find your ancestor on the passenger arrival lists, check for other people who may have traveled from the same village. They may be related to your ancestor, and these names may likely turn up in censuses as your ancestor's neighbors or as witnesses on documents.

From Salvatore Ebetino's passenger list, I learned that he was born in Terlizzi, Italy, he was a *contadino* (farmer), he was going to Harrison, New York, to join his brother-in-law Albino DeBartolo, he paid his own passage, and he was carrying $12 in cash with him. In scanning the rest of the page where I found Salvatore, sixteen lines below his listing was a Felice Vallarelli (the same surname as Salvatore's wife), and he, too, was from Terlizzi and going to Harrison to be with his brother-in-law Albino DeBartolo. There were also five other passengers from Terlizzi with different destinations in the United States. Salvatore probably knew some of these men, if not all of them.

Sometimes the best information is found at the end of the passenger list. This is where births, deaths, and stowaways are generally listed. Had I not turned to the end of the list, I would have missed learning that my great-aunt had given birth at sea. There was no indication on the listing with the rest of the family that this event had occurred.

Two other gems, if extant, that were microfilmed at the end of each passenger list were the "Record of Detained Aliens" and "Record of Aliens Held for Special Inquiry." Many immigrants were detained at Ellis Island and other immigrant receiving stations for a night or two until relatives could come to pick them up. Information on the Record of Detained Aliens included the name of the alien, number in the family who were detained, the cause of detention, their disposition (relationship, name, and address of person picking them up), the date and time of release, and the number of meals they ate during detention. Unescorted women and their children were always held until their husbands or other male relatives claimed them. If the male escort was waiting for them when the boat docked, then the woman and her children will not be listed on the record of detained aliens.

Angelina Ebetino was traveling with her four children, and they were detained overnight at Ellis Island until Salvatore, who was living in Rye, New York, arrived to get them. From the Record of Detained Aliens I know that while she was there, Angelina and her family ate supper that night and breakfast the next morning. They were released from Ellis Island at 9:20 A.M.

The Record of Aliens Held for Special Inquiry noted the cause of the detention, actions taken by the Board of Special Inquiry, date of hearings, the number of meals eaten during detention, and if deported, the date, name of vessel, and port from which they returned to the homeland. The initials L.P.C. under the cause meant "likely public charge" (a person who probably would not be able to support himself and thus be a burden on public tax dollars); L.C.D. referred to "loathsome contagious disease." Both were grounds for deportation.

After searching passenger lists, I hit what looked like a dead end in research. While the passenger lists had given me fabulous information, they had not conveniently led me to other obvious records in this country. The question you need to ask yourself is what other records might this person or family have created or been noted on during their lifetimes? Think of the events and circumstances in your own lifetime that have left a paper trail; you may find these types of records on your ancestors, too: birth, baptism, school, Social Security card, draft registration, employment, marriage, divorce, buying property, death.

CITY DIRECTORIES

City directories can be used to fill in gaps left by other records such as censuses that are usually available only every ten years. A city directory is an alphabetical list of inhabitants in a city. It can be frustrating to use because, like many genealogical sources, there is no standard city directory. Contents and availability vary from city to city and from one time period to another. Most directories are issued annually, others sporadically.

City directories list names of adults, including adult children living with parents. Some also list occupation, name of employer, home address, and spouse's name. Although it is uncommon, I've found directories that list a date of death for someone in the household. More commonly, the spouse is listed as a widow or widower the year following the death. In small communities, directories may tell where a family has relocated to.

City directories became more widely published in the late 1800s, but a few date as early as the late 1700s. Each city is different. You need to learn when directories were published for your area of interest. The local library for that area is the best starting place to find directories. There are major directory collections at the Library of Congress in Washington, D.C.; the Family History Library in Salt Lake City; the Allen County Public Library in Fort Wayne, Indiana; and the New England Historic Genealogical Society in Boston. The Family History Library has an extensive collection on microfilm. To find whether its directory holdings include the time period and locality of your interest, check the Family History Library Catalog at one of their Family History Centers. Look under "United States, Directories," or by the state, then county, then city, then directories.

Gaining access to directories can also be a challenge. Some librarians may be willing to conduct a five- to ten-year search through their directories on a mail request. You may also try obtaining directories on interlibrary loan if they were microfilmed. But you may have to hire a researcher in the area to conduct a more thorough search, especially if you have several names to be checked.

As with all published material, typographical errors occur. Check variant spellings of the surname. Try transposing some of the letters. For example, if you were searching for Carmack, you would also check under Cormack, Karmack, and Cramack.

A helpful feature of some twentieth-century city directories is the Householder's Index or Criss-Cross Directory. It is sometimes found at the back of the directory, or it may be a separate volume. These are alphabetical/numerical listings of streets followed by house numbers and inhabitants instead of an alphabetical listing of individuals. The Householder's Index is a wonderful way to discover your ancestors' neighbors' names.

Here are two examples of how city directories and the Householder's Index can aid in tracking women in particular. Women are sometimes more difficult to trace because their surnames change when they marry (see my book, *A Genealogist's Guide to Discovering Your Female Ancestors*, available spring 1998). I was looking for a woman who lived in Colorado Springs in the late 1970s. I found Mindy McFarland living at 53 Main Street in 1978.

The next year she was not listed. For a clue as to whether she moved or married, I turned to the Householder's Index for Main Street, number 53. The name of the inhabitant, Joe Thayer, was living at that address with a wife named Mindy. I located a marriage record to confirm that I had the right person, then continued to follow her in the city directories to the present under her married name.

In another case, I was trying to determine whether Daisy Hunington was divorced or widowed. It is difficult for someone other than a relative to obtain Colorado death records, so I consulted city directories to eliminate hours of searching through obituaries and divorce indexes. Daisy and Randy Hunington lived in the same house for three years after their marriage. In the fourth year, they were listed in separate households. Randy was listed apart from Daisy for several years, ruling out his death. This also narrowed down the time period in which to search for a divorce record.

In the case of Salvatore and Angelina Ebetino, I was able to locate them in only two city directories—not because they weren't listed in others, but because I only had access to two volumes on a research trip to the Library of Congress. I found them listed in the 1928–29 and the 1932 Port Chester and Rye, New York, city directories. Here's how their listings looked:

> 1928–29
> Ebetino Salvatore (Angelina) gdnr h16 Nursery la
>
> 1932
> Ebetino Salvatore (Angelina) gdnr h15 W Purdy av

From these two listings, I know that Salvatore was a gardener (gdnr), and I can narrow down when they moved from Nursery Lane to West Purdy Avenue. (The *h* stands for "house." Check the beginning of the directory for meanings of the abbreviations.) There was no Householder's Index for these two directories.

City directories offer other valuable information. The business section lists undertakers, providing the names of funeral homes in operation during the time your ancestor died. It will also give you names of churches and cemeteries in the area. To locate ancestors who did not live in a city, you may be able to find county directories. Small or rural communities may be included in directories of large cities.

Once you determine where the directories you need are stored and the time period for which they are available, researching these volumes may provide clues and a great deal more information.

CHURCH RECORDS

The Yellow Pages of the Colorado Springs telephone directory list more than ninety religious denominations. There are probably even more than that throughout the country. Each denomination and individual church will have its own restrictions and rules on public access to church records—and this could change with each minister. For example, when I visited the (Catholic) Church of the Resurrection in Rye, New York, and asked if I might search baptismal records on my ancestors, I was handed the volumes and allowed to look through them at my leisure. Two years later, I wrote and informed a different priest at this same church of an impending visit and asked if I could view the records again. He denied my request.

Many historical church records from previous centuries have been transcribed or microfilmed. The first place to check is the Family History Library or one of its Centers.

When you do find church records, you will gain a good deal of information on your ancestors, and these are a good substitute when no vital records exist. Keep in mind, however, that some denominations do not require infant baptisms but conduct adult baptisms, so a baptism may not indicate an approximate birth year.

Other church records to look for are marriages, burials, confirmations, memberships, and admissions and removals.

Remember the number of children in the Ebetino family?

Children:

1. Frank   b. 21 Nov 1900, Terlizzi, Bari, Italy

2. Fred   b. 25 Feb 1904, Terlizzi, Bari, Italy

3. Stella   b. 27 May 1905, Terlizzi, Bari, Italy

4. Isabella   b. 17 Dec 1911, Rye, Westchester, NY

                   d. 1 Sep 1918

5. Philip   b. 8 Apr 1912, Rye, Westchester, NY

6. Michael   b. 12 Apr 1915, Rye, Westchester, NY

7. Salvatore   b. 4 Apr 1917, Rye, Westchester, NY

                   d. 25 Feb 1920

When I searched the records at the Church of the Resurrection, I found a baptism for two Michaels. One was born 12 February 1914 and was baptized 10 May 1914; the other was born 12 April 1915 and baptized 24 October 1915. Both children had as their parents Salvatore and Angelina. When I questioned my Uncle Mike (the one born in April), he said, "Oh, yeah, there was another son with my name who died as a baby." I asked him if any other children had been born and not survived, "Yes, I think there was another boy named Fred who was born and died in Italy before your Uncle Fred was born." I guess I just hadn't asked the right questions the first time.

SOCIAL SECURITY RECORDS

Social Security records can provide you with some of the same information you would find on a birth or death record: name, date and place of birth, parents' names. They will also give you residence and employment information: name and address of the person's employer when the applicant obtained a Social Security number. This can lead you to potential employment records on an ancestor. The real value in the Social Security record is that the applicant supplied the information, not someone else. On a death record, for example, a relative of the deceased gave the information.

No one in the family knew the names of Salvatore's parents. His death certificate only listed his father as Frank and mother as Stella. His death certificate also gave me Salvatore's Social Security number. The U.S. Social Security Death Index at the Family History Library was not available at that time, so I wrote directly to the Social Security Administration (SSA) to see what records they had on him (Social Security Administration, Office of Central Records, Operation for Genealogy, 300 N. Greene Street, Baltimore, MD 21201; write and ask for the current fee). They sent me his SS-5 Application for a Social Security number. I nearly hit the ceiling when it arrived. Right there on the photocopy of the original form, Salvatore named his parents: Frank Ebetino and Stella Tangara. This is the only American record I have ever found giving his parents' first and last names.

The Social Security Death Index is described in Chapter 7 under the Family History Library, but please keep in mind that the information you get from the computer database is minimal. Follow up by writing to the Social Security Administration and requesting a photocopy of form SS-5. It is important to ask for this specifically; otherwise you may end up with the same computer printout.

When you write to the SSA, having the Social Security number will help speed your request and will be less expensive. So check the Death Index first because you don't need the number to check it. The SSA will only release information on deceased persons.

To summarize, in the search for Salvatore and Angelina (Vallarelli) Ebetino, I've explored the following sources:

- personal knowledge

- oral history interviews with relatives

- published sources

- vital records

- newspaper obituaries

- cemeteries

- census records

- passenger arrival lists

- city directories

- church records

- Social Security records

Let's move on to the next chapter and look at another ancestor and some more records you might explore.

Chapter 9

Researching in Historical Documents: Case Study #2

CASE STUDY #2:
NINETEENTH-CENTURY FRONTIER FARMERS

During this country's expansion during the nineteenth century, thousands of families migrated to new lands further west, hoping for a better way of life. If you had ancestors in America during the nineteenth century, they very likely were a part of this movement. James and Mary Ann Goforth began life in Tennessee and settled in Dade County, Missouri.

INTERVIEWS WITH RELATIVES AND CEMETERY SEARCH

My husband's grandmother is still living, and James and Mary Ann Goforth were her great-grandparents. She did not have any personal knowledge of them, since James died the year after she was born and Mary Ann died four years before she was born. Granny did know their names, however, and where they were buried. She took my husband and me to Sinking Creek Cemetery in Dade County, where I copied the tombstone inscription and was able to get their vital statistics:

James Harry Goforth
1833–1914
Civil War Veteran
son of Charles and Luvina Goforth

Mary Ann Goforth
1835–1909
Wife of James

VITAL RECORDS

According to Kemp's *International Vital Records Handbook,* "The Missouri Bureau of Vital Records [in Springfield] has birth and death records from January 1, 1910." James was born in 1833 and Mary Ann in 1835, so I would not find an official birth certificate for either one of them. Mary Ann died a year before mandatory state recordings of deaths. But James died after 1910, so I sent for his death certificate. Here's what that record told me:

> Place of Death: Dade County, Rock Prairie Township
> Name of Deceased: James Harry Goforth
> Sex: Male
> Color: White
> Marital Status: Widower
> Date of Birth: 14 October 1833
> Age: 80 years, 6 months
> Occupation: Retired farmer
> Birthplace: Tennessee
> Name of Father: Don't know
> Birthplace of Father: Don't know
> Maiden Name of Mother: Don't know
> Birthplace of Mother: Don't know

> The above is true to the best of my knowledge: W. H. Goforth, Everton, MO

> Date of Death: May 3, 1914
> Cause of Death: Pneumonia
> Contributory: Exposure
> Signed: [doctor's signature, which, naturally, is unreadable]

> Place of burial: Grove Cemetery
> Date of burial: May 4, 1914
> Undertaker: J. A. Mason, Everton, MO

Interestingly, the person who supplied the information for the death certificate, W. H. Goforth, who was James's son, didn't know the names of his grandparents.

Maybe James and Mary Ann's marriage license would give me more information, including Mary Ann's parents' names. Kemp's book told me that the best way to get a copy of a Missouri marriage record is to write to the county courthouse where the marriage took place. This is true for many states. Unfortunately, the clerk responded that there was no record of their marriage in Dade County. Johni Cerny and Sandra Luebking give an interesting account of a mail request in their chapter on marriage and divorce records in *The Source: A Guidebook to American Genealogy*: "I made three separate [mail] requests for a single marriage license to the same county. The clerk wrote back each time saying that there was no record on file. Upon visiting that county myself a few years later, I found the document in less than five minutes." The moral of the story: Do the checking yourself whenever possible.

Had I found a marriage license for James and Mary Ann, it might have told me the full names of the bride and groom, their residences, their parents' names, any previous marriages, occupations, and places of birth. An important point to keep in mind is that many couples took out marriage licenses but never got married. Always look for the marriage certificate or some notation on the license that the marriage did take place. These records are usually indexed; however, many are prepared only by the groom's surname.

CENSUS RECORDS

James died in 1914, so the most recent federal census where I could look for him was 1910. He was living alone in Everton, Dade County, Missouri, a seventy-six-year-old widower. This census confirmed the information I found on the tombstone that he was a Civil War veteran, plus it told me that he was in the Union Army. I continued to check censuses, working backward in time, adding more information to my family group sheet. But now I had a new document to obtain: his military records.

MILITARY RECORDS

A helpful book for finding and using military records is James Neagles's *U.S. Military Records*. In this book, Neagles discusses the records created for each war in which America was involved and where to find those documents. These include compiled service records, pensions, and bounty-land warrants. Detailed personal information may be found in enlistment forms, muster rolls, and pension applications. Although most historical military records are housed at the National Archives, there may also be records at the Veterans Administration, in state archives, and historical societies.

Wars have been a part of American history since the late 1600s, most of them creating records of servicemen and women. For all your male ancestors especially, look at their date of birth and figure out the years when they would have reached their late teens through their thirties. Then determine if a war was happening at that time. If so, you have a likely candidate for military records.

James Goforth was about twenty-eight when the Civil War broke out; thus, he likely served (as his tombstone told me he did). I sent for his military service records and pension file directly from the National Archives in Washington, D.C., giving them his name, dates and places of birth and death, and stating that he served in the Union Army either from Missouri or Tennessee. (There are forms to obtain records, which you may order from the National Archives [NATF Form 80: Order for Copies of Veterans Records], and you will need to provide the name of the state from which the veteran served.) From his military record, I learned that James was in the Fifteenth Missouri Cavalry. He enlisted in Melville on 1 November 1863 for twenty months. He was born in Jefferson County, Tennessee. At the time of his enlistment he was a thirty-year-old farmer. He had blue eyes, light-colored hair, a fair complexion, and was 5 feet, 9 inches tall. He was a corporal and was discharged from duty on 30 June 1865.

From his pension record I learned even more. It confirmed his death date of 3 May 1914. He was last paid a pension of $27 on 4 February 1914. On his pension application, James said that he was married to "Mary Ann Goforth late Davidson" (ah, now we have her maiden name!). He stated that he was married on 7 September 1854 by L. L. Carlock, Justice of the Court, but that the record of his marriage was burned with the courthouse during the Civil War. Although the question also asked where he was married, he never gave that information. He further stated that he had "never married but once" and that his children were A. W. Goforth, born 19 September 1855; W. H. Goforth, born 10 March 1857; Levina O. Goforth, born 23 July 1861; James T. Goforth, born 17 February 1864; John B. Goforth, born 23 September 1867; C. N. Goforth, born 18 February 1869; Lillian Goforth, born 16 April 1871; and Homer E. Goforth, born 14 March 1875.

On several occasions James asked for increases in his pension check because of new or additional disabilities. In one disposition dated 30 March 1891, he stated that he had "chronic disease of stomach and bowels and piles. Also rheumatism was incurred at Springfield, State of Missouri, from effects of jaundice about the month of November 1864. . . . Also incurred injury to left wrist at Dadeville, Missouri, by accidental shot of revolver while cleaning up arms. About the month of March or April 1865." On 10 May 1904, he claimed that he had a "lame arm, stomach and liver trouble, kidney trouble, such disabilities render him totally incapable of earning a support by manual labor." In addition to James's testimonies, there are notarized letters from his doctor and people who knew of these injuries. This particular file contained at least twenty-five handwritten legal-size pages. I have heard of files that contain hundreds of pages.

When ordering records from the National Archives and many other repositories by mail, you may receive copies of only part of the file. Always request the complete file and *ask the cost,* which may be beyond your budget. It may be more economical in the long run to wait and make a research trip to the repository, where you can also look at many other records that pertain to several ancestors.

FINDING OTHERS INTERESTED IN THE GOFORTHS

While I was compiling information on James and Mary Ann from original records, I wanted to see if other descendants had already done work on the Goforth line. I found out there was a genealogical column published in one of the Dade County newspapers (check Anita Milner's *Newspaper Genealogical Column Directory*). So I sent a query. My husband's grandmother had also given me the address of a distant cousin in Union, Washington. I looked for people advertising in the *Genealogical Helper* who were also searching Goforths of Missouri and Tennessee. I ended up corresponding with nine Goforth descendants, and each one gave me new information or leads to follow.

Let's summarize the records in the Goforth study:

- oral history interviews with relatives
- tombstone inscriptions
- vital records
- census records
- military records
- genealogical queries

MORE EXAMPLES OF RECORDS

To illustrate the next two types of records, land and probate, I am going to use several examples from other than the Ebetino and Goforth families since these will cover a greater variety of time periods.

LAND RECORDS

For the most part, you can find land records from the beginning of a town or county's settlement. Land has been distributed through many means. During colonial times, land was granted to attract settlers. In Virginia, for example, a person who paid another person's passage to the colony was given fifty acres of land. This was known as a "headright grant." As an incentive to join the military, soldiers were sometimes given "bounty land warrants" after their service was completed. Land has also been transferred from one person to another through instruments known as deeds. Land records may be found in federal archives, state land offices, and county courthouses. *The Source: A Guidebook of American Genealogy* has an excellent chapter on this subject by Sandra Luebking, which is a good starting place. Then you might want to read E. Wade Hone's *Land and Property Research in the United States.*

Land transactions between individuals are generally recorded in deed books in the county where the land is located, and there are usually indexes to these volumes. The Family History Library has a large collection of county courthouse records on microfilm, so be sure to check there, too. Deed books may also contain items like mortgages, gifts of transfer, powers of attorney, marriage property settlements, and bills of sale for slaves and other items. There are usually two types of indexes: one for grantors (persons selling the property), which may be called a direct index in some states; the other is for grantees (persons buying or receiving the property), called an indirect index. Transactions with more than one buyer or seller may be indexed under the first person who is listed in the document, followed by "et al.," which means "and others." You may see after a man's name "et ux.," which means "and wife." If the owner of the property was deceased when the land was sold, and the person's executor was making the transaction, then the deed may be recorded under the executor's name. As with any other index, there may be omissions and errors; you need to take this into consideration if you do not find a land entry for one of your ancestors.

Legal land descriptions are generally given by two methods: the metes and bounds system or the rectangular survey system. The metes and bounds system uses natural and artificial landmarks and adjacent property ("beginning at a white oak . . . bounded on the east by the property that borders William Thomas . . .") and is used in the thirteen original states, as well as Maine, Vermont, West Virginia, Kentucky, Tennessee, Texas, and Hawaii. The rest of the states, known as public domain states, use the rectangular survey system, which divides land into sections ("the West half of the Northeast quarter of Section 15, Township 3 South, Range 4 East").

Here are two deed transcriptions (verbatim copies), one showing the metes and bounds system, the other the rectangular survey system. This first deed is taken from Volume 1, pages 28–29, of the Orange County, Virginia, deeds.

> This Indenture made the nineteenth day of May In the Year of our Lord God One thousand Seven hundred and Thirty five Between Michael Clauro of the County of Orange of the one part And— Michael Oneal of the aforesaid County of Orange of the Other part Witnesseth that the said Michael Clauro for and in consideration of the Sum of five shillings Sterling to him in hand paid by the said Michael Oneal The Receipt whereof is hereby acknowledged Hath granted bargained and Sold And by these presents doth grant bargain and sell unto the said Michael Oneal all that tract or parcel of Land containing one hundred Acres Situate lying and being in the County of Orange in the fork of Robinson being part of Six hundred ninety Eight Acres of Land granted to Michael Clauro and John Clauro beginning at the Lower Corner of the said Land at two red oaks thence North twenty degrees East two hundred poles to two white oaks thence North fifty degrees West to a white and red oak on the River thence down the River to the beginning— And all houses, edifices, buildings, gardens, orchards, meadows, commons—pastures, feedings, trees, woods, underwoods, ways, paths, waters, and watercourse, Easements, profits, commodities, Advantages, Emoluments, Hereditaments, Rights Members and Appurtenances whatsoever to the same belonging or otherwise appertaining or which now are or formerly have been accepted, reputed, taken, known, used, occupied [*sic*] or enjoyed to do with the same or as part parcel or member there of and the Reversion and Reversions Remainder and Remainders Rents and Services of the said premises above mentioned and of every part and parcel thereof with the appurtenances To have and to hold the said Lands Hereditaments and premises above mentioned and every part and parcel thereof with the Appurtenances unto the said Michael Oneal his executors and Adm^s [administrators] and—Assigns from the first of this Instant May for and during and unto the full end and

term of one whole Year from thence next and immediately ensuing and following and fully to be compleat [*sic*] and ended yielding and paying therefore one pepper corn in and upon the feast of St. Michael the Archangel is demanded of To the Intent that by Virtue of these presents and force of the Statute for transferring of Uses into possession he the said Michael Oneal may be in the actual possession of all and—Singular the said premises above mentioned with the appurtenances—and thereby be enabled to accept and take a grant of Release of the Reversion and Inheritance thereof to him and his heirs to the only proper Use and behalf of him the said Michael Oneal his heirs and Assigns forever. In Witness whereof the said Michael Clauro hath hereunto set his hand and seal the day Month and Year first above written.

Sealed and delivered in the presence of Us the above mentioned five Shillings Sterling being first paid

the Words of John Clauro being interline first on the tenth line.

his
Michael X Clauro
mark

At a court held for Orange County on Tuesday, the twentieth day of May 1735 Michael Clauro acknowledged this his Lease to Michael Oneal which on the motion of the said Michael Oneal is admitted to record.

Henry Willis

This next deed came from Book A, page 146, of the Johnson County, Kansas, deeds.

This Indenture made this 16th day of June in the year of our Lord one Thousand Eight Hundred and fifty Eight between George Miller and Margaret his wife of Douglas County Territory of Kansas and Frederick W. Case of Johnson County Said Territory of the second part Witnesseth that the said party of the first part, for and in consideration of the sum of Seven Hundred Dollars to them in hand paid by the said party of the Second part, the receipt whereof is hereby acknowledged, have granted bargained and sold

and by these presents do grant bargain and sell unto the said party of the second part his heirs and assigns all that certain piece or parcel of land in Johnson County aforesaid and described as follows To wit; The North East Quarter of Section Thirty two (32) in Township Thirteen (13) of Range Twenty four (24) Containing one hundred and sixty (160) acres more or less. To have and to hold the said premises with the appurtenances unto the said party of the second part his heirs and assigns forever. And the said partys [*sic*] of the first part do hereby covenant with the said party of the second part, his heirs and assigns, that they are lawfully seized of the premises aforesaid; that the said premises are free and clear from all encumbrances whatsoever, and that they will forever warrant and defend the same, with the appurtenances unto the said party of the second part, his heirs and assigns, against the lawful claim of all persons whomsoever. In Witness whereof the said parties of the first part have hereunto set their hands and seals the day and year first above written
Signed Sealed and delivered
in presence of
E. D. Ladd and Caleb S. Pratt
Territory of Kansas
Douglas County

[signed] George Miller

her
Margaret X Miller
mark

On this 16th day of June A.D. 1858 before me a Notary Public in and for said County came George Miller to me known to be the persons described in and who executed the above conveyance, and acknowledged the same to be their own free act and deed. The said Margaret being by me first made acquainted with the contents of said instrument, upon an examination apart from her said husband acknowledged that she executed, and relinquishes her dower in the real estate therein mentioned freely and without compulsion or undue influence of her said husband.

E. D. Ladd
Notary Public

Delivered for Record June 29th 1858 at 4 P.M.
J. N. Blake Recorder

After reading these two deeds, can you understand why you might want to abstract them (taking notes on the crucial information and leaving out the legal mumbo-jumbo)? Wading through these documents while on a research trip can become tedious; it's better to take along an abstract for reference. Here are the same two documents abstracted:

Orange County, Virginia, Deeds
Volume 1, pp. 28–29
Family History Library Microfilm #0033011

Deed between
    Michael Clauro of Orange County, grantor, and
    Michael Oneal of Orange County, grantee.
Dated 19 May 1735; recorded 20 May 1735

In consideration of the sum of five shillings sterling
Description of property: All that tract or parcel of Land containing one hundred Acres Situate lying and being in the County of Orange in the fork of Robinson being part of Six hundred ninety Eight Acres of Land granted to Michael Clauro and John Clauro beginning at the Lower Corner of the said Land at two red oaks thence North twenty degrees East two hundred poles to two white oaks thence North fifty degrees West to a white and red oak on the River thence down the River to the beginning.
Michael Clauro made his mark: X
Witness: John Clauro

Johnson County, Kansas, Deeds
Book A, page 146
Family History Library Microfilm #1618042

Deed between
    George and Margaret Miller (grantors) of Douglas County, Territory of Kansas, grantors, and

Frederick W. Case (grantee) of Johnson County, Territory of Kansas
Dated 16 June 1858; recorded 29 June 1858

In consideration of the sum of $700
Description of the property: All that certain piece or parcel of land in Johnson County aforesaid and described as follows To wit; The North East Quarter of Section Thirty two (32) in Township Thirteen (13) of Range Twenty four (24) Containing one hundred and sixty (160) acres more or less.
Release of Dower: Margaret relinquished her dower rights.
Signed George Miller; Margaret made her mark: X
Witnesses: E. D. Ladd and Caleb S. Pratt

Do you agree that these are much easier to read and review when necessary? Still, make a photocopy of the original. You may want to recheck it for items missed during your first (or tenth) reading.

WILLS AND PROBATE

Probate is actually a process, not a document, which transfers property and items of the deceased to heirs. Wills or court orders are the documents that name these transfers. When a person dies leaving a valid will, that person is said to have died "testate." When a person dies leaving no valid will, then that person is said to have died "intestate."

Not everyone leaves a will, and not all wills get recorded. Those that are recorded are generally indexed. Wills are usually probated in the court that has jurisdiction where the person died.

Wills usually state family relationships, but they may not always give names. John may leave his estate to "my wife." Everyone at the time knew who his wife was, even though you don't. You may also learn daughters' married surnames since they are likely to be mentioned by their husband's name.

Just because a child is not named in a will does not mean the child died before the testator. That child could have received a share of the estate before the parent's death. Or maybe there was a family disagreement and that child was omitted on purpose. If a will was contested, this fact should be filed with the original probate.

The probate process is as follows:

1. A person makes a will.

2. The person dies.

3. The will is presented to the probate court.

4. The court admits the will to probate.

5. The will is recorded.

6. The executor (person named in the will who will see that all requests and bequeaths are taken care of; executrix if the named person is female) usually makes an inventory of the deceased's estate. Other items in the process may include a notice to heirs of accounts, distributions, sale of property (real and personal).

7. The provisions of the will are carried out after all debts are paid.

In an intestate case the process is similar, except there is no valid will:

1. The person dies.

2. Someone with an interest in the estate petitions the probate court (seeking letters of administration).

3. The court appoints an administrator (administratrix if a woman is appointed), who assumes essentially the same tasks as an executor or executrix.

4. Administrator makes an inventory and pays the deceased's debts.

5. Any remaining estate is distributed.

Probate packets and wills recorded in will books are held at the county courthouse, unless the records have been transferred to a state archive. (If the original will is still on file, you will want to check it since errors could have been made when the will was hand-copied into the will book.) The Family History Library in Salt Lake City may have the will you need on microfilm, and copies can be obtained less expensively than writing directly to a county courthouse. States have different names for probate courts; some places may call it a superior court, a circuit court, a district court, a chancery court, a register of wills, or a surrogate's court. Check *The Handy Book for Genealogists* or *Ancestry's Red Book* for county courthouse addresses and the name of the appropriate jurisdiction.

Here's an example of an eighteenth-century will that came from Stafford County, Virginia, Deed and Will Book 1748–1763, page 391:

In the name of God I Townshend Dade of the County of Stafford and Parish of Saint Pauls being at this time sick & weak but of perfect sense & memory praised be God and as touching such goods & Estate as it hath pleased God to bestow on me, doth think proper to dispose of in the Following manner First I give to my Daughter Elizabeth Washington Dinah Virgin & their increase which she has in her possession, to her, & her assigns forever. Secondly I give to my Grandson Langhorn Dade one negro man named Juba. Thirdly I give to my son Baldwin Dade, two negro men called Solomon & George—Fourthly I give to Sarah Dade widow of Cadwallador Dade two negroes Ben & Sukey. Fifthly I give to my Daughter Frances Stuart the following Negroes Tom, Kate, Nancy, & their increase, which she has in her possession. Sixthly, I give to my son Horatio Dade the Following—negroes Harry, Jolly, Daniel, Moses, Nan & her increase, Seventhly I give to my Loving wife Rose Dade twelve ewes & one ram Lastly I give to my son Horatio Dade all the rest of my estate of what kind soever both real & personal. My will is that the tobacco in Grants Lands and the crop of tobacco I have by me, be equally divided between my wife Rose Dade & my son Horatio Dade. Lastly I constitute and appoint my loving wife, & my son Horatio Dade Executors of this my last will & Testament revoking and disannulling all other wills by me made whereunto I have set my hand & seal this 9th day of April 1761.
Signed, Sealed & Delivered
in presence of us interlined before
[signed]
Townshend Dade
signed Will Young [&] Richard A. McClannen

At a court held for Stafford County June the 9th: 1761—
The within last will & Testament of Townshend Dade, Gent. deced was presented in Court by Horatio Dade, Gent. one of the Exs therein named who made oath thereto according to Law and being further proved by the oath of the witnesses there to is admitted to record; and on motion of the said Exs & be performing what is usual in such cases. Certificate is granted to him for obtaining a probate thereof in due form.

Although the will may have been recorded and preserved, the inventory and other papers in the probate packet may have been destroyed or lost over the years. Still, always check for the inventory. This will detail the deceased's belongings and assign a monetary value to them. You can actually follow the executor or administrator going from room to room in the person's house. Here's a small sampling from an inventory taken in 1682 that was published in Howard Millar Chapin's *Life of Deacon Samuel Chapin of Springfield* (Providence: Snow & Farnham Co., 1908):

An Inventory of ye Estate of Cicely Chapin deceased ye Wife of Deacon Samll Chapin of Springfd taken March 5th 1682, taken by us Jonathan Burt Senr and Benjamine Parsons Senr.

One Rugg at 20ˢ One Coverlitt & blue blancket 15ˢ
One pr of Bodyes, a green apron & a Wascoate at 10ˢ a Cloak &
    Cloath hood 25ˢ
One bed at 30ˢ To 3 pillows & one bolster at 10ˢ
One Cloath Wascoate & one serge Wascoate 20ˢ blue apron, serge
    Neckcloath 5ˢ
To 4 coats at 3ᴸ a Cloath hood at 5ˢ one pr stockings, 2 Wascoats at 6ˢ
To 2 handkerchiefs, one dressing 4ˢ One sheet one slip 2 pillow-
    beirg 12ˢ
To 1 Chest one wheele, 2 Keelers 12ˢ to 3 platters at 12ˢ
To 1 pe of tongs, fire shovell, iron pots 2 pe pot hooks 2 tramels,
    Crooke
To 1 Bedstead 5ˢ one pʳ bitle rings, 3 wedges 10ˢ brass Kettle 5ˢ
To 1 hooe 2 axes a Whifletreechaine a spitt 14 a pot, iron Kettell 28ˢ
To 2 platters at 6ˢ An iron Kettell a pr Brass seales & weights 30ˢ
To a leather jacket a peas hook a frying pan 15ˢ
A debt of Japhet Chapins at 40ᴸ for Land hire of a cow 40ˢ
To a cow hide 8ˢ By pay of two Cows at 6ᴸ 15ˢ
To a steere & a Cow at 6ᴸ 10ˢ fan & grindstone at 12ˢ 6ᵈ
To a debt of John Hitchcocks at 25ᴸ

A more "modern" inventory shows some of Mary Clark's belongings (Greenwich, Connecticut, probate volume 32, pages 493–98, 11 July 1908):

Personal Property

North Bed-Room	
Carpet	$ .25
Bedstead	2.00
3 Mattresses	2.50
1 Bed Spring	.50

2 Pair Curtains	.50
Feather Bed	.05
Bed Spread & Bolsters	2.00
Steamer Chair	.40
Low Chair	.25
Bureau	.25
Wash-stand	.75
Lantern	.20
Trunk	.75
7 Pictures	.75
1 Glass	.25
2 Frames	.20
Small Box	.10
	$12.00

Finally, let's look at an intestate probate, also from Greenwich, Connecticut, probate volume 28, page 622–23, 2 September 1903:

Estate of David Norris
Inventory value of Estate $500.00

To the Court of Probate for the District of Greenwich:
Estate of David Norris late of Greenwich in said District, dec'd.

The subscribers, appointed appraisers on said Estate, having been legally sworn have appraised all the property. Included in the Inventory of the Administratrix of said estate including choices in action, according to its value as follows, viz:—The undivided one half of all that certain tract, piece or parcel of land with the buildings thereon situated in said town of Greenwich, bounded and described as follows; commencing at a point formed by the intersection of the public highway old Post Road so-called and a highway called Grigg Ave., and running thence easterly along land of David Lyon thence southerly along said Post Road to land now or formerly of David Lyon one hundred and seventy (170) feet thence Northerly through land of said Fannie B. Grigg to the south side of Grigg Ave., so-called at a point one hundred and fifty five (155) feet Easterly of the point beginning and thence Westerly along said Grigg Ave., one hundred and fifty five (155) feet to the point of beginning Together with all rights of said Grantor in and to said highways in front of and adjoining said above described premises to the center lines thereof, subject to the right of the public therein.

There is no encumbrance on the property excepting that the deed is given upon the express condition that no intoxicating liquor shall be sold on the premises conveyed by this deed and this restriction shall apply to the heirs and assigns of said grantees and run with the land. Warranty deed of said premises is recorded in Vol. 84, page 462 of Greenwich Town Records.

Amount, $500.

Appraisers under oath: Wm. H. Wessels, Charles E. Grigg

her

Delia   X   Norris Administratrix

mark

NON-POPULATION SCHEDULES

There are four types of federal non-population schedules that are just as fascinating and interesting as the population enumerations: mortality, manufacturing/industry, agricultural, and social statistics. You can use these schedules in the National Archives or obtain them through lending library programs (see Chapter 10); some are available through the Family History Library. State archives or libraries will likely have the schedules that pertain to their state.

Mortality Schedules

These schedules will give you the name of the deceased, sex, age, color, whether free or slave, marital status, place of birth (state, territory, or country), month of death, occupation, disease or cause of death, and the number of days ill.

Mortality schedules list the people who died during the twelve-month period prior to the official census date, or more precisely for the time span of 1 June through 31 May of 1849–50, 1859–60, 1869–70, 1879–80, and 1884–85. Mortality schedules were taken only for the census years 1850, 1860, 1870, 1880, and 1885. Mortality schedules, 1850–80 and for 1885 South Dakota only, are indexed on microfiche and on CD-ROM. If you'll recall from the discussion on vital records, these years predate when most states mandated the reporting of deaths. If your ancestor was considerate enough to die during one of these twelve-month periods for these census years, make sure you check the mortality schedules, even though omissions occurred.

Even if your ancestor did not die at the right time to be included in a mortality schedule, these are still valuable to your research. By scanning the causes of death, you can get a feel for epidemics and types of illnesses people in the same area and time period as your ancestor were dying from. These diseases were listed as the causes of death for some of the inhabitants on the 1870 Boscawen, Merrimack County, New Hampshire, schedule:

- consumption (tuberculosis)

- typhoid pneumonia

- dysentery

- heart disease

- old age

- typhoid fever

- measles

- syphilis

Manufacturing/Industry Schedules

The type of information you may find on the manufacturing/industry schedules varies depending on the year, but generally you will learn about the manufacturing, mining, fisheries, mercantile, commercial, and trading businesses in the community. The name of the company or owner is given along with the kind of business, capital invested, quantity and value of materials, labor, machinery, and products.

The first manufacturing schedule was taken in 1810, but unfortunately, most of these records have been lost. There are a few among the population schedules for this time. The second was taken in 1820. None was compiled in 1830, and for 1840 only statistical information was recorded with nothing but tallies remaining. Between 1850 and 1870 they were referred to as industry schedules, but in 1880 they were called manufacturing schedules again (1880 no longer survives). There were subsequent manufacturing/industry schedules, but these were destroyed by Congressional order.

The 1820 schedule asked for the name of the owner, location of the establishment, number of employees, kind and quantity of machinery, capital invested, articles manufactured, annual production, and general remarks on the business. These schedules are arranged alphabetically by county within each state and are part of National Archives Record Group 29, twenty-seven rolls of microfilm with an index on each roll. There is also a published index: *Indexes to Manufacturers' Census of 1820: An Edited Printing of the Original Indexes and Information* (reprint; Knightstown, IN: Bookmark, n.d.).

The information on the schedules of 1850, 1860, and 1870 includes data on manufacturing, mining, fisheries, and every mercantile, commercial, and trading business with an annual gross product of $500 or more. These list the name of the company or owner, the kind of business, capital invested, quantity and value of materials, labor, machinery, and products.

Here's the listing for John Welch of Coxsackie, Greene County, New York, in 1870. He was a tailor who had $1,000 invested in his business. The kind of power he used was his hands. He had two Singer sewing machines, and in his store he had 200 yards of cloth at a value of $300.

If your ancestor owned a business, these schedules are important to your research. In any case, they're still important. The manufacturing schedules for the area in which your ancestor lived will give you a marvelous sense of the time period. No doubt your ancestor patronized some of these industries. Armed with the names of the businesses in your ancestor's area, you may be able to find some old account books that list your ancestor and purchases.

Agricultural Schedules

Many American ancestors were farmers, so these schedules are extremely valuable to the majority of researchers. The agricultural schedules give you a glimpse of your ancestor's farm life, right down to the numbers and kinds of produce and livestock. The enumerations are especially important if you find two men with the same name living in the same community—after all, no two people would own the same acres of land with the exact same livestock.

Though enumerations were taken from 1850 to 1910, only the 1850, 1860, 1870, and 1880 schedules are available to the public. The 1890 schedule went up in smoke with the 1890 population census. The 1900 and 1910 agricultural schedules were destroyed by Congressional order.

Farms with an annual produce worth $100 or more were enumerated in 1850 and 1860. For the 1870 and 1880 schedules, farms with three acres or more or with an annual produce worth $500 or more were enumerated. The schedules list the name of the owner, agent, or tenant; the kind and value of acreage, machinery, livestock, and produce.

Social Statistics

These were taken from 1850 to 1880. Though you won't find your ancestors listed on these, they will round out the information on the community in which your ancestor lived and are well worth the time to study. For each county, the statistics listed information on the value of estates; annual taxes; wages; colleges, academies, and schools; seasons and crops; libraries; newspapers and periodicals; churches; pauperism; and crime. They also list cemeteries with a general description and addresses. Some may also include a map with the cemeteries marked, the procedures for interment, the cemeteries no longer active, and the reason for closing. You may also find lists of trade societies, lodges, clubs, and other groups, giving the addresses, major branches, and names of executive officers. Churches may be listed with a brief history, a statement of doctrine and policy, and a statistical summary of membership.

On the 1870 social statistics for El Paso County, Colorado, I learned that the average wage per month for a farm hand was $25; the average wage per day of a laborer without board was $2.50, with board it was $1.50; the average wage per day for a carpenter without board was $4.50; and the average wage for a female domestic per week without board was $6.40.

The 1880 social statistics were published by the Government Printing Office, and most government document sections of public or university libraries may have this publication. Otherwise, check at the National Archives, its branches, the lending libraries, or the Family History Library.

SPECIAL FEDERAL POPULATION SCHEDULES

1880 Schedule of Defective, Dependent, and Delinquent Classes

In 1880 a special census was taken of the defective (handicapped), dependent, and delinquent inhabitants in an area. Those who were blind, deaf-mute, idiotic, insane, homeless children, or permanently disabled were recorded with additional information about their condition. Also listed were the inhabitants in prison. If these schedules are still in existence for your area of interest, they will be found among the non-population schedules listed above. Frederick Howard Wines's *Report on the Defective, Dependent, and Delinquent Classes* gives summaries and statistical information based on this census.

Veterans and Military Schedules

Enumerations of veterans were taken by the federal government as a part of the 1840 and 1890 population censuses. On the second page of the 1840 census, along with the enumerations for slaves, you will find information on Revolutionary War pensioners or their widows receiving pensions, giving their full names and ages. Names of these pensioners were published in 1841 and this list was reprinted by the Genealogical Publishing Company in 1967, called *A Census of Pensioners for Revolutionary or Military Services.*

Although the bulk of the 1890 census was destroyed, parts of the veterans schedules survived. There are extant schedules for Union veterans and widows of veterans for half of Kentucky through the states alphabetically thereafter to Wyoming. States beginning with the letter A through the other half of Kentucky were lost in the fire. These are part of the National Archives Microcopy Record Group 15, Microcopy M123, 118 rolls.

If your ancestor fought for the Confederacy, you should still check these rolls. While the enumerators were supposed to count only Union veterans or their widows, some Southern sympathizers may have also recorded those who fought for the South. When the schedule was reviewed in Washington, D.C., a line was simply drawn through the Confederate's name, making it still readable.

The information you will learn from this enumeration includes the name of the veteran or his widow, rank, company, name of regiment or vessel, date of enlistment, date of discharge, length of service, post office address, disabilities incurred, and other remarks such as whether the veteran was receiving a pension.

Remember James H. Goforth from our earlier discussion? He's listed on the 1890 Veterans Schedule for Morgan Township, Dade County, Missouri. He's listed as a private, from Company 2, 15th Regiment Missouri Cavalry. He enlisted 1 November 1864 and was discharged 30 June 1865. His post office address was Dadeville, Missouri, and his disability was listed as lung disease, and he was receiving a pension. Once again, though, we don't know if James himself supplied the information for this enumeration.

A separate military schedule was taken for military personnel, including those at United States bases overseas and on naval vessels as a part of the 1900, 1910, and 1920 federal population censuses. For 1900 these are part of National Archives Microcopy T623, rolls 1838–1842. The Soundex is on Microcopy T1081, rolls 1–32. For 1910 there is no Soundex; the military and naval enumerations are on Microcopy T624, roll 1784. For 1920 the enumerations for overseas military and naval forces are part of Microcopy T625, rolls 2040–41; the Soundex is on Microcopy M1600, rolls 1–18.

Remember, too, that the Dakotas took a veterans enumeration in 1885. It is on National Archives Microcopy GR27, roll 5.

Slave Schedules

Slaves were enumerated on separate schedules in 1850 and 1860. These list the name of the slave owner, not the slaves themselves. They also give the number of slaves the person owned and the number released from slavery.

Also under the slave owner's name will be a line entry for each slave giving the age, color, sex, whether or not a deaf-mute, blind, insane, or idiotic, and whether or not a fugitive from the state. (See *Black Studies: A Select Catalog of National Archives Microfilm Publications* and the Bibliography for other guidebooks on researching African American ancestry.)

Indian Schedules

Special Native American enumerations give the name of the tribe; the federal reservation, the agency, nearest post office, the number in the household, the type of dwelling; and for each member of the household, the person's Native American name and an English translation, the relationship to the head of the household, marital status, tribal status, occupation, health, education, and land ownership.

Technically, the 1870 federal population census was the first to designate Indians in the "color" column with an "I." Prior to that census year, enumerators for 1850 and 1860 were instructed to record only White ("W"), Black ("B"), or Mulatto ("M"), although you may find exceptions in these censuses where an "I" is recorded.

Native Americans were enumerated on the 1880 federal census just like the general population, but for the 1900 and 1910 censuses, special schedules are found among the regular population schedules that enumerate Native Americans. These are called "Inquiries Relating to Indians." In 1920 Native Americans were enumerated on the general population schedules and in a "Supplemental Schedule for Indian Population." These schedules are usually at the end of the censuses of the general population for each enumeration district.

From 1885 to 1940 Native American censuses were taken by agents on each federal reservation. These were taken randomly, not annually. They are part of National Archives Record Group 75, Microcopy M595, 692 rolls. An Indian Census Card Index for 1898 to 1906 was compiled by the Dawes Commission to verify rights to tribal status for the Five Civilized Tribes (Cherokee, Chickasaw, Choctaw, Creek, and Seminole). The index is available at the Family History Library and at the National Archives regional branch in Fort Worth, Texas.

From 1910 to 1939 the Bureau of Indian Affairs took Native American school censuses. These list the names of children between the ages of six and eighteen years, their sex, tribe, degree of Native American blood, distance from home to school, parent or guardian, and attendance in school during the year. Often they also include the maiden name of the mother. These schedules are housed in the National Archives regional branch for the region where the tribe was located. (See *American Indians: A Select Catalog of National Archives Microfilm Publications* and the Bibliography for other guidebooks on researching Native American ancestry.)

Even if you don't have Native American ancestry, these rolls are interesting. The Indian names and their English translations are fascinating: *Na ka wo sa a* or Agnes Fatwolf; *Vi ho a wo a* or American Horse; *Ha stu na goo* or Bear Behind; and *Na ka ya ta* or Alfred Brown.

There are many more types of records that you can find about your ancestors; you should leave no stone unturned when searching for your heritage. You never know what a record will tell you about someone. Here is a sampling of other documents:

- Family bibles

- Church records (baptisms, confirmations, marriages, burials, admissions, transfers of membership)

- Tax rolls

- Employment records

- School records

- Divorce records

- Other court records (guardianships, indentures, civil and criminal cases)

- Prison records

- Funeral home and mortuary records

- Coroner's records

- Visas and passports

EVALUATING HISTORICAL DOCUMENTS FOR ACCURACY

After you begin searching for records on your ancestors, you will discover that sometimes they are easy to find in the documents and sometimes they aren't. Once you gather the records, you need to begin another phase of your research: evaluating the information each document gives you. I have yet to meet a genealogist who has found one document after another with consistent and matching data. One record will tell you one thing, another will say something slightly or totally different. Remember how the immigration data for Salvatore Ebetino on the 1920 federal census and the 1925 New York State census were different? Which one should I believe? Obviously, I needed to go to records that would give me more accurate information, like his naturalization and passenger list. But suppose these documents did not exist?

All of your sources need to be evaluated for accuracy. Most genealogists label sources as either "primary" or "secondary," which helps them evaluate the source. A primary source is a record created at the time of an event or shortly after the event occurred. It involves the personal knowledge or testimony of a person who was involved in or closely related to the event. A secondary source is one that is copied or compiled from the original or microfilmed records. Hence, a marriage certificate, which is generally created at or close to the time of the marriage, would be considered a primary source. If I were to transcribe a number of nineteenth-century marriage records and publish them in a book, that book would be considered a secondary source. The book was created long after the marriages took place, and I did not witness any of them. Such a book is also prone to transcription errors. Granted, there could also be errors in the original marriage documents, but they are still the original record.

A record is either primary or secondary; it cannot be both. It was either created at the time of the event or it wasn't. The majority of death certificates are created at or near the time of death. The information they contain, however, may be accurate or inaccurate. That's where evaluating comes into play.

Information on any record comes from either firsthand knowledge or secondhand knowledge. You need to look at each document and ask yourself, "Who supplied this information?" In many cases you won't be able to answer that question. On a death certificate it is usually indicated. On a census it is not. The reason death certificates are so bothersome to evaluate is that they contain both first- and secondhand knowledge. The data about the death—cause, attending physician, length of illness, and so on—is firsthand knowledge provided by the doctor or whoever knew about the death. The other information—the deceased's age, birth date, parents' names—came from secondhand knowledge, probably that of the widow or the deceased's offspring.

You would think the widow or a son or daughter would provide accurate data, wouldn't you? Keep in mind that the widow is probably distressed and may not be thinking clearly. She may inadvertently give her mother's maiden name instead of her mother-in-law's. Or maybe she doesn't even know her mother-in-law's maiden name. Remember the death certificate for James H. Goforth? His son supplied the information; he reportedly did not know the names of his grandparents. For whatever reason, he didn't know or didn't care to report this information.

Researchers usually ask themselves some of these questions to determine the accuracy of information on a record:

- How close to the original record is the copy you are looking at? Is it a photocopy of the original document? An abstract? A transcription?

- Who supplied the information contained in the document?

- If known, did that person have any reason to lie or stretch the truth? (An underage bride whose parents did not approve of the husband-to-be may lie about her age. A woman may fudge about her marriage date if a child was conceived before the ceremony took place. A man might say he's older than he is if he wants to enlist in the military. There are hundreds of reasons to distort the truth. There are many "legitimate" reasons for lying.)

- How close to the event is the information being supplied? (The 1920 census says an immigrant came to this county in 1908, but the 1910 census says he came in 1909. The 1910 census may be more accurate since it was taken closer to the time of immigration.)

- Does the record tell you something directly or do you have to draw a conclusion? (Does Jacob Simon's will state, "I leave to my son Josiah . . . ," leaving no doubt in your mind that Josiah is Jacob's son? Or does the record require you to make an assumption, as does the 1850 census? It lists a group of people living in the same household: a man age 40, a woman age 38, a boy age 16, a girl age 14, and another girl age 12. Nothing on this record tells us that this is a husband, wife, and their three children. It could be a brother and sister and her children. We make an assumption based on other information that we find or have found that this is a husband, wife, and their children.)

- When was the record created and when was it recorded? (A deed or a will could have been created several years before it was recorded in the county courthouse. Make sure you take note of both dates.)

Some records have their own idiosyncrasies to consider, such as Bibles. Don't assume that the entries were written at the time of the event. Are all the entries done in the same hand and in the same color ink? That may be a clue that they were all written at the same time. I know that sometimes I print words and sometimes I write in script, and I rarely pick up the same pen from one year to the next. What about the date the Bible was published? If the first entry is for an event in 1886 but the Bible wasn't published until 1910, then something's wrong. The entries should postdate the publication.

Frankly, the biggest issue is not whether a record is a primary source or a secondary one, it's evaluating the information. All sources are prone to mistakes, even tombstones. The point is to compare all the data from all the records you search, then come to a conclusion based on all the evidence. Just because five records say that Isaac Kensington was born in 1856 doesn't mean this is true. You may find another, single record that you will deem to be more accurate and reliable that says he was born in 1854. It's not the quantity of data, but the quality. Johni Cerny and Arlene Eakle in *Ancestry's Guide to Research: Case Studies in American Genealogy* give excellent examples of how they evaluate records as they trace a lineage.

Because of gaps, discrepancies, and inconsistencies in records, you will see in many published genealogies sentences such as, "He was born *probably* in 1875." "He died *circa* 1788–89." "She *likely* immigrated with her husband." "She lived to be *about* 98 years old." "He was born *sometime between* 1910 and 1915." And one of my favorites, "Sarah was *almost certainly* the daughter of William." All of these statements tell us that the researcher can't be absolutely sure of the information. Good genealogists follow these sentences with a footnote or endnote explaining the reason for the vagueness and how they arrived at a particular date or conclusion, or they include the explanation in the text.

I think Mark Twain hit it right on the head, however, when he wrote about accuracy of information. (He would have made a good genealogist.) When he was a cub reporter, his editor told him he should never state as a fact anything he could not personally verify. He followed this instruction to the letter when he wrote an account of a local social event:

> A woman giving the name of Mrs. James Jones, who is reported to
> be one of the social leaders of the city, is said to have given what
> was purported to be a party yesterday to a number of alleged ladies.
> The hostess claims to be the wife of a reputed attorney.

As you can see from this chapter and the previous one, there is a wealth of records out there, and each contains a variety of information about your ancestors. Your ancestors have left a wonderful paper trail just waiting for you to follow.

Chapter 10

Researching from a Distance

Simla, Colorado, has a population of about five hundred people; the only thing between this town and the next one fifteen miles away is cattle. The closest public library with a genealogical collection is fifty-five miles to the west in Colorado Springs; the closest LDS Family History Center is sixty miles (also in the Springs); the closest Regional Branch of the National Archives is 110 miles away in Denver; and the county courthouse is thirty-five miles from my house.

When we lived in Colorado Springs, I had always considered myself a diehard genealogist—one who would get up long before my usual 8 A.M. to be at a research repository when it opened, so I wouldn't have to wait for a microfilm reader. But now the thought of getting up by 5 A.M. to be there at 7:30 A.M. no longer appeals to me.

Being the type of person who seeks the easiest way of doing something, I discovered a solution to my distance problem. I found that I could do quite a bit of research at home. One way is to write letters to obtain photocopies of documents from record repositories. Another is to research original records myself on microfilm.

ORDERING RECORDS BY MAIL

By now you know that there are at least five guidebooks that will give you addresses and information on where to write for records: Thomas Kemp's *International Vital Records Handbook, Ancestry's Red Book, The Handy Book for Genealogists,* and Elizabeth Bentley's *The Genealogist's Address Book* and her *County Courthouse Book.* These works tell you where to write and which repositories or jurisdictions contain which records. Kemp also provides forms that are ideal when ordering birth, marriage, and death records. These books don't tell you how to write letters that get results, however. Librarians and clerks are busy people, and their duties are not limited to answering letters and looking up genealogical records. I've spoken to clerks who told me that unless a letter is brief and to the point, it goes directly into the trash. So I'd like to give you some points on successful letter writing.

Keep your letter brief. If you've ever taken a journalism class, you know that all newspaper articles must capture six elements within the first paragraph: who, what, where, when, why, and how. When you write a letter requesting, say, a probate packet on your ancestor, you need to state the first four of these elements: who, what, where, and when. Librarians, archivists, and clerks don't care about the why and how. A sample letter is shown in Figure 10.1.

Short and sweet; that's what your goal is. In the opening of the letter, if you do not know the name of a person, use "Dear Madam or Sir." Starting with just "Dear Sir" is no longer acceptable. Many clerks or librarians who open your letter will be women. Don't start off by insulting them.

In the letter I've given the clerk the *who*: Catlett Conway; the *what*: probate packet; the *where*: Orange County; and the *when*: about 4 September 1827. Unless asked to prove or state a relationship (which some repositories insist upon), you do not need to clutter your letter with "please send me a copy of my great-great-great-great-great grandfather's will." Generally, the clerk doesn't care how you are related to the person. Nor do you need to state that you are doing genealogy or family history research. So what? And as mentioned in Chapter 6, when you get a clerk who is especially helpful, follow up with a thank-you note.

Always, *always, always* include a self-addressed, stamped business-sized envelope (SASE); if writing overseas, send two International Reply Coupons (IRC) purchased from your post office. If you don't, your letter will probably get trashed. Whenever you are requesting information include a SASE— whether you're writing to a courthouse, library, archive, genealogy cousin,

FIGURE 10.1

P. O. Box 338
Simla, CO 80835
5 February 1996

Clerk of Circuit Court
Orange County Courthouse
P.O. Box 230
Orange, VA 22960

Dear Madam or Sir:

Please inform me if you have a probate packet for Catlett Conway
who died in Orange County about 4 September 1827.

I've enclosed a self-addressed, stamped envelope for your convenience
to inform me of the cost of obtaining a photocopy of the probate.
Thank you.

Sincerely,

Sharon DeBartolo Carmack

---

or a professional researcher. The only time I don't send a SASE is when I include a check for the payment or I'm writing to a federal agency, unless I am asked to do otherwise. My feeling is that the fee is established to include postage, and our tax dollars pay for the government to answer letters.

Students have asked me whether they need to obtain certified copies of records. No. Some places will only issue certified copies, however. Certified copies usually cost a few dollars more, and you don't need that official seal. The only client I have had who needed certified copies was one applying for membership in the Colonial Dames of America. For some reason, that organization insists on official copies, and there may be a few other lineage societies that do, too.

Another correspondence tip is to make sure you do your homework by checking the guidebooks. Don't waste your postage and the clerk's time by writing for a birth record when the birth took place in 1846 but vital records were not kept until 1902. Make sure you are writing to the appropriate jurisdiction and that the time frame fits the records they have. One genealogist told me that she accidentally wrote to the wrong office when requesting a probate. The letter was returned to her in her SASE, giving her the correct place to direct her letter. When the genealogist finally had the opportunity to visit the courthouse, she discovered that the correct office was across the hall from where she wrote originally!

Unless you are writing to a relative for family information, a typed letter is easier to read and will get a better response. When I am writing to a distant relative whose address I received from another relative, I start with a handwritten letter. It's less formal and less intimidating. We all know a lot of bogus genealogical letters come in the mail, and a handwritten one will separate yours from the typical form letter. It's best not to include a family group sheet or other form for people to complete in the first letter. Make contact first, see what kind of response you get, then decide whether to send a family group sheet. Some people find these forms confusing, so it may be better to generate a question-and-answer format on your computer. Include a SASE with this type of correspondence also.

LENDING LIBRARIES

One of the problems with ordering records by mail is that you do not know if the clerk or librarian checked thoroughly for your ancestor in the indexes. If you were doing the search yourself, you would check spelling variations of the surname and perhaps look for other relatives. Busy clerks will check only what you've asked for in your letter, if anything at all. Moreover, the clerk doesn't know your family like you do and may miss something that you would catch. The ideal situation is to look for records yourself. If you can't make a trip to the courthouse or repository, you can check at the Family History Center to see if those records have been microfilmed and order them. If you live at a distance from a repository, you can obtain many microfilmed records from one of the lending libraries. (The addresses are listed in the Appendix.)

AMERICAN GENEALOGICAL LENDING LIBRARY

American Genealogical Lending Library (AGLL) has a program where you can rent or purchase records on microfilm or microfiche for use in your home or at a local library. AGLL has the largest collection of genealogical and historical records available on microfilm/fiche for rental, with more than 200,000 titles. Their record holdings include:

- All federal census records, 1790–1920, including indexes

- Selected state censuses and slave schedules

- Military records

- Ship passenger lists

- Vital records, deeds, probates

- County and local histories

- Family histories and genealogies

- Ethnic collections

- Special collections

To participate in AGLL's program, you must become a member. A one-year membership at this writing is $47.50; renewal membership is slightly cheaper. When you join, you will receive a free subscription to AGLL's *Genealogy Bulletin* and their catalog of holdings in your choice of format: printed, microfiche, computer diskette, or CD-ROM.

Once you are a member, you will be sent order forms to rent records on microform. The rental cost per roll of microfilm or fiche title is currently $3.25, and you may keep the rolls for one month from the date you receive them. If you order ten or more items at the same time, the rolls are just $2.75 each. It usually takes a week to ten days to receive the items you've ordered.

AGLL also offers census indexes on CD-ROM. These are available for purchase at $49.95 each. Each CD-ROM contains a full copy of their film/fiche catalog as well. If the bulk of your family was in, say, Pennsylvania in 1870, the census index on CD-ROM could be a great time-saver for you.

NATIONAL ARCHIVES MICROFILM RENTAL PROGRAM

Similar to the AGLL program, the National Archives offers a microfilm rental service, too. The main difference is that the National Archives offers only its federal records, whereas AGLL has records from other repositories.

Microfilms may be rented for thirty days. The current rental price is $2.25 per roll for orders of ten rolls or more, $2.75 each for orders of five to nine rolls, and $3.25 per roll for orders up to four rolls. There is also a $3 shipping charge on all orders. The start-up price is $25.

Viewing Rented Microfilm

Of course, in order to view loaned microfilmed or fiched media, you will need the appropriate type of reader. Holding the film or fiche up to the light will only give you an aching neck. You can either take the rented film to your local public library that has microform readers or purchase your own machine. I was able to buy used microfilm and microfiche readers through my local Family History Center when they bought new ones. Also contact your public library; they may be able to give you the name of a dealer who sells used machines.

The main drawback I have found in using this home method of research is not being able to make photocopies. But this is easily remedied by taking the roll of film to a library with a microprinter. Aside from the space problems—a microfilm reader is not small or light—it really has been a time-saver to be able to order microfilms by mail and view them at my leisure in my home. I don't have to wake up before dawn to be at a library when it opens.

There's also no limit on the amount of time I sit in front of the reader. Many libraries have two- or three-hour time limits when others are waiting to use the readers. I disliked having to drive a total of three hours round-trip for just two hours of research. The money I save on gas I now use to rent microfilms.

For someone who lives many miles from a research repository, obtaining microfilmed records to research at home is a real advantage. You may want to consider investing in a used microfilm reader and joining AGLL or the National Archives Rental Program.

NGS LIBRARY LOAN SERVICE

Members of the National Genealogical Society may take advantage of its Library Loan Service, offering thousands of book titles that include family histories and genealogies, county and town histories, guidebooks, record transcriptions, and more. You may borrow books by mail; the fee is based on a zone rate system that accompanies the book order forms. There are three zones with costs ranging from $10 to $12. This charge includes postage and the loan fee. You may keep the books for two weeks after you receive them.

While the *1988 NGS Library Booklist* is no longer available for purchase, you may borrow it from the NGS library, and you may still purchase the *1989 Booklist Supplement* and collected acquisitions pages from the *NGS Newsletter* from 1990. The cost for these is $12. NGS is planning to convert their catalog to electronic format. Updates and details on this project will be published in the *NGS Newsletter*.

NEHGS CIRCULATING LIBRARY

The New England Historic Genealogical Society also has a lending library for its members. Currently, you may order up to three books at a time by mail for $14. This fee covers shipping by the U.S. Postal Service. The fee varies if you elect to have the books sent by UPS. You may borrow the books for fourteen days from the date you receive them. You pay the return postage.

About 20,000 books circulate. The *Circulating Library Catalog*, a two-volume set, must be purchased first. The current cost is $15 for the set plus $2.50 shipping. Books listed in the catalog are family genealogies; state, county, and town histories for most states; extensive town vital records for New England; and many other reference works, including British, Canadian, and Caribbean sources, plus microfilms of selected references.

Orders may be placed by mail, fax, e-mail, on CompuServe, or from the NEHGS Web site. See the Appendix for these numbers.

THE PUBLIC LIBRARY AND INTERLIBRARY LOAN

Many genealogical collections are part of a public library, but even if your public library does not have a genealogical section, it will have an interlibrary loan (ILL) system. Although you may not be able to obtain published genealogies and family histories via ILL, you can get general history and genealogy books that circulate and microfilms of newspapers. One of the wonderful aspects of the computer age is that more and more libraries are making their catalog holdings available through databases that you can access from your home computer and modem. From the comfort of your computer chair, you can browse library catalogs from across the nation. Just yesterday, in fact, I went to the Library of Congress.

Once you find a book that interests you, call or visit your local librarian to see if it can be requested on ILL. Though the librarian may get the book from a different library than the one you found it in, it will help if you provide the full citation for the book and in which database you found it. Most books you order on ILL will be checked out to you, so you can take them home and read them at your leisure.

Microfilms of newspapers, on the other hand, usually must stay in the library, even though you may have your own reader at home. Here is another place where some homework will expedite your request. Try to track down where the microfilms of the newspapers you're interested in are housed, and find out whether the repository will loan them. Providing the ILL librarian with this information will be advantageous to everyone involved.

RESEARCHING ON THE INTERNET

As you will notice by glancing through the Appendix, many genealogical societies, book vendors, and libraries have Web sites or Internet access. The sites available for genealogists are numerous, to say the least. As mentioned in Chapter 3, you can also look for "non-genealogical" sites that offer information of a genealogical or historical nature. Examples of some of the areas you can explore from your home computer and an Internet server: genealogical databases (such as the 1871 Ontario census index, Texas Confederate pension records index, and Kentucky vital records index), ethnic sources (such as Sources of Genealogical Information in Ireland and Frequently Asked Questions [FAQs] for German, Austrian, and Slavic genealogy), references (U.S. Geological Survey/Geographic Names Information System Database of Locations and Yahoo's current U.S. maps), newsgroups, and library catalogs, to name a few. The Journal of Online Genealogy <http://www.tbox.com/jog/jog.html> is an organized attempt to gather articles focusing on Internet-related genealogical topics.

Whether you visit record repositories in person or research from the comfort of your home, you will find lots of materials that are useful in the search for your ancestors. Sometimes, however, you may need to hire someone to conduct the research for you because you cannot get it done any other way. I'm sure you want to spend your research dollars wisely, so let's see how you go about finding and hiring a professional genealogist.

Chapter 11

When and How
to Hire a
Professional Genealogist

There comes a time during the course of a genealogical research project when just about everyone (professionals included) needs to hire a professional genealogist. Sometimes you cannot make a trip to the locality where your ancestors lived in order to do the research yourself. Sometimes you find yourself at a "brick wall" in your research and don't know where to turn or what to do next. Before I get into the ins and outs of hiring someone to conduct research for you, I want to discuss some "brick-wall strategies," since this may save you the expense of hiring a researcher.

BRICK-WALL STRATEGIES

One day, you'll be happily researching your ancestors, then boom! You've slammed against a brick wall. You just can't find anything further on that ancestor or family. You've hit a dead end. You may not know whether the family or a particular ancestor was still in the area, moved, or died. There's nothing in the records anymore. You're stumped, not sure where to turn next. Be comforted in knowing that you're not alone. It's what we genealogists have come to know as a "brick-wall problem," and everyone hits one sooner or later.

BROADEN RESEARCH TO RELATIVES AND NEIGHBORS

Several strategies can help you tackle your case. If one strategy doesn't work, try another. The most common technique for breaking through the brick wall is to broaden your search to include the ancestor's or family's relatives, neighbors, associates, and friends. When you can find no records on your family, perhaps other relatives or neighbors may have generated documents that will refer to your family or give you clues for new avenues to pursue.

I was at a dead end in researching the origins in Ireland of my great-grandmother Delia (Gordon) Norris, who immigrated to America about 1885 and settled in Greenwich, Connecticut. None of the records I found for her, her husband, or her children gave me any clues as to where in Ireland she originated. So I turned to Delia's relatives.

From family stories I knew Delia had a twin sister, Mary, who married a man with the last name of Clark. No one knew much more than that. Neither woman was buried with her husband; Mary was interred with Delia in Greenwich. From the tombstone, I had at least a death year for Mary with which to begin working. Based on the brick-wall strategy of expanding research to other relatives, I began looking for records on Mary Clark, hoping that a document on her might lead me to the native origins of her and her sister Delia. So far, I have found a ton of records created on or about Mary, her husband, and a son. Although none of them has yet revealed their homeland in Ireland, I'm still pursuing this avenue of research. The point is, though my research had hit a dead end with Delia, it's now blossoming since I took a look at a different branch of the family.

STUDY THE SOCIAL HISTORY

Another strategy for breaking the wall is to broaden your research to social histories of the ethnic group, time period, and place. Social histories, such as books like David Hawke's *Everyday Life in Early America,* give accounts of everyday people and their lives. Such books won't list your ancestors by name, but they will give you clues and insight into the lifestyles of people like your ancestors and what motivated them to behave in a certain manner, and this knowledge may affect your research direction.

For example, I learned from social histories on Italian Americans that it was quite common for the man to immigrate first and then bring his family to America up to five or ten years later. Many of these men originally had no intention of staying in America; their goal was to earn enough money to go back to Italy and buy land. Dubbed "birds of passage," they had a high return migration rate; in other words, they went back and forth between Italy and America.

Once I found Albino DeBartolo on a passenger arrival list for 1905, and learned that his family did not arrive until 1913, I went back to the passenger arrival lists' index to see if he fit the pattern of a returnee. Sure enough, he did. He made two more trips back and forth to Italy between 1905 and 1913. Had I not broadened my research to social histories and learned the typical migration pattern for this ethnic group, I might have missed these records on him.

IGNORE THE PROBLEM

One of the best strategies I have found for overcoming brick-wall situations is to ignore the problem, and it will probably go away. Put your research on that particular family or ancestor away for at least six months to a year. Don't think about it. I like to work on other family lines while I'm waiting for the time to elapse, so I won't go through withdrawal and need more therapy.

It is amazing what you will see with fresh eyes when you pull out the information after a long break. You'll be slapping your head and saying: "Why didn't I notice *that* before?" You'll find clues and sometimes blatant data staring you in the face that you were blind to while in the heat of the search. Sometimes it really helps to step away from the problem in order to see it clearly; then go back and try, or retry, the brick-wall strategies.

Plus, your knowledge has changed and grown during that six to twelve months of abstinence. If you have been working on other family lines in the interim, your experience from that research may help you with your brick-wall case.

READ CASE STUDIES

Another good strategy for tough research blocks is to study how others have overcome their obstacles. In scholarly genealogical journals such as the *National Genealogical Society Quarterly, The American Genealogist,* and others, you may find ideas on how to approach your own problem through case-study articles, even if these do not pertain directly to your family. A case may relate to your research because the family in the article is from the same geographical area or is of the same ethnic background. Or the articles may help you to see how other genealogists think and approach difficult research cases. From the footnotes or endnotes, you may learn about record groups or sources that you may not have known of or had not considered. Even reading book reviews may help. I discovered a book by John A. Brayton titled *The Five Thomas Harrises of Isle of Wight, Virginia,* while reading book reviews. This book was highly recommended by the reviewer and deals with a topic that every researcher encounters sooner or later: sorting out different men with the same name, who were about the same age and lived in the same community. Reading a book like this, though it does not deal with your family, will give you ideas and methods for tackling this type of problem.

SHOW THE PROBLEM TO ANOTHER GENEALOGIST

Having someone with a fresh outlook study the problem may help solve your research brick wall. Remember, since everyone's family history is different, everyone's research experience and knowledge is somewhat different. Another genealogist may home in on something you've overlooked completely. This is an important reason to network at society meetings, conferences, and on the Internet. Professionals do this kind of networking all the time. When they are truly stumped, they will turn to a colleague for advice. The old adage of "two heads are better than one" certainly applies to genealogical research.

When all of these strategies fail, however, you may have to face the fact that some research brick walls never come crumbling down. But you don't know until you have tried different strategies for breaking through them. I've often encountered people who have spent twenty years searching for a woman's maiden name; eventually they discovered it. Solutions to brick-wall problems take time, patience, and the willingness to follow hunches and try different strategies. Whatever you do, don't give up without a good fight. And, when all else fails, maybe it's time to call a pro.

FINDING A PROFESSIONAL GENEALOGIST

There are several ways to find a professional genealogist. One of the best ways is to look in the *Association of Professional Genealogists Directory.* It is available in most genealogical libraries, or you may purchase a copy from the Association of Professional Genealogists (see Appendix). Published biennially, this directory lists all the APG's members, their specialties, and brief biographies. It is indexed, so you can find researchers by locality or research specialty such as ethnic group, adoption, deeds, and religious groups. APG is an international membership society, but it is not a certifying or accrediting body. Members do not need to "prove" their qualifications, and there is no prerequisite for joining. They simply pay membership dues. Each member must, however, sign and uphold a code of ethics (see Chapter 12). A member who violates this code will have his or her membership revoked, either for a certain time period or permanently, depending on the indiscretion.

Another good method for finding a professional is writing for the rosters of the Board for Certification of Genealogist's (BCG) and the Accredited Genealogists (AG) (see Appendix). Both of these organizations have screening processes that genealogists must undergo before they become certified or accredited. (See the next chapter for the requirements.) You can be assured that if you hire any of these genealogists, they have passed rigorous requirements.

You also may be able to obtain a list of professionals in the area in which you need research by writing to the local library and historical or genealogical society. Usually these repositories supply only a list of names. They will add a disclaimer that they do not recommend anyone in particular and that they are not responsible should problems arise.

Many professional genealogists advertise in magazines such as *Everton's Genealogical Helper* and *Heritage Quest.* Currently there are no mandatory licensing agencies. Becoming certified or accredited is voluntary; thus, anyone may hang out a shingle announcing that he or she will do research for hire. Engaging the services of a noncertified or nonaccredited genealogist can be risky. If you go this route, be sure to ask for their credentials, education, professional affiliations, publications, and their access to records. You may also want to ask for references or a sample research report. If you engage the services of a multistaffed research company (there are many, especially in Salt Lake City and other major metropolitan areas), ask for the credentials of the person assigned to your case.

Another good way to find a reputable researcher is to ask people in your genealogical society or those with whom you network. They will tell you honestly whether they liked the work of professionals they have used.

RESEARCH COSTS

Professional genealogists generally charge an hourly rate, anywhere from $10 to $75, depending on the specialty and locality. The average rate is about $15 to $35 an hour. A researcher in New York City or Washington, D.C., will be more expensive than one in Elbert County, Colorado. Likewise, a researcher with a unique specialty or one who has a national reputation for problem-solving will charge more than one who is simply searching census records. This hourly fee covers not just the time to conduct the research, but also the time it takes to analyze the problem and write a research report. In short, you're paying for the researcher's time and skill, not the amount of information he or she may find. A researcher may spend ten hours searching for your great-great-grandmother's parents and come up empty-handed. This is not bad research; the records just are not there or do not give the right information. Everyone's ancestry is unique, and no researcher can predict how long it will take to solve a problem, especially one that you've been working on for twenty years. I've had cases that opened up in the first hour, and others that I was never able to solve.

In addition to the hourly fee, you can expect to pay all out-of-pocket expenses: telephone charges, postage, photocopying, cost to obtain records, and, if travel is required, lodging and transportation (parking, tolls, mileage). Always ask initially what expenses will be billed. When you write to inquire about a researcher's services and availability, always send a self-addressed, stamped envelope.

The method of payment depends on each individual researcher. When I was taking clients, I required new clients to commit to a minimum of five hours, of which I requested a retainer of half up front. At the time, my hourly rate was $20. Five hours would be $100 total, but I asked the client to send $50 before I would start on the project. The balance was due when I sent the research report. At that time I let the client know what other research was needed (if any), and told the client that I would be happy to continue the work on receipt of their payment and authorization for another set number of hours. From there, I billed my client after five to ten hours.

Always set a limit on the number of hours, including time to write the report. In fact, sometimes writing the report can take up as much time— maybe more—as doing the actual research. This is not because professionals are bad writers, but because a lot of analysis goes into the report. If you do not set an hourly limit, you could end up with a $1,000 bill rather quickly. To help cut the cost, you may want to find one or more relatives who would be willing to share expenses.

Many genealogists use written agreements when a client engages their services. This is in both of your interests. The agreement should state the hourly rate, what expenses you're responsible for, and how frequently reports will be made to you. You need also to make it clear whether you want photocopies of all documents or abstracts.

Ask the researcher if he or she will be doing all the work on your case. Let's say you have hired a Virginia specialist, but in the course of the research, the genealogist discovers that your ancestor moved to Tennessee. Will the Virginia researcher be able to continue with the project, either from microfilm records, by mail, or by making a trip, or will you need to hire someone in Tennessee? Or will your Virginia genealogist subcontract with a Tennessee specialist? If the case is subcontracted, you will absorb the cost if the hourly rate is higher than the Virginia researcher's. For example, suppose your Virginia person charges $20 an hour, but the Tennessee one charges $30. You will be billed the extra $10 an hour as an expense. On the other hand, if the Tennessee researcher charges less—say, $15 an hour—the professional usually makes the profit. I know it doesn't sound fair, but the Virginia researcher is essentially taking the responsibility for whether the Tennessee researcher conducts research accurately and comprehensively. Some genealogists bill their clients the actual expense of hiring a subcontractor, whether the fee is more or less. The advantage to having your Virginia researcher subcontract is that you do not have to start all over again with a new researcher. The Virginia person can assign the Tennessee person only that part that needs to be done, whereas you would have to start from square one, explaining what has been done.

Another aspect to consider is the ownership of the research. Many professionals use clients' research (with permission) as the basis of articles, as case studies in books, or as examples in their classes and lectures. If you are planning to publish the results of the research done by a professional, make sure this is clear before you begin.

COMMUNICATING WITH THE RESEARCHER

Before a professional genealogist can begin work on your problem, he or she will need to know all the records you have already checked. This will save you money and the researcher time. If you'll recall from Chapter 1, it took me twenty-five hours to organize one woman's genealogy just so I could tell what she had done before I began my work. This is why it is so important for you to be organized and to keep some kind of research log. You never know when you will need someone's help.

When you write to a professional, summarize your research problem, followed by a bibliography of sources you've checked. Include photocopies or abstracts of any documents you have acquired that pertain to the problem, or at least let your researcher know what you have and let the professional decide whether he or she needs to see the photocopy. Never send originals, only photocopies.

Once the researcher has this material, depending on the amount of documents and previous research, it will take the professional an hour or more to analyze the problem and determine which direction the research needs to go.

Be specific in what you ask the researcher to do. You can say, "I want to know everything there is to learn about Henry Owen," or "I want the Davidson line traced back to the immigrant." I wouldn't ask for "my entire genealogy," however. That's too overwhelming and broad. If you do this, the researcher will ask you, "Which lines are you most interested in?"

Communicate your goals. Are you planning to use the research in a family history to distribute to relatives at a family reunion? If so, then you have a deadline about which you need to forewarn your researcher. I've had clients call me a month before they were planning a trip to Italy to ask me to find out the name of their great-grandpa's birth village. A month simply isn't enough time, even if I devoted eight hours a day, five days a week, to the problem. It takes time to order records, either by mail or on microfilm. (By the way, waiting time is not billable, but the time to write a letter or order microfilms is.)

THE RESEARCH REPORT

The report you receive should be typed, easy to follow, and documented. If you don't understand the report, jot down questions and query the researcher. Every source the professional checked, regardless of results, should be completely cited: name of record, repository where the record was found, the book and page number or microfilm number. You should be able to find that record yourself if need be. Photocopies of documents the researcher sends you should also contain the citation information somewhere (usually on the back). The report should detail the research, evaluate the sources and findings, and give you suggestions for further research (if any is needed). You may decide at that point to either continue or terminate the research. When you decide that you no longer need to engage the researcher's services, send a letter informing the professional.

DISPUTES

Sometimes misunderstandings occur, or you are not happy with the professional's services. Talk it over with the researcher first and try to resolve the problem. The Association of Professional Genealogists recommends this course of action in their brochure "So You're Going to Hire a Professional Genealogist":

> In the unlikely event that a difficulty between you and your genealogist is not resolved, notify the organization or person who referred the professional to you and tell your genealogist you have done so. The Association of Professional Genealogists offers a confidential arbitration service for both clients and professionals. The Board for Certification will serve as an arbiter when a certified professional is involved.

This is the big advantage in hiring a researcher who is a member of APG or who is certified. If there is a problem, these organizations will help. If you have hired someone who does not belong to one of these groups and a problem arises, you may be out of luck. This is another reason to get involved in genealogy by attending national conferences, seminars, and institutes, and by reading the major journals. Through these media and networking with others, you will learn who specializes in the areas of your interest as well as the professional's reputation.

Chapter 12

Becoming a
Professional

You may be thinking, "Why is there a chapter on how to become a professional in a beginners' book?" Frankly, I think that's when it dawns on people that such an animal as a professional genealogist exists. When I attended my first genealogy class, the beginner's track of Samford University's Institute of Genealogy and Historical Research, I was awed by my instructors, Sandra Hargreaves Luebking and Ann Dallas Budd. I was also impressed by the banquet speaker, Elizabeth Shown Mills. These women were not only making money at doing something they loved, but they brought an air of sophistication and professionalism to genealogy that I had not known existed. From that moment on, though I was just a baby genealogist, I knew I wanted to be one of them. But how?

I searched the libraries for books on how to become a professional. I found only one: Donald Lines Jacobus's *Genealogy as Pastime and Profession*. It was written in 1930 and revised in 1968. As highly acclaimed as it was, it was out of date and didn't answer all my questions. Are there courses I should take? How do I become certified? What fee should I charge? How do I get clients? How do I write a research report?

EDUCATION

I basically had to learn on my own how to become a professional. I knew I needed education, so I attended as many courses as I could (see Chapter 4). I went to Samford two years in a row, read all the how-to books available, and took classes sponsored by my local genealogical society. Another way to prepare for your new career is to take the NGS Home Study Course or BYU's Independent Study classes. They are all good; the point is, you need to take classes and learn as much as you can about researching. Courses, as opposed to workshops and short-term classes, will assign homework, giving you research experience and feedback from the instructors.

In addition, you should attend national conferences or at least purchase lecture tapes. If you attend a lecture during every conference session, you will be getting eighteen to twenty hours of instruction per conference. If you also purchase tapes of some of the lectures you did not attend, you will get even more.

Self-instruction includes more than just reading how-to guidebooks. As discussed in Chapter 4, budding professionals should be reading and studying the major journals: the *National Genealogical Society Quarterly*, the *New England Historical and Genealogical Register*, and *The American Genealogist*, to name a few.

If you plan to specialize in a particular locality or ethnic group, you need to do additional research for that area. You need to be an "expert," the one person everyone says, "Oh, for New Mexico research, you need to call . . . ."

Samford University's Institute of Genealogy and Historical Research now has a professionals' one-week track, "Genealogy as a Profession," as does the Salt Lake Institute of Genealogy, "Professional Genealogy."

RESEARCH EXPERIENCE

Researching your own family will give you excellent experience, but it may be limited. For example, if all your ancestors were recent immigrants, you won't have research experience with the records of colonial America. If you want to conduct research for hire, you need to have a broad-based research knowledge, unless you plan to specialize. Although you could start charging for your services right away, many genealogists feel more comfortable volunteering their time until they acquire confidence in their abilities. As mentioned in Chapter 3, many people find it extremely beneficial to volunteer to answer research questions by mail or to help patrons in person.

When I first set foot in our local Family History Center, I was overwhelmed and had no clue what I was doing. After a few visits, I discovered that if I volunteered one day a week, they would put me through a special course on how to use the collection. Not only did this benefit my research, but by helping other people, I learned about many sources that were not covered in the volunteer training.

Ask a few friends if you can research their family history. Tell them you'll conduct the research for free if they'll reimburse you for the expense of ordering microfilms and making photocopies. Here's the part you skip when you research your own family: writing a report. Write your friend a detailed report of your research findings. This is a crucial part of becoming a professional. You need to be able to communicate to a client what you did, why you did it, and what you found. By testing the waters with a few friends who are non-genealogists, you can determine whether your reports are clear and understandable.

JOINING A PROFESSIONAL ORGANIZATION

When I was aspiring to be a professional researcher, I also joined the Association of Professional Genealogists (see Appendix for address). Even if you are just contemplating a career in genealogy, join APG. Their quarterly journal has articles that will answer many of your questions about the profession, show you the hot topics in the field, and help you make informed decisions on setting fees, office hours, paying taxes, buying office equipment, and so on. Some APG members have formed chapters in these areas: Colorado, Louisiana, Washington, D.C., New York Metro area, Salt Lake City, and Southern California. Write to APG or consult a recent edition of the *Association of Professional Genealogists Quarterly* for contact persons.

Those who join APG are asked to sign the following code of ethics:

ASSOCIATION OF PROFESSIONAL GENEALOGISTS CODE

As a member of the Association of Professional Genealogists, I agree that professionalism in genealogy requires ethical conduct in all relationships with the present or potential genealogical community. I therefore agree to abide by the following standards:

The professional genealogist promotes a coherent, truthful approach to genealogy, family history, and local history. The professional presents research results and opinions in a clear, well-organized manner; fully and accurately cites sources; and does not withhold, suppress, or knowingly misquote or misinterpret sources or data.

The professional genealogist promotes the trust and security of genealogical consumers. The professional honestly advertises services and credentials; explains without concealment or misrepresentation all fees, charges, and payment structures; abides by agreements regarding project scope, number of hours, and deadlines or reporting schedules; keeps adequate, accessible records of financial and project-specific contacts with the consumer; and does not knowingly violate or encourage others to violate laws and regulations concerning copyright, right to privacy, business finances, or other pertinent subjects.

The professional genealogist supports records access and preservation. The professional is courteous to research facility personnel and treats records with care and respect; supports efforts to locate, collect, and preserve the records by compiling, cataloging, reproducing, and indexing documents; and does not mutilate, rearrange, or remove from its proper custodian any printed, original, microform, or electronic record.

The professional genealogist promotes the welfare of the genealogical community. The professional gives proper credit to those who supply information and provide assistance; does not knowingly supplant another researcher; encourages applicable education, accreditation, and certification; and refrains from public behavior, oral remarks, or written communications that defame the profession, individual genealogists, or the Association of Professional Genealogists.

BECOMING CERTIFIED OR ACCREDITED

As mentioned in the last chapter, there is no mandatory licensing of genealogists, although unsuccessful attempts have been made in a few states. If you choose to become certified or accredited, it is because you care about the quality of work you do, you believe that your skills are at a high level, and you want to show your clients that you are part of a special and respected group of professionals.

BOARD FOR CERTIFICATION OF GENEALOGISTS

The Board for Certification of Genealogists (BCG) was founded in 1964 and has the reputation of having the highest standards of competence and ethics in genealogical research (address is in the Appendix). There are six categories of certification. According to the BCG brochure "Genealogical Certification: Who? What? Why? How?" here are the definitions of each category:

Certified Genealogical Record Specialist (CGRS): One who searches original and published records, understands all sources of a genealogical nature relating to the chosen areas of specialization, and provides accurately detailed information concerning the contents of the records examined.

Certified Genealogist (CG): One who is proficient in all areas of genealogical research and analysis, is qualified to resolve pedigree problems of sundry types, and is experienced in the compilation of well-crafted family histories.

Certified American Indian Lineage Specialist (CAILS): One who conducts research to determine descent from a historical Native American tribe indigenous to North America, being well versed in the pertinent materials and applicable standards within this specialized field.

Certified American Lineage Specialist (CALS): One who reconstructs a single line of descent and prepares hereditary [lineage/patriotic] society applications. The work of a CALS is based upon a sound knowledge of pertinent resources and a skilled appraisal of the authenticity and acceptability of both original source records and compiled printed material. American, as used here, is not limited to the United States.

Certified Genealogical Instructor (CGI): One who plans and conducts a full course of genealogical instruction, covering all aspects of genealogical methodology and sources. The CGI must also pass the requirements for CG.

Certified Genealogical Lecturer (CGL): One who gives public addresses of an educational nature on specific genealogical topics or on related subjects pertinent to the tracing of family relationships. The CGL must also pass the requirements for CGRS or CG.

If you think you might be interested in certification, request and complete the BCG's preliminary application, indicating in which category you would like to apply. BCG will then send you a copy of its "Application Guide" and the testing materials. You may change your category at any point during the one year allotted for completing the application. Each category has its own specific requirements; you will be also asked to furnish the following:

1. Background information on your education, both genealogical and general, and educational activities, such as attending conferences.

2. A bibliography of any articles or books you have had published. If you have not published, state this; publications are not a requirement.

3. Why you seek certification.

4. What your intended specialization will be.

5. How accessible the records are to you; what research repositories you will use most frequently.

6. Reading and interpreting documents. The Board will supply you with two historical documents. You must transcribe and abstract them, write a brief essay on the records' genealogical value, and write a brief research plan for further research based on the information in the documents.

7. Use and interpretation of secondary sources. The Board will ask you to choose two books, articles, or other printed sources and to discuss their strengths and weaknesses.

8. Sign the BCG's Code of Ethics (which is similar to APG's given earlier, only more detailed).

9. Complete the qualifications for the specific category for which you are applying. These include different types of research reports. Basically, you will need to demonstrate that you exhibit an excellence in research skills and the ability to communicate your findings.

Once you have completed your portfolio, it will go to at least three judges who are experts in the area in which you are applying. The judges act independently and anonymously. You will receive a written evaluation when your application and portfolio are returned; this usually takes about three to four months. Two-thirds of the applicants pass the requirements.

Certification is granted for five years, at which time you may renew. The requirements for renewal are not as in-depth, but each renewal application must show evidence of continued quality and growth. You pay a nonrefundable fee when you initially apply for certification and when you renew.

THE ACCREDITATION PROGRAM OF THE FAMILY HISTORY LIBRARY

Beginning in the early 1960s, the Family History Library (then known as the Genealogical Library) developed a program to accredit professional researchers so that they could refer inquiries for research to them. Unlike the BCG, which has certification categories unrelated to locality, the Accredited Genealogist (AG) program is geographically divided and subdivided, and candidates may choose subdivisions in which to specialize (see Appendix for address).

United States: The six New England states; the four eastern states (New York, Pennsylvania, New Jersey, and Delaware); the fifteen southern states (from Texas and Oklahoma east to Maryland and Florida); the eight midwestern states (from Minnesota, Iowa, and Missouri east to Ohio)
Canada: (French- or English-speaking areas)
British Isles: England, Wales, Isle of Man, Scotland, Ireland
Scandinavia: Norway, Sweden, Denmark, Finland
Europe: Belgium, Czechoslovakia, France, Italy, Germany, Netherlands, Switzerland, Poland
Asia: Japan, Korea

There are also exams for Mexico, Polynesia (non-English speaking), American Indians, and records of the LDS Church. To date there are no exams for the western part of the United States.

When you apply for accreditation you should have completed about one thousand hours of research in the geographical area in which you are applying. You are asked to submit with your application a case study of three to four generations in your chosen geographical area. AGs also have a code of ethics, which applicants must sign and abide by.

There is no charge to take the two-part examination, written and oral. The exam must be taken at the Family History Library in Salt Lake City. The written test consist of six parts and takes about eight hours to complete. The six parts are as follows and are based on your area and time period of specialty:

1. Handwriting: Your ability to read genealogical documents

2. Document recognition: Your ability to identify important genealogical documents and reference sources

3. LDS Church records: Your knowledge of the content and application to research of LDS records

4. Brief pedigree evaluations: Your ability to evaluate a genealogical pedigree, listing sources you would search to extend the pedigree and what you would expect to find in those sources

5. Pedigree problem: Your ability to take a pedigree problem, carry out research in the library, and write a report detailing the results of your research and suggestions for further research

6. General questions and answers: Your knowledge of the facts pertaining to the history and records of your area of specialty

The oral examination covers two points and takes about one and a half hours:

1. A review of the written examination

2. Your defense of the pedigree case study you completed

If you fail to pass the written exam, you may retake it after three months have elapsed, and you will have to demonstrate to the Accreditation Committee that you have overcome your weaknesses in the previous test.

Sound like a lot of work to become certified or accredited? You bet it is. But you will definitely feel a great sense of accomplishment when you pass the requirements. And you'll be doing yourself, your clients, and the genealogical community a great service.

FELLOWS

Somewhere in your genealogical studies you will run across not only the certification or accreditation initials after someone's name, but also the initials FASG, FNGS, FUGA, and so forth. The *F* in all of these means "fellow":

Fellow of the American Society of Genealogists, Fellow of the National Genealogical Society, Fellow of the Utah Genealogical Association. These are honorary designations to people who have contributed greatly to the field of genealogy and the sponsoring organization. One fellowship in particular, however, deserves more attention and detail: FASG.

The American Society of Genealogists is an honorary organization formed in 1940 by three prominent genealogists: John Insley Coddington, Meredith B. Colket, Jr., and Dr. Arthur Adams. Other well-known genealogists were invited to join, among them Donald Lines Jacobus, who is often referred to as the "father of modern American genealogy." According to David L. Greene in his article for the *Association of Professional Genealogists Quarterly*, "What Is F.A.S.G.? Notes on the American Society of Genealogists," the founders' goals were to "improve the standing of genealogy by promoting the highest standards within the field."

The ASG is limited to fifty members, who are known as Fellows. ASG members elect new fellows based on candidates' published genealogical scholarship. The emphasis is on compiled, well-documented genealogies that resolve difficult research problems. Articles and books that are primarily record transcriptions, abstracts, or methodology do not qualify a candidate.

The election process is confidential; the candidates themselves do not even know that they are being considered until they are notified of their election. A Fellow nominates someone with the recommendation of two other Fellows. The membership committee reviews the candidate's bibliography and qualifications; these are then forwarded to the entire membership for consideration. If the candidate receives more than four-fifths of the ballots cast, the person is elected for life. Those elected have included homemakers, ministers, college professors, archivists, librarians, and lawyers, who have ranged in age from their twenties to their nineties.

In 1950 the ASG established the National Institute for Genealogical Research at the National Archives and in 1964 helped create the Board for Certification of Genealogists. It also funded the publication of a scholarly journal, *The Genealogist*. Each year the ASG presents the Donald Lines Jacobus Award for an outstanding genealogy published within the preceding five years, as well as certificates of appreciation for other genealogical works. Anyone involved in genealogy who strives for genealogical excellence and scholarship should become familiar with the recent Jacobus award winners and the works of the Fellows (look for the FASG initials after a genealogist's name).

DONALD LINES JACOBUS AWARDS, 1990–96

1990   no award
1991   Doris F. Poinsett, *Valentin Pfost/Post, 1740–1800, of Hardy County (West) Virginia and Some of His Descendants* (1989)
1992   no award
1993   Dean Smith and Melinde Lutz Sanborn, *The Ancestry of Samuel Blanchard Ordway* (1992) and *The Ancestry of Emily Jane Angell* (1993)
1994   Paul Heinegg, *Free African Americans of North Carolina and Virginia* (1993)
1995   Lewis Bunker Rohrbach, *Höffelbauer Genealogy, 1585–1993: The American Families of Helfelbower, Heffelbower, Heflebower, Hefflebower, Heflybower, Hefflibauer, Hefibauer and Heffelbauer Together with Their German and Austrian Ancestry* (1995)
1996   no award

SETTING FEES

If you've read the previous chapter on "When and How to Hire a Professional Genealogist," you know that most genealogists charge by the hour, anywhere from $10 to $75, with the average being about $15 to $35. If you are interested in becoming a professional, query other genealogists in your area or specialty and find out what they charge per hour. This will give you an idea of what your fee range should be. Start low, so that you are able to justify raises of $5 to $10 an hour as your research knowledge grows.

Remember that all your time spent on a client's case is billable to the client: actual research, analysis, and writing the report. Many genealogists also charge their hourly fee plus charges for telephone consultations. Another billable time is travel. Some genealogists do not charge when they have to commute to a repository; some prorate the cost among the clients they researched for that day. When professionals do charge for travel time, some bill at half their hourly rate. You will also need to decide whether you will charge your client directly for tolls, mileage, or transportation fares, or whether you will deduct them on your taxes at the end of the year.

This brings us to a complicated issue: paying taxes and taking home-office deductions. In fact, I won't touch on this topic since there are so many ins and outs and new rules every year. You will need to consult an accountant or tax advisor.

Can you support yourself as a genealogist? Probably not. There are quite a few who do, but they live in large cities that offer good research opportunities: Washington, D.C., Salt Lake City, New York City, Chicago, Denver, to name a few. Can you make a decent second income from genealogy? Absolutely. Most genealogists, however, supplement their research income with a part-time job or with other genealogical-related activities, or they have a working spouse.

FINDING CLIENTS

I know quite a few genealogists who have never advertised their services. They are kept busy full-time by word-of-mouth referrals. How do they do that? They get to know the librarians, clerks, and archivists where they conduct most of their research. They get on the referral lists these people send to those who seek research by mail. They also have earned a reputation for quality research from their fellow researchers in the area and across the nation.

The majority, however, get started by advertising for clients in magazines such as *Everton's Genealogical Helper* and *Heritage Quest* until they have a sufficient client base and are also getting referrals. Clients also find genealogists by checking the *Association of Professional Genealogists Directory* and the rosters of the Board for Certification of Genealogists and Accredited Genealogists (see previous chapter).

Another method is networking at conferences and on the Internet. Getting to know other professionals and having them get to know you and your research skills and expertise will gain you referrals from colleagues.

Publishing your research results is one of the best ways to become known in the field and is a good way to get clients. This is how I became known as an Italian American specialist. Just about everything I had published dealt with Italian Americans. By lecturing about the topic at national conferences and regional seminars, I also became known as a specialist in writing family history narratives that place ancestors into historical perspective. Practically all of my lectures have the same theme: how studying the social history will help you put your ancestors into their historical times. Although I no longer take clients for research projects (only writing and editing), I still get requests from people who have read my articles or attended my lectures.

PROFESSIONAL OPPORTUNITIES
BESIDES CLIENT WORK

Many of the Fellows and other professionals do not take on clients for paid research. They pursue other avenues in the field of genealogy that provide supplemental income, and combined with client work, these can provide a decent salary.

WRITING

Genealogical writing pays poorly, if at all. A few genealogical magazines pay for articles; the scholarly journals offer no monetary compensation. Genealogical book publishers usually pay a 10 percent royalty if they print your manuscript, but they do not offer any advance. Some genealogists abstract or transcribe historical documents, then self-publish a book. This requires a monetary investment in advance before you can begin to recoup or make a small profit. Writing and publishing may bring you a little extra spending money sporadically, but that's about it. The real value of writing and being published is in becoming known.

TEACHING

Genealogists who love to teach offer genealogical classes. Many of these instructors have not had formal teaching experience, but they have had extensive research experience (although research experience alone does not make one a good teacher). Actually, often the best way to learn a subject is to teach it. If you have been volunteering at your local genealogical library, you are also a teacher.

I started teaching genealogical classes in my home. Besides making announcements at genealogical society meetings that I was going to teach a beginners' class, I also hung up flyers in the two genealogical libraries in town. I held six- to eight-week sessions and took up to eight students at a time since that was all I could fit around my living room table. Taking into consideration reproducing handout material for each student, I set a fee of $25 plus $5 for handouts for each student.

This was an excellent way for me to start teaching and to learn more about genealogy, since I had to prepare classroom lectures about all aspects of research. Teaching at home was less formal than a classroom situation: I had no monetary overhead, and all my books and supplies were right there when I needed them. It got old after a year or so, however. I had to make sure my house (primarily the living room and a bathroom) was always clean, and my family had to be quiet and stay upstairs during classes. I also had no teaching aids like a blackboard or overhead projector. Another consideration was additional insurance coverage in case someone slipped and fell while in my home or coming up the walkway.

It is better to find a place to hold classes, even if you have to rent a classroom at a public school or in a church. You will have the teaching equipment you need, plus it "feels" more like a class. Remember that you will have to account for this rental fee in your cost to the students.

LECTURING

For advanced researchers, lecturing can provide a supplemental income. Genealogical lecturing is somewhat competitive. You have to become a successful public speaker, and you need a repertoire of lectures that have a wide appeal to general audiences. Most genealogical societies who bring in out-of-town speakers are looking for speakers who have a national reputation for proven audience appeal and attraction. They primarily select speakers based on word-of-mouth referral from members who have heard popular speakers at national conferences. Genealogical speakers charge from $75 to $200 a lecture. The average is about $100 to $150.

Lecturing is extremely time-consuming. The top genealogical speakers put countless hours into researching, preparing, and rehearsing a single one-hour lecture. Even for lectures that a speaker presents over and over again to different audiences, there is time involved for keeping abreast of the latest sources in the field and updating the lecture. Another consideration is visual aids. Audiences do not want someone who will stand behind the lectern and read from a script. They want lively presentations with attractive, useful visual aids (slides and overhead transparencies).

If you think you'd like to become a genealogical lecturer eventually, you may want to join the Genealogical Speakers Guild (see the Appendix). This is a good way to learn more about the genealogical lecturing world, and to market your availability. The GSG produces a quarterly newsletter and a biennial membership directory that is widely distributed among genealogical societies.

OTHER WAYS TO SUPPLEMENT INCOME

Some genealogists supplement their client earnings by offering charts, forms, and books for sale. Others look for unique specialties and raise their hourly rates. Be creative. Study issues of *Everton's Genealogical Helper* and *Heritage*

Quest and see if you can find an avenue of research or service that isn't being offered. There are ads for research travel guides to ancestral homelands; people who will hunt down your ancestors' tombstones and photograph them; people who will cross-stitch your pedigree chart; people who will reproduce old photographs; people who will make T-shirts and mugs for family reunions. There are also people who live in major research areas like Salt Lake City or Washington, D.C., who turn their homes into bed-and-breakfast inns for genealogists.

When I got the idea for my business, the Genealogists' Literary Service, I first studied issues of the genealogical magazines and found that there was only one person advertising editing and proofreading services to genealogists. But I knew that I was able to offer some things that this person did not: first, I had a national reputation in the field as a genealogical editor, having edited two internationally circulated genealogical periodicals; second, besides offering editing and proofreading, I also advertised manuscript critiquing (advice on the content and arrangement of a book or article manuscript) and ghostwriting (taking the client's research notes and writing an article or family history for them).

Even if an idea is already being done, discover an angle on how you would do it a little differently or more professionally. Then give it all you've got!

Chapter 13

Leaving a Family History Legacy

Your family history is incomplete if all you have done is spend count-less hours finding genealogical documents, dutifully recording the information on your charts and forms, or entering the data into a computer. That is an accomplishment, of course, but all you have left for your descendants is a couple of file cabinets and notebooks full of charts and forms. What do you think they'll do with it when you die? I imagine they'll have a lovely bonfire. If you think I am exaggerating, I promise you that when you start talking to people involved in genealogy, you'll hear the same horror stories I've heard.

Charts and forms are pretty dull, especially to non-genealogists. After you're gone, your family will take a quick look at the charts, see how far back the lineage is traced, then they'll probably pitch the stuff. If you're lucky, they'll pass your charts on to Cousin Mandy, who's also kind of crazy and interested in dead relatives. But what happens when she dies?

While the main thrust of this chapter is to show you how to turn your charts and forms into a treasured legacy, let's first take a look at how you can protect your work in case you have a heart attack while you're researching in some courthouse and never get a chance to "complete" your family history.

The way to ensure that your hard work won't get destroyed after you die is to bequeath it to someone who will appreciate it and perhaps will do something with it in the future. That someone could be an interested member of the family, another genealogist, or a genealogical library or historical society. Determine who that someone will be, then add your genealogical items to your will. My will states that:

> I give, devise and bequeath, in fee simple absolute, all genealogical data, books, and photographs to my daughter, Laurie or her children, to be held in trust by my spouse, Stephen, until Laurie turns 21 years old. In the event she or her children do not want them or if they predecease me, this gift of genealogical data shall go to the local genealogical society where I reside at the time of my death.

If you leave your genealogical materials to a genealogical or historical society or library, they will make the material available to other researchers through microfilming or as a manuscript collection. It would be courteous, however, to prearrange with the repository or society where you'll be donating your genealogy and to have a genealogical friend sort through your materials before the truckload arrives at the society or library door.

Though I cringe when I think of it, technically a lot of my genealogical files could be tossed; in particular those pertaining to the Ebetino family. Why? Because I have compiled all of that information into a published book that has been distributed to genealogical libraries, relatives, and other Italian American genealogists. Compiling your research into a book is so important. If something were to happen to my files (fire, flood, earthquake, or other natural disaster), at least I could reconstruct my research and reorder documents based on the information in my book. (This is another good reason for citing your sources!)

WRITING YOUR FAMILY HISTORY

Obviously, you cannot write or compile a book on every family line you research. You will have to pick the ones that are nearest and dearest to you. You will never live long enough to research all of your ancestors *and* write books about them. At some point, however, you will need to stop researching and start writing. This is the best way to ensure that if your charts and forms get destroyed after you've died, something will be left behind and all of your research efforts won't be in vain. Many genealogists choose the option of compiling their family history and publishing it as a way of leaving a legacy.

When I say, "write your family history," I'm not talking about a *New York Times* best-seller that has hundreds of pages. My Ebetino family history was completely self-published. It contained only 120 pages. The point was to compile all the information into one readable format—not just a book of names and dates or a bound version of my charts and forms. It began with a twelve-page narrative on the lives of the immigrant ancestors Salvatore and Angelina (Vallarelli) Ebetino. Then I compiled "genealogical summaries" that followed all the descendants of this couple. I concluded with short biographies of most of the descendants.

Most family histories are simply genealogical summaries that look like the one in Figure 13.1. Notice that there are references showing where all the data came from. This is not optional when you are compiling a family history, whether it is just for relatives or to be distributed widely. Another part of your family history that is not optional is an index. If you leave out either of these two items, your genealogy will be considered practically worthless, no matter how much time you put into it or how good the research is.

Within these summaries, genealogists usually add biographical information and data gleaned from records, such as immigration facts, land transactions, abstracts or transcripts of wills, census enumerations, and so on. These summaries generally begin with the progenitor, or the first known ancestor in a line, then they come forward in time listing in more summaries everyone who is descended from this person.

There are several excellent books that will guide you when you decide to write and publish your family history. For the mechanics of writing and compiling your genealogy, seek Patricia Law Hatcher's *Producing a Quality Family History* and Kirk Polking's *Writing Family Histories and Memoirs* (others are listed in the Bibliography).

You also need a guide that will show you how to number your genealogy. Too many amateur genealogists naively think that they have invented a better numbering system than the ones that have been tried, tested, and accepted by the scholars in the field of genealogy. You don't need to reinvent the wheel. Three articles published in the *National Genealogical Society Quarterly* (see Bibliography) explain everything you need to know about numbering everyone in your genealogy: Joan Ferris Curran, "Numbering Your Genealogy: Sound and Simple Systems"; Madilyn Coen Crane, "Numbering Your Genealogy—Special Cases: Surname Changes, Step Relationships, and Adoptions"; and John H. Wray, "Numbering Your Genealogy: Multiple Immigrants and Non-emigrating Collaterals."

Then you will need to cite your sources. Cite the name of the record, to whom it pertains, the repository where you found the record, and the specific book, volume, and page number (or microfilm information). Although dated, Richard S. Lackey's *Cite Your Sources* is still the most widely used guide for referencing genealogical documents and books. A new book, however, may replace it: Elizabeth Shown Mills' *Evidence: Citation and Analysis for the Family Historian*. For documenting formats covering CD-ROMs and other electronic media, see *The Chicago Manual of Style*, 14th edition, Chapters 15 and 16.

To help you create the index, you'll need Patricia Law Hatcher and John V. Wylie's *Indexing Family Histories*.

Most family histories are self-published because they simply do not have a wide enough readership in which a commercial publisher would want to invest. Self-publishers, some of which are listed in the Appendix, specialize in small-print runs of books. When I published my Ebetino book, I had 100 copies printed. You will need to pay for the publishing of your book up front, then try to recoup your investment when you sell the book to relatives. Before you publish, however, you should contact several small-press publishers to get cost estimates and to learn how to prepare the camera-ready pages and photographs for offset printing.

WRITING ARTICLES

Although you may have done quite a bit of research on a particular line or family, when you get ready to write your family history you may find that it only fills a dozen pages or less. That's when you may want to consider making it into an article for one of the genealogical journals. Ideally, the article should emphasize the research methodology you used to compile the information, but several journals will publish just the genealogical research you've collected, as long as it is written in an article-type format. This assures that your genealogy will have a wide readership and be preserved. It will also be indexed in *PERSI* so that other descendants may find your material. To learn which journals publish the kind of article your genealogy would be suited for, see my "The Genealogical Writer's Market" that was published in three installments in the *Association of Professional Genealogists Quarterly* from September 1993 to March 1994.

FAMILY ALBUMS

If writing an article or writing and publishing a family history sounds like a lot of work (and it certainly is) and not something that appeals to you, you may want to compile a family album instead. Family albums are generally one of a kind, although some genealogists make two or more albums to give to family members. A family album is a good way to get all the documents you've collected out of the file cabinet and into a treasured family artifact that will be passed on to the next generations.

Start with a binder, preferably one that is archival quality, which can be purchased from one of the archival-preservation catalogs listed in the Appendix. Then you will want to choose archival-quality pages and sheet protectors. Yes, you will invest quite a bit of money in this album, but its purpose is to outlive you. You want this to be similar to the family bible that everyone treats with the utmost care and respect. You want your album to last for many, many lifetimes.

Once you have these supplies, you can fill your family album with narrative summaries of your family history, photographs, original and photocopied documents, and charts and forms. You may want to have an album that starts with each of your four grandparents as children and then follows their lineage back to the immigrant to America or further. If you are really ambitious, you may make an album for each surname that you have accumulated considerable research on. In this case, start with the earliest known ancestor, followed by family group sheets and documents on all the descendants. You can begin or end all the albums with a pedigree/ancestor chart. Obviously, there are many ways in which you may organize your family history album.

I compiled a sample family album to show my classes. In a three-ring binder with acid-free sheet protectors, I started with a five-generation pedigree chart. Then I used subject dividers, labeling each with the surnames from my pedigree chart. After each surname tab, I put a family group sheet with source citations, starting with the most recent generation and working backward. Then came photographs of the people on the family group sheet. The labels describing the pictures were affixed to the upper or lower corners of the sheet protector, not to the photographs. After the pictures, I included photocopies of birth, marriage, and death certificates and any other historical records I found on that family. Then I did the same with the next family.

The idea is to gather in one place everything that pertains to a particular family, ancestor, or lineage. Leaving everything piecemeal in a file cabinet will be overwhelming for your descendants. They won't know what is important to keep and what to throw away—and they may not care. If your important documents, photographs, and final draft charts and forms are organized into an album, you eliminate this problem. Your family will know that this is a valuable family heirloom. The main advantage is that you can continue to add information.

The main disadvantage of this method of preserving your family history is that you will probably make only one album. Although it will be unique and special, it can be shared by only a limited number of people. And suppose it gets lost as it's handed down from one generation to the next? Suppose Cousin Joey has the album, but won't share. Or suppose your unmarried Great-Aunt Sylvia has the album, shows it off, but neglects to bequeath it when she dies. It becomes part of her estate, descendants fight over it—or, worse, Aunt Sylvia's best friend can't track down the descendants, so she keeps the album. Now it's out of the family's possession. Too much can go wrong here if you're not careful.

Although I think the family album idea is a good one, I would still write a family history or genealogical summaries. Even if you never publish, but simply send photocopies to the Family History Library in Salt Lake City for microfilming, your research and genealogy will be preserved.

In short, do *something* with your genealogy! The research and gathering of information is only half of the process. Pull it all together in a manuscript, article, book, or album. That's what your descendants will keep—not your file cabinets and charts.

FIGURE 13.1

Genealogical Summary

1. MARY FITZHUGH STUART, daughter of David Stuart, was b. ca. 1810,[1] King George Co., Virginia; d. 31 Aug 1881, Albemarle Co., Virginia;[2] m. 19 July 1830 in King George Co. to JAMES MADISON FITZHUGH.[3] James, son of Henry and Elizabeth (Conway) Fitzhugh, was b. 25 Apr 1809, Virginia; d. 20 Feb 1845, Orange Co., Virginia.[4] His will was dated 8 May 1844 and was recorded 24 Mar 1845 in Orange Co., Virginia.[5]

Issue:

2.   i. CATLETT CONWAY, b. 25 Apr 1831, King George Co., Virginia.[6]
3.   ii. JOHN STUART, b. ca. 1835, Virginia;[7] (served CSA).[8]
4.   iii. BATTAILE, b. ca. 1837, Virginia.[9]
5.   iv. FRANCIS CONWAY, b. 1839, Virginia;[10] (served CSA).[11]
6.   v. LOUISA CONWAY, b. ca. 1841, Virginia.[12]
7.   vi. OSCAR STUART, b. 1842, Virginia;[13] (served CSA).[14]
8.   vii. JAMES MADISON, b. ca. 1844, Virginia.[15]

---

[1] 1850 federal population census, Orange Co., Virginia, p. 260, line 7; 1860 federal population census, Orange Co., Virginia, p. 71, line 16; 1870 federal population census, Orange Co., Virginia, p. 226, line 35.

[2] Obituary for Mary Fitzhugh (Stuart) Fitzhugh, typed transcript from the *Washington Star* (no place, date, or page number cited) sent to the compiler by Mary Eleanor Fitzhugh Hitselberger, Fon du Lac, Wisconsin.

[3] King George Co., Virginia, marriages, 1786–1850, p. 32; Family History Library [FHL] microfilm #0032053.

[4] *Genealogies of Virginia Families from The Virginia Magazine of History and Biography*, vol. 2 (Baltimore: Genealogical Publishing Co., 1981), p. 864.

[5] Will of James Madison Fitzhugh, dated 8 May 1844, recorded 24 March 1845, Orange County, Virginia, Will Book 10, pp. 263–64.

[6] *Genealogies of Virginia Families from The Virginia Magazine of History and Biography*, vol. 2, p. 864; tombstone inscription, Catlett Conway son of James M. and Mary S. Fitzhugh, Old Fork Episcopal Church, Ashland, Hanover Co., Virginia, transcribed October 1985.

[7] 1850 federal population census, Orange Co., Virginia , p. 260, line 8; 1870 federal population census, Orange Co., Virginia, p. 226, line 34.

[8] Confederate States of America, Virginia, Index, FHL #0029786 and FHL #0881413.

[9] *Genealogies of Virginia Families from The Virginia Magazine of History and Biography*, vol. 2, p. 864.

[10] 1850 federal population census, Orange Co., Virginia, p. 260, line 9.

[11] Confederate States of America, Virginia, Index, FHL #0029786.

[12] 1850 federal population census, Orange Co., Virginia, p. 260, line 10.

[13] 1850 federal population census, Orange Co., Virginia, p. 260, line 11; 1860 federal population census, Orange Co., Virginia, p. 71, line 17.

[14] Confederate States of America, Virginia, Index, FHL #0029786, and FHL #0881413.

[15] 1850 federal population census, Orange Co., Virginia, p. 260, line 12.

Chapter 14

When You Become an Ancestor: Leaving Your Life Story

Okay, so you've done an excellent job in researching your ancestors. You've even gone that extra step and written and published your family history. That's quite an accomplishment, and I'm proud of you. But you've neglected one part: you. Sure, you included genealogical data on your charts or as part of your family history book, maybe even added a short bio of your own accomplishments. Keep in mind that one day you, too, may be an ancestor. What are you leaving behind so that your descendants will be able to find *you*? What record of yourself are you preserving for all eternity? A name, a date, a place? Hasn't there been more to your life than the day you were born and the day you will die?

The Golden Rule of Genealogy is to leave for your descendants what you wish your ancestors had left for you. What do you wish you could find on one of your ancestors? Old love letters between your grandparents? A diary detailing Great-Great-Grandpa's life during the Civil War? An autobiography written by your great-grandmother, telling you how she felt about traveling in a covered wagon?

Though we can easily see how different life was for our parents, grandparents, great-grandparents, and so on, it's harder to see how different our lives will be from our children's, grandchildren's, great-grandchildren's. My daughter thinks that microwave ovens and blow dryers were around when I was a child. They weren't. My daughter also thinks that color televisions were in every room in every household when I was a child. They weren't. Think of all the inventions my daughter has come to know in just her short fifteen years of life: home computers, video cameras, VCRs, fax machines, modems, home-office photocopy machines, cordless telephones, cellular phones, answering machines, caller ID, personal pagers (can I stop now?). If all this has become available in the last decade or so, what will life be like in the next decade, or the next, or the next?

By recording in some method what life was like for *you* growing up, coming of age, getting married, going through midlife, aging, you will be leaving a document that shows how different each generation is. The following are some easy, painless ways to leave a record of yourself and your immediate family for future generations.

LET'S LEAVE 'EM SOMETHIN' TO TALK ABOUT

> *July 23, 1965: I played school with fat Karen. Me and Karen had a*
> *fight.*

> *July 24, 1965: I played Barbies with fat, fat-so Karen. Me and fat*
> *Karen went to the toy store.*

I was nine when I wrote those entries in my first diary—a habit that has produced almost twenty volumes ever since. I'm so glad my notations have matured.

> *February 5, 1997: Marcia and I had an argument today. We went*
> *shopping for new dresses, and when I told her that*
> *the one she liked best made her look fat, she got*
> *upset.*

Notice how my grammar improved, too.

Aaron Boylan began his 1911 autobiography with, "If anyone should read this story of my life (which I much doubt) . . ." Even though he didn't think anyone would read it or be interested in his life story, he continued to fill page after page about growing up in the mid-1800s. "I have went back in my life story to record these . . . pleasing incidents much more for my own pleasure than with any expectation that they will ever be read or appreciated by anyone else." Fortunately, Aaron had a descendant who was thrilled when she found his autobiography—so thrilled that she published it as *Frontier Farmer: Autobiography and Family History of Aaron A. Boylan, 1827–1923* (edited by Katherine L. Sharp; Baltimore: Gateway Press, 1993).

What do Aaron Boylan—a man who lived and died before I was born and who is not related to me—and I have in common? We are leaving a written account for future generations. We are telling our descendants about our lives because no one else will be able to tell it better. We are telling them things that they won't find in the course of genealogical research into records like censuses, birth certificates, land records, or the like. We are giving them a glimpse into our personalities—our souls.

Love letters, diaries, and autobiographies are the stuff on which social history is based, recounting for us firsthand what it was like to come of age and live during a given time period and at a particular place. If your ancestor had kept these gems and they survived the years for you to appreciate, wouldn't you be overcome with joy? Trust me, your descendants will feel the same way.

DIARIES AND JOURNALS

"But my life is so routine, so boring," is a common response I hear when I get on my soapbox about this subject during genealogical classes and lectures. Generally, I jokingly say, "Then make things up like I do. In my diaries, I've broken all ten commandments and committed all of the seven deadly sins." I got scared, though, when someone took me seriously. You may lie to your friends, you may lie to your spouse, but please don't lie to your diary.

Yes, our lives do seem routine and boring to us. Many of my diary entries read, "Did laundry. Cleaned house. Read a historical romance novel." Yawn. I felt better, though, when I read one of Louisa May Alcott's diary entries: January 9, 1886, "Great storm and cold. Read." Now here is the author of *Little Women,* and that's all she could think of to write on January 9?

Wouldn't you just love to find your great-great-grandmother's diary that recorded such daily activities? Her life was no more exciting than ours; certainly she wouldn't have considered it exciting. Most of the women diarists on the overland trail documented tedious activities like washing, baking, unpacking and packing, the number of miles they traveled, the presence or absence of grass for the cattle. I'm sure these women wouldn't consider this exciting—but modern women would. And these diaries tell us what life was like during that time. Knowing how thrilled you would be to find an ancestor's diary, it would be a sin to deprive your descendants of that joy.

Make the decision to start today. Although you may find it easier to record your daily activities and thoughts on a computer-generated diary, keep in mind that your descendants will want to see your handwriting. That's part of the ambiance of a diary. A computer-generated diary is better than none at all, but consider some of the problems. Technology changes awfully fast these days. Remember the Commodore 64 just ten years ago? Do you have a computer today that can read those disks? Always make a printout of your diary entries and put them in a notebook binder. And for heaven's sake, don't put a password on your diary files. What if you forget the password? What if you die? Doesn't that defeat the whole purpose of leaving it for your descendants after you're gone? If you're worried that someone will read it— because after all, you are baring your soul in your diary—then hide it so that it won't be discovered until you're long gone.

Once you discipline yourself to set aside five or ten minutes a day for this invaluable activity, you will find that it isn't a chore after all. I used to write in my diary in the evenings before I went to bed, but I found I was too tired to write much. Now I write about the previous day's activities the next morning while I have a cup of tea.

Consider how much to tell in your diary. Some people feel that they don't want certain aspects of their lives known by future generations; some experiences are just too personal. But those personal items will probably be the most interesting parts. Above all, you need to make sure you don't come across in your diaries as a saint. Everyone has flaws; everyone has regrets about things they've done. That's what makes each one of us unique and interesting. I don't want my descendants to think I was perfect; I'm not. I don't want my descendants to think I made all the right decisions all the time; I haven't. Essentially, I want to be a "colorful" ancestor—one of the ones some great-great-great-great-grandchild of mine will say, "Wow! I wish I had known her. Wasn't she fascinating?" So I record *everything* in my diary (so my friends don't panic when they read this, I've used initials instead of names).

And there's another consideration. Someday, someone may publish your diary. Now that's a scary thought. Perhaps you want to use only initials for people you refer to in your diary so that your descendants won't be confronted with a lawsuit by the descendants of the people you named as partners in crime. Using only initials for people also lends an air of mystery to your diary. I've read a number of historical diaries where the diarist used only initials for friends and acquaintances, and the absence of full names does not detract from the diary's interest. (Besides, if the person reading the diary is a genealogist, he or she will be able to research the initials and figure it out.)

In the winter 1996 *Authors Guild Bulletin* it was reported that 84-year-old Edward Robb Ellis has kept a diary for sixty-seven years, writing more than 20 million words so far. (This book, by comparison, contains about 80,000 words—the average length of an "adult" book.) Ellis started when he was a sophomore in high school. He selected passages (about 1 percent of the entire collection) and published them in a book titled *A Diary of the Century*. Can you imagine all the history and everyday life experiences his diaries contain? And won't his descendants jump for joy?

Although there are books offering advice on how to keep a diary or journal (see Bibliography), I don't think you need a manual on this one. Basically, if you write about your daily activities and (perhaps more importantly) your feelings and thoughts about things, you'll be doing great.

LOVE LETTERS

What about all those old love letters? You did keep them, didn't you? For some reason, I find that women are more inclined than men to throw out their former lovers' letters when they get married. If you still have any love letters, hang on to them!

Here's a love letter I just love. Mrs. Sarah Austin was writing to her lover in the late 1830s. She wrote this to him right before she departed on a short trip from home and would be away from the daily arrival of her lover's letters:

> Do not laugh at me as I bid you farewell somewhat solemnly and as if we were parting. Here I have lived in a sort of half presence of what I love. Here I have received your letters. Here hangs your picture. Here are a thousand things . . . which remind me that you are not all a dream.

Why is it that if we found out that our mother was having a secret affair, it would be a scandal, but if we found out our great-grandmother had a secret lover—ah, now that's romance!

Remember the "Golden Rule"? Wouldn't you be ecstatic if you found an ancestor's love letters? Your descendants will feel the same when they find yours. I'm a pack rat, so I've kept every letter a boyfriend has ever written me. When my husband went on a remote tour to Korea for a year, we wrote to each other daily. I still have every letter he wrote, and he kept every letter I wrote. One of these days (perhaps in my next life if it hasn't already been filled with things to do), I'll arrange the letters chronologically, with one of my letters, then one of his answering it, and so on, and put them on the computer. I wouldn't dream of throwing away the originals, but typed copy will be easier and less tedious for my daughter or grandchildren to read.

Love letters, of course, are not just between lovers. One easy way to get parts of your life on paper is to write a love letter to the youngest person in your family—a child, grandchild, great-grandchild, niece, nephew, whomever it may be. Write it for a special event, like the person's birthday. Describe what life was like when you were that age. You can also include memories of your parents, grandparents, or whoever was the oldest family member that you remember. What did that person look like? What is your fondest memory of that person? What did that person teach you about life? Keep a copy for your family memorabilia.

You can also write a love letter to someone who was close to you who has died. Tell them all the things you wished you had told them. Tell them about your life now. Tell them how they touched your life and what they meant to you. In the letter, include details about the person: looks, personality, idiosyncrasies. Then file the letter with your genealogical materials.

Perhaps you send out a Christmas letter with your cards every year. It's a wonderful way to summarize your family's happenings over the year. Make sure you keep a copy of each one for your genealogical files, or start a Christmas letter notebook.

By writing these letters, you are creating the future generation's artifacts and historical documents. Letter writing, unfortunately, is becoming a thing of the past. It's easier to pick up the phone and call. But every time you do this instead of writing a letter, you are losing a part of your family history. Letters can be saved and treasured. Phone conversations are gone when you hang up (unless you tape them, of course). Now do you understand why conversations are called "sweet nothings"? There's nothing left!

What about e-mail and faxes? They certainly are a sign of our times and daily lives, but only if they're kept. Are you downloading, printing, and saving every e-mail letter you get or every fax you receive? If you do save faxes, they had better be saved on bond paper at the least. Thermal fax paper has a very short lifespan—about three to five years. Somehow, though, I find it hard to imagine that typed faxes and e-mail messages will have the same impact when your descendants find them in the attic tied up with a pretty ribbon.

AUTOBIOGRAPHIES

Your autobiography or memoir does not have to be a daily recounting of your entire life. It doesn't have to start on the day you were born and end today. That's overwhelming for anyone, even a teenager! Write about episodes in your life. When a memory comes to you, write about it. The beauty of doing it on a computer is that you can later arrange these vignettes chronologically.

Writing about your life is also therapeutic. Remember Aaron Boylan at the beginning of the chapter? He wrote his autobiography mostly for his own pleasure. It gave his life meaning. In a lot of ways, each of us is the culmination of our culture's history. By recording your life, thoughts, dreams, and feelings, and leaving them for future generations, you are giving our culture some continuity. Each of us has a slightly different, though very common, life experience. My grandmother, if she was still alive, could tell me what life was like before washing machines, television, indoor plumbing. I can't do that. I don't know from experience what that was like. I can only read about it. But I can't read about it if someone doesn't write it down.

Several guidebooks cover writing your life story and memoirs. I recommend these, and you'll find several in the Bibliography. But if writing about your life seems too time-consuming and overwhelming, here are some other ways to get information on paper for your descendants.

The least painful way of recording the past twenty, thirty, forty, fifty or more years is to simply start making a chronological summary of your life. On notebook paper or on the computer, start with the year you were born and list each year thereafter to the present. Next to each year, in parentheses, write the age you were in that year or the grade you were in school. These times will usually jog your memory better than asking yourself, "Gee, what *was* I doing in 1975?" Now jot down one or more significant things that you remember happening that year. And be sure to put your name at the top so that someone later will know who this chronology is about!

SHARON DeBARTOLO CARMACK

1956	I was born on Wednesday the 17th of October at 9:18 P.M. at United Hospital in Port Chester, New York.
1957 (1)	My father changed our last name from DeBartolo to Bart.

1958 (2)	
1959 (3)	
1960 (4)	One of the nuns made me sit in the corner at pre-school because I refused to finger-paint.
1961 (5)	We moved from New York to La Habra, California.
1962 (6)	
1963 (7)	President Kennedy was shot, and I remember my teacher and parents being upset, but I didn't understand why. My Uncle Jack O'Conner died a few weeks after the President.
1964 (8)	
1965 (9)	
1966 (10)	We moved from La Mirada, California, to Mineral Wells, Texas.
1967 (11)	Our house was burglarized while we were visiting relatives in New York. A few months later, we moved back to La Mirada.

If you include national historical events like I did about President Kennedy, be sure to record what impact they had on you. We can read in the newspapers how an event affected the nation, but we won't find in the newspaper how it affected *you*. Only you can tell us that.

After you have filled in as many years as you can, put it aside. Things will gradually come back to you to add. If you want to pursue writing an autobiography later, this will serve as an excellent outline.

To accompany your chronology, draw some floor plans of all the houses you've lived in. Draw in the placement of furniture. Note the house's street address if you can remember it. Describe the house: what color was it, how many stories? If you have a picture, include that with the floor plan.

Remember I talked about episode writing? This means recording significant experiences in your life, then combining them chronologically. One way to trigger your memory is to use interlibrary loans to obtain newspapers from special days in your life, such as the day you were married (or divorced), the day one of your children was born, or the day you graduated from high school. I discussed this method under oral history interviews, too, but you can certainly apply a lot of those same methods to recording your own life.

Kem Luther, author of *Cottonwood Roots* (Lincoln: University of Nebraska Press, 1993), claims that there are three ways to ensure that you'll leave some kind of record of yourself for the future. The first is to buy land. There has never been any statute of limitations as to how long land records are kept. He's right. In researching your own ancestry, you may find an ancestor's land record from the 1600s or 1700s.

The second way to leave a record of your life is to get arrested. Do you realize the amount of records that are created when you're arrested? Now that I think about it, you actually may be wasting your time going to all of those genealogical society meetings. You could be out causing trouble, creating great fodder for your diary, plus leaving a record of yourself.

The final way to become immortal is to get your name in the newspaper (if you get arrested, you'll be killing two birds with the same stone). Even though newsprint is highly acidic and doesn't last very long, practically all newspapers are preserved on microfilm. They are among our nation's most well-preserved documents because they record history in the making. If you get your name in the newspaper, you've become immortalized.

A PARTING THOUGHT

By choosing genealogy as your hobby or profession, you are doing something out of the ordinary. You are recording information about everyday people from the past—the silent ones who "wait quietly for someone to listen"—the ones who don't fill the pages of the history books, but the ones who did indeed make history. But in that process of recording your family history, please don't neglect yourself.

Someday you'll be an ancestor someone is looking for. Your descendants will want to know more about that crazy person who spent untold hours glued to a microfilm reader looking for dead relatives. They'll want to know more about you than what they'll find in a census record or on a marriage certificate. They'll want to know the real you: what you thought, how you reacted to things, what you felt. They won't find that in the records.

Tell them—because no one, *absolutely no one,* can tell them about your life better than you. Only you can do that. It's your turn to leave a legacy. Why not leave 'em somethin' to talk about?

Glossary of Genealogical Terms

abstract	a summary of the important aspects of a document
administrator/ administratrix	person appointed by the probate court to administer an intestate estate; administrator (male), administratrix (female)
Ahnentafel	German for "ancestor table"
allied families	surnames connected by marriage into one's lineage
ancestors	parents, grandparents, great-grandparents, and so on; the people from whom one is descended
ancestor chart	see *pedigree chart*
biography	written narrative of someone's life
brick wall	an apparent dead end in research
census	a periodic enumeration or count of the population

collateral	those relatives other than one's ancestors: aunts, uncles, cousins, etc.
compiled records	records that have been transcribed, abstracted, or indexed into a compilation, which may or may not be published
correspondence log	form to keep track of letters requesting genealogical data from relatives and research repositories
deed	legal transfer of property title from one individual to another
descendant	a person who descends from an ancestor
dower rights	under common law, a life interest in one-third of the real property owned by a woman's husband
et al.	Latin meaning "and others"
et ux.	Latin meaning "and wife"
executor/executrix	a person or persons named in a will to carry out the terms in the will; exectuor (male), executrix (female)
family bible	bible belonging to a family that records the family's births, marriages, and deaths
family group sheet	form used to record genealogical information on a whole family—parents and children
family history	the history of one's family; the study of whole families and incorporating historical perspective
family tradition	stories and legends verbally handed down through generations
"final papers"	petition for U.S. citizenship
"first papers"	declaration of intention filed by an alien who wants to become a U.S. citizen

forebears	ancestors
gazetteer	dictionary of geographic localities
genealogy	the study of one's lineage or ancestry
generation	individuals born and living at about the same time
grantee	a person buying or receiving real property
grantor	a person selling real property
guardian	a person appointed by the court to manage property or protect the rights of someone who is unable to do so, such as a minor child
heir	a person who inherits or who is entitled to inherit
historical perspective	learning about the community, history, and time period in which ancestors lived
immigrant ancestor	the first person in an ancestral line to settle in America
interlibrary loan	borrowing books or microfilms from a distant library through your local public library
intestate	describing a case where a person dies leaving no valid will
issue	children of a couple
lineage	some people refer to this as the "direct" line: parents, grandparents, great-grandparents, and so on
metes and bounds	method of surveying and measuring land using natural and artificial landmarks and adjacent lands
microfiche	a flat sheet of film
microfilm	a roll of 16 or 35mm film

naturalization records	documents produced when an alien becomes a citizen of the United States
oral history	a verbal account of a person's life or ancestry
original source	a historical document in its original form
pedigree	one's ancestry or lineage
pedigree chart	form used to record genealogical information on an ancestral line
population schedules	see *census*
primary source	a record created at the time of an event or close to the time of an event, usually (but not necessarily) by someone with personal knowledge; see also *original source*
probate	the legal process of transferring items of a deceased person's estate to heirs
progenitor	the earliest known ancestor in one's lineage
query	a question; an ad placed in genealogical magazines seeking information on ancestors
rectangular survey system	method of land surveying and measurement dividing the land into sections
research log	form to keep track of searches made in record repositories
research or record repository	a place that retains historical documents and is open to the public; e.g., library, archive, courthouse
research report	a detailed account of research done by a professional genealogist for a client
secondary source	a record or group of records that have been copied or compiled from the original and put into another form; or one that was created long after an event,

usually by someone who had no personal knowledge of the event

social history   history that focuses on the everyday lives of ordinary people in a society

Soundex   indexing code based on the way a name sounds as opposed to the way it is spelled

surname   last name

testate   describing a case where a person dies leaving a valid will

testator   a person who left a valid will

transcribe   to make a verbatim copy of a record; see *transcript*

transcript   a verbatim copy of a record

vital records   records of births, marriages, divorces, and deaths; also known as "VRs"

will   legal document providing for the disposition of a person's property

Acronyms and Abbreviations

Once you've been doing genealogy for any length of time, you will undoubtedly run across the deluge of initials unique to the family history world. Like any disciplined field, genealogy has its own language and abbreviations for multiple words or phrases that are repeatedly used.

SOCIETIES AND ORGANIZATIONS

AG	Accredited Genealogist
APG	Association of Professional Genealogists
ASG	American Society of Genealogists
BCG	Board for Certification of Genealogists

Certification Categories:

CG	Certified Genealogist
CGRS	Certified Genealogical Record Specialist
CGL	Certified Genealogical Lecturer
CALS	Certified American Lineage Specialist
CGI	Certified Genealogical Instructor
CAILS	Certified American Indian Lineage Specialist

FASG	Fellow, American Society of Genealogists
FGS	Federation of Genealogical Societies
FNGS	Fellow, National Genealogical Society
FUGA	(pronounced "foo-ga") Fellow, Utah Genealogical Association
G&B	The New York Genealogical and Biographical Society
GSG	Genealogical Speakers Guild, or simply The Guild
HisGen	(pronounced "hiss-jen") The New England Historic Genealogical Society, also referred to as NEHGS
IGI	The Family History Library's International Genealogical Index
NGS	National Genealogical Society

BOOK DEALERS, LENDING LIBRARIES, AND RESEARCH REPOSITORIES

AGLL	American Genealogical Lending Library
FHL	Family History Library
Fort Wayne	the Allen County (Indiana) Public Library
GPC	Genealogical Publishing Company
NARA	National Archives and Records Administration, also known as "The Archives"
Salt Lake	the Family History Library in Salt Lake City

THE INSTITUTES

GIM	(pronounced "jim") Genealogical Institute of Mid-America
IGHR	Institute of Genealogy and Historical Research; may also be referred to as "Samford" for the university where it is held
NIGR	National Institute on Genealogical Research

Magazines and Other Publications

APGQ	*Association of Professional Genealogists Quarterly*
The Helper	*Everton's Genealogical Helper*
NGSQ	*National Genealogical Society Quarterly*
NUCMC	(pronounced "nuck-muck") *National Union Catalog of Manuscript Collections*
PERSI	(pronounced "purr-see") *Periodical Source Index*
The Record	*The New York Genealogical and Biographical Record*
The Register	*The New England Historical and Genealogical Register*
TAG	*The American Genealogist*
TG	*The Genealogist*

Appendix of Addresses

The following is by no means a comprehensive listing of addresses. Readers should consult Elizabeth Petty Bentley's *The Genealogist's Address Book* for more listings. As with any directory, addresses and telephone numbers change. The ones listed here are current as of this publishing.

GENEALOGICAL SOCIETIES

Federation of Genealogical Societies
P.O. Box 830220
Richardson, TX 75083-0220
Phone/fax: (972) 907-9727
Internet:
103074.1721@compuserve.com
Web site:
http://www.connect.net/beau/fgs/
fgs.htm

National Genealogical Society and National Genealogical Society Computer Interest Group
4527 17th St. N
Arlington, VA 22207-2399
Phone: (703) 525-0050
Fax: (703) 525-0052
Web site:
http://www.genealogy.org/~ngs/
BBS: 703-528-2612 (modem settings 8/N/1)
CompuServe: GO GENSUP

The New England Historic Genealogical Society
99/101 Newbury St.
Boston, MA 02116
Phone: (617) 536-5740
Fax: (617) 536-7307
CompuServe: 74777,3612
Internet:
74777.3612@compuserve.com

PROFESSIONAL ORGANIZATIONS

Accredited Genealogists
Family History Library
35 North West Temple
Salt Lake City, UT 84150

Association of Professional Genealogists
P.O. Box 40393
Denver, CO 80204-0393
e-mail: apg-admin@apgen.org
Web site:
http://www.apgen.org/~apg/

Board for Certification of Genealogists
P.O. Box 14291
Washington, DC 20044

Council of Genealogy Columnists
c/o Regina Hines Ellison, CGRS
158 Lafayette Circle
Ocean Springs, MS 39564

Genealogical Speakers Guild
2818 Pennsylvania Ave. NW, Suite 159
Washington, DC 20007

LINEAGE/PATRIOTIC SOCIETIES

General Society of Mayflower Descendants
4 Winslow St.
P.O. Box 3297
Plymouth, MA 02361

Jamestowne Society
P.O. Box 7389
Richmond, VA 23221

National Society, Daughters of the American Revolution
1776 D St. NW
Washington, DC 20006-5392
Phone: (202) 628-1776
Web site: http://www.dar.org/~revolt

The National Society of the Sons of the American Revolution
1000 S. Fourth St.
Louisville, KY 40203

REPOSITORIES WITH NATIONAL OR INTERNATIONAL GENEALOGICAL COLLECTIONS

Allen County Public Library
Genealogy Department
900 Webster St.
P.O. Box 2270
Fort Wayne, IN 46802
e-mail: mclegg@everest.acpl.lib.in.us

Dallas Public Library
Genealogy Section
1515 Young St.
Dallas, TX 75201
Phone: (214) 670-1433

Daughters of the American Revolution Library
(see address under *Lineage/Patriotic Societies*)
Phone: (202) 879-3229

Denver Public Library
Genealogy Division
1357 Broadway
Denver, CO 80203-2165
Phone: (303) 571-2190

Family History Library of The Church of Jesus Christ of Latter-day Saints
35 North West Temple
Salt Lake City, UT 84150
Phone: (801) 240-2331
Consultation by telephone:
    United States and Canada
        (801) 240-2364
    British Isles, Australia, New Zealand
        (801) 240-2367
    Other international areas
        (801) 240-3433
    FamilySearch
        (801) 240-2584
Consultation by fax:
    (801) 240-1584
Online computer consultation:
    FHL@BYU.EDU

Immigration and Naturalization Services
Historical Reference Library
425 "I" St. NW
Washington, DC 20536

Library of Congress
Local History and Genealogy Reading Room
10 First St. SE
Washington, DC 20540

Los Angeles Public Library
History and Genealogy Department
433 S. Spring St.
630 W. Fifth St. (mailing address)
Los Angeles, CA 90071
Phone: (213) 612-3317

National Archives and Records Administration
8th and Pennsylvania Ave. NW
Washington, DC 20408
Web site: http://www.nara.gov/

Newberry Library
60 W. Walton St.
Chicago, IL 60610
Phone: (312) 943-9090

New England Historic Genealogical Society
(see address under *Genealogical Societies*)
For circulating library orders and information:
Fax: (617) 624-0325
CompuServe:
74777.361@compuserve.com
e-mail: nehgs@nehgs.org
Web site: http://www.nehgs.org

New York Public Library
U.S. History, Local History, and Genealogy Division
Fifth Ave. and 42nd St.
Grand Central Station, P.O. Box 2237
New York, NY 10017
Phone: (212) 930-0828

NATIONAL INSTITUTES, HOME-STUDY COURSES, SELECTED EXTERNAL DEGREE PROGRAMS

Brigham Young University's Independent Study
236 Harman Bldg.
P.O. Box 21514
Provo, UT 84602-1514
Phone: 1-800-298-8792
e-mail: indstudy@coned1.byu.edu
Web site:
http://coned.byu.edu/is/indstudy.htm

Genealogical Institute of Mid-America
Continuing Education
Sangamon State University
Springfield, IL 62794-9243
Phone: (217) 786-7464
Fax: (217) 786-7279

Institute on Genealogy and Historical Research
Samford University Library
Birmingham, AL 35229
Phone: (205) 870-2846
Fax: (205) 870-2642
e-mail: mbthomas@samford.edu
Web site:
http://www.samford.edu/schools/ighr/ighr.html

National Genealogical Society's American Genealogy: A Basic Course
(see address under *Genealogical Societies*)

National Institute for Genealogical Research
P.O. Box 14274
Washington, DC 20044-4274

Regis University
School for Professional Studies
3333 Regis Blvd.
Denver, CO 80221-1099
Phone: 1-800-967-3237

Salt Lake Institute of Genealogy
Utah Genealogical Association
P.O. Box 1144
Salt Lake City, UT 84110
Phone: (888) 463-6842

The University of Alabama
New College External Degree Program
P.O. Box 870182
Tuscaloosa, AL 35487-0182

Vermont College of Norwich University
Adult Degree Program
Montpelier, VT 05602
Phone: 1-800-336-6794

NATIONAL CONFERENCES

Association of Professional Genealogists
(see address under *Professional Organizations*)

Federation of Genealogical Societies
(see address under *Genealogical Societies*)

GENTECH, Inc.
P.O. Box 28021
Dallas, TX 75228-0021
Phone and fax: (972) 495-1569
Web site:
http://www.gentech.org/~gentech

National Genealogical Society
(see address under *Genealogical Societies*)

Utah Genealogical Association
P.O. Box 1144
Salt Lake City, UT 84110
Phone: (888) 463-6842
Web site: http://www.infouga.org

FAMILY HISTORY PUBLISHERS

Anundsen Publishing Co.
108 Washington St., Box 230
Decorah, IA 52101
Phone: (319) 382-4295

Closson Press
1935 Sampson Dr.
Apollo, PA 15613-9209
Phone: (412) 337-4482
Fax: (412) 337-9484
e-mail: rclosson@nb.net

Family History Publishers
845 S. Main St.
Bountiful, UT 84010
Phone: (801) 295-7490

Frontier Press
(see address under *Genealogical Books and Supplies*)

Gateway Press, Inc.
1001 N. Calvert St.
Baltimore, MD 21202
Phone: (410) 837-8271

Heritage Books, Inc.
(see address under *Genealogical Books and Supplies*)

Newbury Street Press
(see address under *New England Historic Genealogical Society*)

Picton Press
P.O. Box 250
Rockport, ME 04856-0250
Phone: (207) 236-6565
Fax: (207) 236-6713

Southern Historical Press
(see address under *Genealogical Books and Supplies*)

Archival and Preservation Catalogs
Light Impressions
439 Monroe Ave.
P.O. Box 940
Rochester, NY 14607-3717
Phone: 1-800-828-6216
Fax: 1-800-828-5539

Restoration Source
P.O. Box 9384
Salt Lake City, UT 84109-0384
Phone: (801) 278-7880
Fax: (801) 278-3015

University Products Inc.
P.O. Box 101
South Canal St.
Holyoke, MA 01041-0101
Phone: 1-800-628-1912

GENEALOGICAL BOOKS AND SUPPLIES (BOOKS, FORMS, CHARTS, AND CONFERENCE TAPES)

Ancestry Incorporated
P.O. Box 476
Salt Lake City, UT 84110
Phone: 1-800-262-3787
Fax: (801) 531-1798
e-mail: info@ancestry.com
Compuserve: 76400,2667
Prodigy: GBDC96A@prodigy.com
Web site: http://www.ancestry.com

Association for Gravestone Studies
278 Main St., Suite 207
Greenfield, MA 01301
Phone: (413) 772-0836
e-mail: ags@berkshire.net

Everton Publishers
P.O. Box 368
Logan, UT 84321
Internet: catalog@everton.com

Frontier Press
P.O. Box 3715
Galveston, TX 77552
Phone: 1-800-772-7559
Fax: (409) 740-0138
e-mail: KGFrontier@aol.com
Web site: http://www.doit.com/frontier

Genealogical Books in Print
6818 Lois Dr.
Springfield, VA 22150

Genealogical Publishing Co., Inc.
1001 N. Calvert St.
Baltimore, MD 21202
Phone: 1-800-296-6687
Fax: (410) 752-8492

Heritage Books, Inc.
1540 E. Pointer Ridge Place, Suite 140
Bowie, MD 20716
Phone: 1-800-398-7709

National Archives Trust Fund
NEPS Dept. 735
P.O. Box 100793
Atlanta, GA 30384
e-mail: inquire@nara.gov
Web site: http://www.nara.gov

Oldstone Enterprises
(sells tombstone rubbing kits and wax)
186 Lincoln St.
Boston, MA 02111
Phone: (617) 271-0498
Fax: (617) 271-0499

Repeat Performance
(national genealogical conference tapes)
2911 Crabapple Lane
Hobart, IN 46342
Phone: (219) 465-1234

Southern Historical Press
P.O. Box 738
Easley, SC 29641-0738
Phone: (803) 233-2346

Virginia Book Company
114 S. Church St.
P.O. Box 431
Berryville, VA 22611
Phone: (540) 955-1428
Fax: (540) 955-1162

GENEALOGICAL SOFTWARE DISTRIBUTORS

Broderbund Software
Banner Blue Division
39500 Stevenson Place
Fremont, CA 94539-3103
Phone: 1-800-474-8696
Web site:
http://www.familytreemaker.com

Brother's Keeper
John Steed
6907 Childsdale Ave.
Rockford, MI 49341
Phone: (616) 364-5503
Fax: (616) 866-3345
e-mail: 75745,1371@compuserve.com
Web site:
http://ourworld.compuserve.com/
   homepages/Brothers_Keeper

Family Gathering
Commsoft, Inc.
Palladium Interactive, Inc.
P.O. Box 1200
Windsor, CA 95492
Phone: (707) 836-9000
Fax: (707) 838-6343
e-mail: familygathering@cmmsft.com
Web site:
http://www.palladiumnet.com/Family
Gathering

Family Tree Maker
(see *Broderbund Software* listed above)

The Master Genealogist
Wholly Genes Software
6868 Ducketts Lane
Elk Ridge, MD 21227
Phone: 1-800-982-2103
e-mail: LISSA.SOERGEL@Wholly.
   Genes.permanet.org

Personal Ancestral File
Salt Lake Distribution Center
1999 W. 1700 S.
Salt Lake City, UT 84104
Phone: 1-800-346-6044

Reunion
Leister Productions
P.O. Box 289
Mechanicsburg, PA 17055
Phone: (717) 697-1378
Fax: (717) 697-4373
e-mail: 7477,1626@compuserve.com

Roots V
Commsoft, Inc.
P.O. Box 310
Windsor, CA 95492-0310
Phone: 1-800-327-6687
e-mail: info@cmmsft.com

LENDING LIBRARIES

American Genealogical Lending Library
P.O. Box 329
Bountiful, UT 84011-0329
Phone: 1-800-760-AGLL
Fax: (801) 298-5468
e-mail: sales@agll.com
Web site:
http://www.xmission.com/~agll/

National Archives Microfilm Rental Program
P.O. Box 30
Annapolis Junction, MD 20701-0030

National Genealogical Society
(see address listed under *Genealogical Societies*)

**New England Historic and
Genealogical Society**
(see address listed under *Genealogical
Societies*)

GENEALOGICAL JOURNALS AND MAGAZINES

The American Genealogist
P.O. Box 398
Demorest, GA 30535-0398

Ancestry
P.O. Box 476
Salt Lake City, UT 84110-0476
Phone: 1-800-531-1790
Fax: (801) 531-1798
CompuServe: 76400,2667
Prodigy: GBDC96A

*Association of Professional
Genealogists Quarterly*
(see address listed under *Professional
Organizations*; membership in APG
includes subscription)

Everton's Genealogical Helper
Everton Publishers
P.O. Box 368
Logan, UT 84321
Phone: 1-800-443-6325
Web site: http://www.everton.com

Genealogical Computing
P.O. Box 476
Salt Lake City, UT 84101
Phone: 1-800-531-1790
e-mail: gceditor@ancestry.com
CompuServe:
76400.2667@compuserve.com
Prodigy: gbdc96d@prodigy.com

Genealogical Journal
Utah Genealogical Association
P.O. Box 1144
Salt Lake City, UT 84110

The Genealogist
25 Rodeo Ave. #22
Sausalito, CA 94965

Heritage Quest
P.O. Box 329
Bountiful, UT 84011-0329
Phone: 1-800-658-7755

*National Genealogical Society
Quarterly*
(see address listed under *Genealogical
Societies*; membership in NGS
includes subscription)

*New England Historical and
Genealogical Register*
(see address listed under *Genealogical
Societies*; membership in NEHGS
includes subscription)

Reunions Magazine
P.O. Box 11727
Milwaukee, WI 53211-9727
Fax: (414) 263-6331
e-mail: reunions@execpc.com
Web site:
http://www.execpc.com/~reunions

Bibliography

GENERAL GENEALOGICAL GUIDEBOOKS

Arnold, Jackie Smith. *Kinship: It's All Relative.* Baltimore: Genealogical Publishing Co., 1994; reprint 1996.

Baltheizen, Ann Ross. *Searching on Location: Planning a Research Trip.* Salt Lake City: Ancestry Inc., 1992.

Bentley, Elizabeth Petty. *The County Courthouse Book.* 2d ed. Baltimore: Genealogical Publishing Co., 1995.

Carmack, Sharon DeBartolo. *A Genealogist's Guide to Discovering Your Female Ancestors.* Cincinnati: Betterway Books, 1998.

Cerny, Johni, and Arlene Eakle. *Ancestry's Guide to Research: Case Studies in American Genealogy.* Salt Lake City: Ancestry Inc., 1985.

Crandall, Ralph. *Shaking Your Family Tree.* Dublin, N.H.: Yankee Publishing Co., 1987.

Croom, Emily Anne. *The Genealogist's Companion and Sourcebook.* Cincinnati: Betterway Books, 1994.

———. *Unpuzzling Your Past: A Basic Guide to Genealogy.* 3d ed. Cincinnati: Betterway Books, 1995.

Davenport, Robert R. *Hereditary Society Blue Book*. Baltimore: Genealogical Publishing Co., 1994.

Doane, Gilbert, and James B. Bell. *Searching for Your Ancestors: The How and Why of Genealogy*. 5th ed. Minneapolis: University of Minnesota, 1980.

Dollarhide, William. *Managing a Genealogical Project: A Complete Manual for the Management and Organization of Genealogical Materials*. Rev. ed. Baltimore: Genealogical Publishing Co., 1991.

Drake, Paul E. *What Did They Mean by That? A Dictionary of Historical Terms for Genealogists*. Bowie, Md.: Heritage Books, 1994.

Eichholz, Alice, ed. *Ancestry's Red Book: American State, County, and Town Sources*. Salt Lake City: Ancestry Inc., 1989.

Evans, Barbara Jean. *A to Zax: A Comprehensive Dictionary for Genealogists and Historians*. 3d ed. Alexandria, Va.: Hearthside Press, 1995.

Everton, George B., comp. *The Handy Book for Genealogists*. 8th ed. Logan, Utah: Everton Publishers, 1991.

Greenwood, Val D. *The Researcher's Guide to American Genealogy*. 2d ed. Baltimore: Genealogical Publishing Co., 1990.

Helmbold, F. Wilbur. *Tracing Your Ancestry*. Birmingham, Ala.: Oxmoor House, 1985.

Luebking, Sandra Hargreaves, and Loretto Dennis Szucs. *Family History Made Easy: A Step-by-Step Guide to Discovering Your Heritage*. Salt Lake City: Ancestry Inc., 1998.

Meyer, Mary Keysor. *Directory of Genealogical Societies in the USA and Canada*. 8th ed. Pasadena, Md.: M. K. Meyer, 1992.

Meyerink, Kory. *Printed Sources: A Guide to Published Genealogical Records*. Salt Lake City: Ancestry Inc., 1997.

Rillera, Mary Jo. *The Adoption Searchbook*. Westminster, Calif.: Triadoption Publishers, 1981.

Rose, Christine. *Nicknames: Past and Present*. 2d ed. San Jose, Calif.: Rose Family Association, 1995.

Rubincam, Milton. *Pitfalls in Genealogical Research*. Salt Lake City: Ancestry Inc., 1987.

Stevenson, Noel C. *Genealogical Evidence*. 2d ed. Laguna Hills, Calif.: Aegean Park Press, 1989.

Stratton, Eugene A. *Applied Genealogy*. Salt Lake City: Ancestry Inc., 1988.

Stryker-Rodda, Harriet. *How to Climb Your Family Tree*. Baltimore: Genealogical Publishing, 1987.

Szucs, Loretto Dennis, and Sandra Hargreaves Luebking, eds. *The Source: A Guidebook of American Genealogy*. Rev. ed. Salt Lake City: Ancestry Inc., 1997.

Vandagriff, G. G. *Voices in Your Blood: Discovering Identity Through Family History.* Kansas City, Mo.: Andrews and McMeel, 1993.

Whitaker, Beverly DeLong. *Beyond Pedigrees: Organizing and Enchancing Your Work.* Salt Lake City: Ancestry Inc., 1993.

Willard, Jim and Terry. *Ancestors: A Beginner's Guide to Family History and Genealogy* (a companion to the PBS series). New York: Houghton Mifflin Co., 1997.

COMPUTER GENEALOGY AND THE INTERNET

Cosgriff, John and Carolyn. *Turbo Genealogy: An Introduction to Family History Research in the Information Age.* Salt Lake City: Ancestry Inc., 1997.

Crowe, Elizabeth Powell. *Genealogy Online: Researching Your Roots.* New York: Windcrest/McGraw-Hill, 1994.

Kemp, Thomas Jay. *Virtual Roots: A Guide to Genealogy and Local History on the World Wide Web.* Wilmington, Del.: Scholarly Resources, 1997.

Murray, Suzanne. "Genealogy on the Internet: An Online Course." *Association of Professional Genealogists Quarterly* 12 (June 1997): 50–52.

Przecha, Donna, and Joan Lowrey. *A Guide to Genealogy Software.* Baltimore: Genealogical Publishing Co., 1994.

Rowland, Robin, and Dave Kinnaman. *Researching on the Internet: The Complete Guide to Finding, Evaluating, and Organizing Information Effectively.* Rocklin, Calif.: Prima Publishers, 1995.

GENEALOGY, GENETICS, AND FAMILY HEALTH HISTORIES

Krause, Carol. *How Healthy Is Your Family Tree: A Complete Guide to Tracing Your Family's Medical and Behavioral History.* New York: Simon and Schuster, 1995.

Lustenberger, Anita A. "How to Be a Family Heath Historian." *National Genealogical Society Quarterly* special issue, *Your Family's Heath History: An Introduction* 82 (June 1994): 85–96.

Mitchell, Joan Kirchman. "A Genetics Resource Guide for the Family Health Historian." *National Genealogical Society Quarterly* special issue, *Your Family's Heath History: An Introduction* 82 (June 1994): 131–43.

Nelson-Anderson, Danette L., and Cynthia V. Waters. *Genetic Connections: A Guide to Documenting Your Individual and Family Health History.* Washington, Mo.: Sonters Publishing, 1995.

Pollen, Daniel A. *Hannah's Heirs: The Quest for the Genetic Origins of Alzheimer's Disease.* New York: Oxford University Press, 1993.

Saxbe, William B. "Heredity and Health: Basic Issues for the Genealogist." *National Genealogical Society Quarterly* 84 (June 1996): 127–33.

HOME SOURCES, ARTIFACTS, AND ARCHITECTURE

Note: American Association for State and Local History is herein abbreviated as AASLH.

Horridge, Patricia, et al. *Dating Costumes: A Checklist Method.* Nashville: AASLH, 1977.

Howard, Hugh. *How Old Is This House? A Skeleton Key to Dating and Identifying Three Centuries of American Houses.* New York: Farrar, Straus and Giroux, 1989.

Kyvig, David E., and Myron A. Marty. *Nearby History: Exploring the Past Around You.* Nashville: AASLH, 1982.

McAlester, Virginia and Lee. *A Field Guide to American Houses.* New York: Alfred A. Knopf, 1993.

Montgomery, Erick D. "Historic Site Documentation." *Association of Professional Genealogists Quarterly* 4 (Winter 1989): 77.

Paulsen, Deidre M., and Jeanne S. English. *Preserving the Precious.* Rev. ed. Salt Lake City: Restoration Source, 1989.

Sagraves, Barbara. *A Preservation Guide: Saving the Past and the Present for the Future.* Salt Lake City: Ancestry Inc., 1995.

PHOTOGRAPHS

Davies, Thomas L. *Shoots: A Guide to Your Family's Photographic Heritage.* Danbury, N.H.: Addison House, 1977.

Frisch-Ripley, Karen. *Unlocking the Secrets in Old Photographs.* Salt Lake City: Ancestry Inc., 1992.

Noren, Catherine. *The Way We Looked: The Meaning and Magic of Family Photographs.* New York: Lodestar Books, 1982.

Severa, Joan. *Dressed for the Photographer: Ordinary Americans and Fashion, 1840–1900.* Ohio: Kent State University Press, 1995.

Shull, Wilma Sadler. *Photographing Your Heritage.* Salt Lake City: Ancestry Inc., 1988.

Sturm, Duane and Pat. *Video Family History.* Salt Lake City: Ancestry Inc., 1989.

Weinstein, Robert A., and Larry Booth. *Collection, Use, and Care of Historical Photographs.* Nashville: AASLH, 1977.

ORAL HISTORY

Allen, Barbara, and Lynwood Montell. *From Memory to History.* Nashville: AASLH, 1981.

Baum, Willa. *Transcribing and Editing Oral History.* Nashville: AASLH, 1977.

Davis, Cullom, Kathryn Back, and Kay MacLean. *Oral History: From Tape to Type.* Chicago: American Library Association, 1977.

Epstein, Ellen, and Jane Lewit. *Record and Remember: Tracing Your Roots Through Oral History.* Lanham, Md.: Scarborough House, 1994.

Fletcher, William. *Recording Your Family History: A Guide to Preserving Oral History Using Audio and Video Tape.* Berkeley, Calif.: Ten Speed Press, 1989.

CORRESPONDENCE

(Also see General Genealogical Guidebooks and Vital Records Guidebooks)

Bentley, Elizabeth Petty. *Directory of Family Associations.* 3d ed. Baltimore: Genealogical Publishing Co., 1996.

————. *The Genealogist's Address Book.* 3d ed. Baltimore: Genealogical Publishing Co., 1994.

Everton's Genealogical Helper. Magazine published every other month by Everton Publishers.

Hinchliff, Helen. "Using Direct Mail in Family History Projects." *Association of Professional Genealogists Quarterly* 7 (March 1992): 3.

Smith, Juliana Szucs. *Ancestry's Address Book: A Comprehensive List of Addresses of Local, State, and Federal Agencies and Institutions.* Salt Lake City: Ancestry Inc., 1997.

RESEARCH IN LIBRARIES AND ARCHIVES

(See also National Archives and Federal Records, below)

America History and Life—A Guide to Periodical Literature. Santa Barbara, Calif.: ABC-Clio, Inc., annual.

Bell, Mary McCampbell, and others. "Finding Manuscript Collections: NUCMC, NIDS, RLIN." *National Genealogical Society Quarterly* 77 (December 1989): 208–18.

Bentley, Elizabeth Petty. *The Genealogist's Address Book.* See in particular the sections on National Addresses, State Addresses, and Ethnic and Religious Organizations/ Research Centers. Baltimore: Genealogical Publishing Co., 1991.

Directory of Archives and Manuscript Repositories in the United States. 2nd ed. National Historical Publications and Records Commission, 1988.

"Directory of Genealogical Societies and Libraries." Published annually in the July–August issue of *Everton's Genealogical Helper.*

Filby, P. William. *A Bibliography of American County Histories.* Baltimore: Genealogical Publishing Co., 1985.

———. *Directory of American Libraries with Genealogy and Local History Collections.* Wilmington, Del.: Scholarly Resources, 1988.

Genealogical Periodical Annual Index. Bowie, Md.: Heritage Books. Annual since 1962.

Genealogies Cataloged in the Library of Congress Since 1986. Washington, D.C.: Library of Congress, 1991.

Grundset, Eric G. "One Hundred Years at the DAR Library." *NGS Newsletter* 22 (July/August 1996): 98–101.

Grundset, Eric G., and Steven B. Rhodes. *American Genealogical Research at the DAR.* Washington, D.C.: National Society, Daughters of the American Revolution, 1997.

Hoffman, Marian, comp. *Genealogical and Local History Books in Print.* 5th ed. Baltimore: Genealogical Publishing Co., 1996.

Horowitz, Lois. *Knowing Where to Look: The Ultimate Guide to Research.* Cincinnati: Writer's Digest Books, 1984.

Jacobus, Donald Lines. *Index to Genealogical Periodicals.* 3 vols. Baltimore: Genealogical Publishing Co., 1963–65 (reprinted in one volume, 1978).

Kaminkow, Marion J., ed. *Genealogies in the Library of Congress: A Bibliography.* 2 vols. Baltimore: Magna Carta Book Co., 1972. Suppl. for 1972–76 publ. 1977; 2d suppl. 1976–86 publ. 1987.

———, ed. *A Complement to Genealogies in the Library of Congress: A Bibligraphy.* Baltimore: Magna Carta Book Co., 1981.

———, ed. *United States Local Histories in the Library of Congress: A Bibliography.* 5 vols. Baltimore: Magna Carta Book Co., 1975.

Mann, Thomas. *A Guide to Library Research Methods.* New York: Oxford University Press, 1987.

Moody, Suzanna, and Joel Wurl. *The Immigration History Research Center: A Guide to Collections.* New York: Greenwood Press, 1991.

National Union Catalog of Manuscript Collections. Washington, D.C.: Library of Congress, annual since 1959.

Neagles, James C. *The Library of Congress: A Guide to Genealogical and Historical Research.* Salt Lake City: Ancestry Inc., reprint 1996.

Parker, J. Carlyle. *Going to Salt Lake City to Do Family History Research.* Turlock, Calif.: Marietta Publishing Co., 1996.

Periodical Source Index (PERSI). Fort Wayne, Ind.: Allen County Public Library, annual since 1986.

Schaefer, Christina K. *The Center: A Guide to Genealogical Research in the National Capital Area.* Baltimore: Genealogical Publishing Co., 1996.

Schreiner-Yantis, Netti., comp. *Genealogical and Local History Books in Print.* 4th ed. 1st supp. 1990; 2d supp. 1992. Springfield, Va.: Genealogical Books in Print, 1992.

————. *Genealogical and Local History Books in Print.* 3d ed. Springfield, Va.: Genealogical Books in Print, 1981.

CEMETERY RESEARCH

American Blue Book of Funeral Directors. New York: National Funeral Directors Association, biennial.

Carmack, Sharon DeBartolo. "Carved in Stone: Composition and Durability of Stone Gravemarkers." *NGS Newsletter* 17 (May–June 1991): 69–70.

————. *Communities at Rest: An Inventory and Field Study of Five Eastern Colorado Cemeteries.* Simla, Colo.: privately published, 1993.

————. "There's More Here Than Meets the Eye: A Closer Look at Cemetery Research and Transcribing Projects," Federation of Genealogical Societies *Forum* 7 (Fall 1995): 1, 16–17.

Duval, Francis. *Early American Gravestone Art.* New York: Dover Publishing, 1979.

Forbes, Harriette Merrifield. *Gravestones of Early New England and the Men Who Made Them.* Princeton, N.J.: Pyne Press, 1927.

Jackson, Kenneth T., and Camilo José Vergara. *Silent Cities: The Evolution of the American Cemetery.* New York: Princeton Architectural Press, 1989.

Jacobs, G. Walker. *Stranger Stop and Cast an Eye: A Guide to Gravestones and Gravestone Rubbing.* Brattleboro, Vt.: Stephen Greene Press, 1974.

Jordon, Terry G. *Texas Graveyards: A Cultural Legacy.* Austin: University of Texas, 1982.

Kot, Elizabeth Gorrell. *United States Cemetery Address Book, 1994–95.* Vallejo, Calif.: Indices Publishers, 1994.

National Yellow Book of Funeral Directors. Youngstown, Ohio: Nomis Publications, annual.

Schafer, Louis S. *Tombstones of Your Ancestors.* Bowie, Md.: Heritage Books, 1991.

Sloane, David Charles. *The Last Great Necessity: Cemeteries in American History.* Baltimore: Johns Hopkins University Press, 1991.

Strangstad, Lynette. *A Graveyard Preservation Primer.* Nashville: American Association for State and Local History, 1988.

Weitzman, David. *Underfoot: An Everyday Guide to Exploring the American Past.* New York: Charles Scribner's Sons, 1976.

CHURCH RECORDS AND RELIGION

Berry, Ellen Thomas, and David Allen Berry. *Our Quaker Ancestors: Finding Them in Quaker Records.* Baltimore: Genealogical Publishing Co., 1987; reprint 1996.

Humling, Virginia. *U.S. Catholic Sources: A Diocesan Research Guide.* Salt Lake City: Ancestry Inc., 1996.

Kirkham, E. Kay. *A Survey of American Church Records.* Logan, Utah: Everton Publishers, 1978.

Melton, J. Gordon. *National Directory of Churches, Synagogues, and Other Houses of Worship.* Detroit: Gale Research. 1994.

Rottenberg, Dan. *Finding Our Fathers: A Guidebook to Jewish Genealogy.* Baltimore: Genealogical Publishing Co., 1977; reprint 1995.

Suelflow, August R. *A Preliminary Guide to Church Records Repositories.* St. Louis: Church Archives Committee, Society of American Archivists, 1969.

NEWSPAPER RESEARCH

Brigham, Clarence S. *A History and Bibliography of American Newspapers, 1690–1820.* 2 vols. Worcester, Mass.: American Antiquarian Society, 1947.

Gale Directory of Publications and Broadcast Media (formerly *Ayer Directory of Publications,* Fort Washington, Pa.). Detroit: Gale Research Co., annual.

Gregory, Winifred, ed. *American Newspapers, 1821–1936.* New York: H. W. Wilson Co., 1937.

Horowitz, Lois. *Knowing Where to Look: The Ultimate Guide to Research.* See in particular chapter 11, "Research Tools for Daily Living: Newspapers." Cincinnati: Writer's Digest Books, 1984.

Library of Congress. *Newspapers in Microform: United States.* Washington, D.C.: Library of Congress, Catalog Publications Divisions, 1948 and supplements.

———. *Newspapers in Microform: Foreign Countries.* Washington, D.C.: Library of Congress, 1948 and supplements.

Milner, Anita Cheek. *Newspaper Genealogical Column Directory.* Bowie, Md.: Heritage Books, 1989.

———. *Newspaper Indexes.* 3 vols. Metuchen, N.J.: Scarecrow Press, 1977–82.

VITAL RECORDS GUIDEBOOKS

Kemp, Thomas J. *International Vital Records Handbook.* 3d ed. Baltimore: Genealogical Publishing Co., 1996.

"Where to Write for Vital Records." U.S. Department of Health and Human Services Publication No. (PHS) 93-1142. Write to the U.S. Government Printing Office, Superintendent of Documents, Washington, DC 20204 for current price.

CENSUS RESEARCH

1790–1890 Federal Population Census: A Catalog of Microfilm Copies of the Schedules. Washington, D.C.: National Archives Trust Fund Board, 1979.

1900 Federal Population Census: A Catalog of Microfilm Copies of the Schedules. Washington, D.C.: National Archives Trust Fund Board, 1978.

1910 Federal Population Census: A Catalog of Microfilm Copies of the Schedules. Washington, D.C.: National Archives Trust Fund Board, 1982.

1920 Federal Population Census: A Catalog of Microfilm Copies of the Schedules. Rev. ed. Washington, D.C.: National Archives Trust Fund Board, 1991.

200 Years of U.S. Census Taking: Population and Housing Questions, 1790–1990. Washington, D.C.: U.S. Department of Commerce, Bureau of the Census, 1989.

A Century of Population Growth. Washington, D.C.: Government Printing Office, 1909; reprint Baltimore: Genealogical Publishing Co., 1989.

Lainhart, Ann S. *State Census Records.* Baltimore: Genealogical Publishing Co., 1992.

Pierce, Alycon Trubey. "In Praise of Errors Made by Census Enumerators." *National Genealogical Society Quarterly* 81 (March 1993): 51–55.

———. "Update: More Praise for Census 'Errors.'" *National Genealogical Society Quarterly* 82 (September 1994): 216–220.

Prechtel-Kluskens, Claire. "American Indian Censuses, 1880–1920." *The Record: News from the National Archives and Records Administration* 3 (May 1997): 21–23.

Thorndale, William, and William Dollarhide. *Map Guide to the U.S. Federal Censuses, 1790–1920.* Baltimore: Genealogical Publishing Co., 1988.

Wines, Frederick Howard. *Report on the Defective, Dependent, and Delinquent Classes.* Washington, D.C.: Government Printing Office, 1888.

NATIONAL ARCHIVES AND FEDERAL RECORDS

Elliott, Wendy. "Your Right to Federal Records." *NGS Newsletter* 14 (July–Aug 1988): 85–88.

Guide to Genealogical Research in the National Archives. Washington, D.C.: National Archives Trust Fund Board, 1982.

Guide to Federal Records in the National Archives of the United States. 3 vols. Washington, D.C.: National Archives and Records Administration, 1996.

Luebking, Sandra Hargreaves, and Loretto Dennis Szucs. *The Archives: A Guide to the National Archives Field Branches.* Salt Lake City: Ancestry Inc., 1988.

Microfilm Resources for Research: A Comprehensive Catalog. Washington, D.C.: National Archives Trust Fund Board, 1990.

LAND RECORDS AND MAPS

Andriot, Jay, comp. *Township Atlas of the United States.* McLean, Va.: Document Index, Inc., 1991.

Bockstruck, Lloyd D. *Revolutionary War Bounty Land Grants Awarded by State Governments.* Baltimore: Genealogical Publishing Co., 1996.

Bureau of Land Management. *Manual of Instructions for the Survey of the Public Lands of the United States.* Washington, D.C.: Department of the Interior, 1973, Technical Bulletin 6.

Greenwood, Val D. *The Researcher's Guide to American Genealogy.* 2d ed. See particularly chapters 16 and 17, "Government Land: Colonial and American" and "Local Land Records."

Hone, E. Wade. *Land and Property Research in the United States.* Salt Lake City: Ancestry Inc., 1997.

Luebking, Sandra Hargreaves. "Research in Land and Tax Records." *The Source: A Guidebook of American Genealogy.* Loretto Dennis Szucs and Sandra Hargreaves Luebking, eds. Salt Lake City: Ancestry Inc., 1996.

Makower, Joel, ed. *The Map Catalog: Every Kind of Map and Chart on Earth and Even Some Above It*. New York: Vintage Books, 1992.

Salmon, Marylynn. *Women and the Law of Property in Early America*. Chapel Hill: University of North Carolina Press, 1986.

PROBATE RESEARCH, INHERITANCE, AND HANDWRITING

Fischer, David Hackett. *Albion's Seed: Four British Folkways in America*. New York: Oxford University Press, 1989.

Greenwood, Val D. *The Researcher's Guide to American Genealogy*. 2d ed. See in particular chapter 13, "Understanding Probate Records and Basic Legal Terminology"; chapter 14, "What About Wills?"; chapter 15, "The Intestate—Miscellaneous Probate Records—Guardianships"; and chapter 18, "Abstracting Wills and Deeds." Baltimore: Genealogical Publishing Co., 1990.

Kirkham, E. Kay. *The Handwriting of American Records for a Period of 300 Years*. Logan, Utah: Everton Publishers, 1973.

Shammas, Carole, Marylynn Salmon, and Michel Dahlin. *Inheritance in America: From Colonial Times to the Present*. New Brunswick, N.J.: Rutgers University Press, 1987; reprint, Galveston, Tex.: Frontier Press, 1997.

Stryker-Rodda, Harriet. *Understanding Colonial Handwriting*. Baltimore: Genealogical Publishing Co., 1986.

MILITARY RECORDS

A Census of Pensioners for Revolutionary or Military Services. Washington, D.C.: Department of State, 1841; reprint, Baltimore: Genealogical Publishing Co., 1967.

Allen, Desmond Walls. *Where to Write for Confederate Pension Records*. Bryant, Ark.: Research Associates, 1991.

Beers, Henry Putney. *The Confederacy: A Guide to the Archives of the Confederate States of America*. Washington, D.C.: National Archives Trust Fund Board, 1986.

Bockstruck, Lloyd DeWitt. *Revolutionary War Bounty Land Grants Awarded by State Governments*. Baltimore: Genealogical Publishing Co., 1996.

Bunnell, Paul J. *Research Guide to Loyalist Ancestors: Archives, Manuscripts, and Published Sources*. Bowie, Md.: Heritage Books, 1990.

Coldham, Peter Wilson. *American Loyalist Claims: Abstracted from the Public Record Office, Audit Series 13, Bundles 1–35 & 37*. Washington, D.C.: National Genealogical Society, 1980.

DAR Patriot Index. 3 vols. Washington, D.C.: Daughters of the American Revolution, 1990.

Dorubusch, Charles E. *Military Biography of the Civil War*. 3 vols. New York: New York Public Library, 1971.

Groene, Bertram. *Tracing Your Civil War Ancestor*. New York: Ballantine Books, 1989.

Johnson, Richard S. *How to Locate Anyone Who Is or Has Been in the Military*. 4th ed. Burlington, N.C.: Military Information Enterprises, 1991.

Index of Revolutionary War Pension Applications in the National Archives. Washington, D.C.: National Genealogical Society Special Publication 40, 1976.

Military Service Records: A Select Catalog of National Archives Microfilm Publications. Washington, D.C.: National Archives Trust Fund Board, 1985.

Munden, Kenneth W., and Henry Putney Beers. *The Union: A Guide to Federal Archives Relating to the Civil War*. Washington, D.C.: National Archives Trust Fund Board, 1986.

Neagles, James C. *Confederate Research: A Guide to Archive Collections*. Salt Lake City: Ancestry Inc., 1986.

———. *U.S. Military Records: A Guide to Federal and State Sources*. Salt Lake City: Ancestry Inc., 1994.

Purdy, Virginia C., and Robert Gruber. *American Women and the U.S. Armed Forces: A Guide to the Records of Military Agencies in the National Archives Relating to American Women*. Originally compiled by Charlotte Palmer Seeley. Rev. ed. Washington, D.C.: National Archives Trust Fund Board, 1992.

White, Virgil D. *Genealogical Abstracts of Revolutionary War Pension Files*. 4 vols. Waynesboro, Tenn.: National Historical Publishing Co., 1990—. There is also a cumulative index to this set.

———. *Index to War of 1812 Pension Files, 1815–1926*. 3 vols. Waynesboro, Tenn.: National Historical Publishing Co., 1989.

PASSENGER LISTS, IMMIGRATION, AND NATURALIZATION

Allan, Morton. *Morton Allan Directory of European Passenger Steamship Arrivals*. 1931; reprint, Baltimore: Genealogical Publishing Co., 1993.

Anuta, Michael J. *Ships of Our Ancestors*. Menominee, Mich.: Ships of Our Ancestors, 1983.

Carmack, Sharon DeBartolo. "Ordering Records from the Immigration and Naturalization Service." *Reunions Magazine* (Summer 1994): 12.

Colletta, John Philip. *They Came in Ships.* Rev. ed. Salt Lake City: Ancestry Inc., 1993.

Immigrant and Passenger Arrivals: A Select Catalog of National Archives Microfilm Publications. Rev. ed. Washington, D.C.: National Archives Trust Fund Board, 1991.

Newman, John J. *American Naturalization Processes and Procedures, 1790–1985.* Indianapolis: Indiana Historical Society, 1985.

Schaefer, Christina K. *Naturalization Records of the United States.* Baltimore: Genealogical Publishing Co., 1997.

Sigrist, Paul E. "The Complete Ellis Island Oral History Project Interview List." Unpublished manuscript. Washington, D.C.: U.S. Department of the Interior, National Parks Service, n.d. (Available at the Family History Library in Salt Lake City, and at the Ellis Island Research Library.)

Szucs, Loretto Dennis. *They Became Americans: How to Discover Your Family or Ancestors in Naturalization Records.* Salt Lake City: Ancestry Inc., 1997.

Tepper, Michael. *American Passenger Arrival Records: A Guide to the Records of Immigrants Arriving at American Ports by Sail and Steam.* Baltimore: Genealogical Publishing Co., 1993.

ETHNIC RESEARCH

American Indians: A Select Catalog of National Archives Microfilm Publications. Washington, D.C.: National Archives Trust Fund Board, 1984.

Baxter, Agnes. *In Search of Your Canadian Roots.* Baltimore: Genealogical Publishing Co., 1994, reprint 1995.

Black Studies: A Select Catalog of National Archives Microfilm Publications. Washington, D.C.: National Archives Trust Fund Board, 1984.

Carmack, Sharon DeBartolo. *Italian-American Family History: A Guide to Researching and Writing About Your Heritage.* Baltimore: Genealogical Publishing Co., 1997.

————. "Researching Ethnic Origins." *Reunions Magazine* 2 (Spring 1992): 4.

Chapman, Colin R. *Tracing Your British Ancestors.* Baltimore: Genealogical Publishing Co., 1993, reprint 1996.

Choquette, Margarita. *Beginner's Guide to Finnish Genealogical Research.* Bountiful, Utah: Thomsen's Genealogical Center, 1985.

Chorzempa, Rosemary A. *Polish Roots.* Baltimore: Genealogical Publishing Co., 1994, reprint 1996.

Cole, Trafford. *Italian Genealogical Records: How to Use Italian Civil, Ecclesiastical, and Other Records in Family History Research*. Salt Lake City: Ancestry Inc., 1995.

Colletta, John Philip. *Finding Italian Roots: The Complete Guide for Americans*. Baltimore: Genealogical Publishing Co., 1993, reprint 1996.

Cory, Kathleen B. *Tracing Your Scottish Ancestry*. Baltimore: Genealogical Publishing Co., 1990, reprint 1996.

Epperson, Gwenn F. *New Netherland Roots*. Baltimore: Genealogical Publishing Co., 1994, reprint 1995.

Flores, Norma, and Patsy Ludwig. *A Beginner's Guide to Hispanic Genealogy*. San Mateo, Calif.: Journal Press, 1993.

Grenham, John. *Tracing Your Irish Ancestors*. Baltimore: Genealogical Publishing Co., 1993, reprint 1996.

Hill, Edward E. *Guide to Records in the National Archives Relating to American Indians*. Washington, D.C.: National Archives Trust Fund Board, 1984.

Mokotoff, Gary. *How to Document Victims and Locate Survivors of the Holocaust*. Teaneck, N.J.: Avotaynu, 1995.

Moody, David. *Scottish Family History*. Baltimore: Genealogical Publishing Co., 1989, reprint 1994.

Moulton, Joy Wade. *Genealogical Resources in English Repositories*. Columbus, Ohio: Hampton House, 1988, reprint 1992.

Rowlands, John, ed. *Welsh Family History: A Guide to Research*. Baltimore: Genealogical Publishing Co., 1995, reprint 1996.

Ryan, James G. *Irish Records: Sources for Family and Local History*. Salt Lake City: Ancestry Inc., 1988.

Shea, Jonathan. *Following the Paper Trail: A Multilingual Translation Guide*. New Milford, Conn.: Language and Lineage Press, 1991, reprint 1994.

Smelser, Ronald. *Finding German Ancestors*. Salt Lake City: Ancestry Inc., 1991.

Streets, David H. *Slave Genealogy: A Research Guide with Case Studies*. Bowie, Md.: Heritage Books, 1986.

Thernstrom, Stephen, ed. *Harvard Encyclopedia of American Ethnic Groups*. Cambridge, Mass.: Belknap Press, 1980.

Thomsen, Finn A. *Beginner's Guide to Danish Genealogical Research*. Bountiful, Utah: Thomsen's Genealogical Center, 1984.

———. *Beginner's Guide to Norwegian Genealogical Research*. Bountiful, Utah: Thomsen's Genealogical Center, 1984.

———. *Beginner's Guide to Swedish Genealogical Research*. Bountiful, Utah: Thomsen's Genealogical Center, 1984.

Walton-Raji, Angela. *Black Indian Genealogy Research: African American Ancestors Among the Five Civilized Tribes.* Bowie, Md.: Heritage Books, 1993.

Wellauer, Maralyn A. *Tracing Your Czech and Slovak Roots.* Milwaukee: Wellauer, 1980, reprint 1995.

———. *Tracing Your Swiss Roots.* Milwaukee: Wellauer, 1979.

GENERAL SOCIAL HISTORIES

Earle, Alice Morse. *Home Life in Colonial Days.* Reprint of 1898 ed. Stockbridge, Mass.: Berkshire House, 1993.

Green, Harvey. *The Uncertainty of Everyday Life, 1915–1945.* New York: HarperCollins, 1992.

Hawke, David Freeman. *Everyday Life in Early America.* New York: Harper and Row, 1988.

Larkin, Jack. *The Reshaping of Everyday Life, 1790–1840.* New York: Harper and Row, 1988.

Mintz, Steven, and Susan Kellogg. *Domestic Revolutions: A Social History of American Family Life.* New York: Free Press, 1988.

Schlereth, Thomas. *Victorian America, 1876–1915: Transformations in Everyday Life.* New York: HarperCollins, 1991.

Sutherland, Donald M. *The Expansion of Everyday Life, 1860–1876.* New York: Harper and Row, 1989.

MISCELLANEOUS ARTICLES AND CASE STUDIES

Brayton, John A. *The Five Thomas Harrises of Isle of Wight County, Virginia.* Winston-Salem, N.C.: the author, 1995.

Burroughs, Tony. "A Lazy Man's Way to Research." *NGS Newsletter* 22 (May/June 1996): 66–67.

Carmack, Sharon DeBartolo, comp. "The Genealogical Writer's Market." Three parts. *Association of Professional Genealogists Quarterly.* (Part 1: The Five U.S. National Journals, vol. 8, September 1993, pp. 61–63; Part 2: Regional Journals, vol. 8, December 1993, pp. 93–95; Part 3: U.S. National Newsletters, vol. 9, March 1994, pp. 15–17).

———. "New College: External Degree Program." *Association of Professional Genealogists Quarterly* 8 (September 1993): 68–70.

Eichholz, Alice. "The Adult Degree Program." *Association of Professional Genealogists Quarterly* 8 (June 1993): 37–38.

Geiger, Linda A. Woodward. "Techniques for Transcribing and Abstracting Documents." *Association of Professional Genealogists Quarterly* 10 (September 1995): 87–88.

Macy, Harry Jr. "Recognizing Scholarly Genealogy and Its Importance to Genealogists and Historians." *The New England Historical and Genealogical Register* 150 (January 1996): 7–28.

Mills, Elizabeth Shown. "The Search for Margaret Ball: Building Steps over a Brick-wall Research Problem." *National Genealogical Society Quarterly* 77 (March 1989): 43–65.

———. "In Search of 'Mr. Ball': An Exercise in Finding Fathers." *National Genealogical Society Quarterly* 80 (June 1992): 115–33.

Peña, Lydia M. "The Adult Undergraduate Degree Program at Regis University." *Association of Professional Genealogists Quarterly* 9 (March 1994): 8–9.

Pence, Richard A. "Which Jacob Pence? A Case Study Documenting Identity." *National Genealogical Society Quarterly* 75 (June 1987): 77–123.

Rising, Marsha Hoffman. "Accumulating Negative Evidence." *Association of Professional Genealogists Quarterly* 4 (Fall 1989): 66–68.

———. "Problematic Parents and Potential Offspring: The Example of Nathan Brown." *National Genealogical Society Quarterly* 79 (June 1991): 85–99.

PROFESSIONAL GENEALOGY

Billingsley, Carolyn Earle, and Desmond Walls Allen. *How to Become a Professional Genealogist.* Bryant, Ark.: Research Associates, 1991.

Greene, David L. "What Is F.A.S.G.?: Notes on the American Society of Genealogists." *Association of Professional Genealogists Quarterly* 5 (Summer 1990): 33–34.

"Guidelines for the Use of Credentials and Postnominals in Professional Genealogy." *Association of Professional Genealogists Quarterly* 12 (March 1997): 35.

Jacobus, Donald Lines. *Genealogy as Pastime and Profession.* Baltimore: Genealogical Publishing Co., 1986.

Leary, Helen F. M. "Certification for Genealogists: A Consumer Report." *National Genealogical Society Quarterly* 79 (March 1991): 5–18.

McMahon, Ruth. "The Path Toward Accredited Genealogist." *Association of Professional Genealogists Quarterly* 11 (September 1996): 76–77.

McVetty, Suzanne. "Profile of Two Professionals: Paula Stuart Warren, CGRS, and James W. Warren." *Association of Professional Genealogists Quarterly* 8 (September 1993): 64–67.

Meyerink, Kory L. "The Accreditation Program of the Family History Library." *Association of Professional Genealogists Quarterly* 7 (March 1992): 12–15.

Wyett, Marcia K. "From Hobbyist to Professional: Three Steps in Making the Transition." *Association of Professional Genealogists Quarterly* 10 (December 1995): 121–22.

WRITING AND PUBLISHING GUIDES

Akeret, Robert U. *Family Tales, Family Wisdom: How to Gather the Stories of a Lifetime and Share Them with Your Family.* New York: Henry Holt and Company, 1991.

Alexander, Dana Jordan, and Amy Shea. *Lasting Memories: A Guide to Writing Your Family History.* Charlotte, N.C.: Generations Publications, 1996.

Barnes, Donald R., and Richard S. Lackey. *Write It Right: A Manual for Writing Family Histories and Genealogies.* Ocala, Fla.: Lyon Press, 1983.

Carmack, Sharon DeBartolo. "A Reviewer's Look at Published Genealogies." *Everton's Genealogical Helper* 51 (May–June 1997): 22–23.

———. "Putting the Two Together: Social History and Family History." *Ancestry* 13 (Nov/Dec 1995): 23, 27.

———. "Words Immortal: Writing Your Family History." *Reunions Magazine* 5 (Summer 1995): 36–37.

———. "Words Immortal: Publishing Your Family History." *Reunions Magazine* 5 (Autumn 1995): 34–36.

Gerard, Philip. *Creative Nonfiction: Researching and Crafting Stories of Real Life.* Cincinnati: Story Press, 1996.

Gouldrup, Lawrence P. *Writing the Family Narrative.* Salt Lake City: Ancestry Inc., 1987.

———. *Writing the Family Narrative Workbook.* Salt Lake City: Ancestry Inc., 1993.

Hatcher, Patricia Law. *Producing a Quality Family History.* Salt Lake City: Ancestry Inc., 1996.

Hoffman, William. *Life Writing: A Guide to Family Journal and Personal Memoirs.* New York: St. Martin's Press, 1982.

Hughes, Ann Hege. "Preparing Manuscripts for Offset Printing." *Association of Professional Genealogists Quarterly* 8 (June 1993): 31.

———. "Publishing Genealogical Research: Commercially and Privately." *Association of Professional Genealogists Quarterly* 5 (Fall 1990): 60.

Ledoux, Denis. *Turning Memories into Memoirs: A Handbook for Writing Lifestories.* Lisbon Falls, Maine: Soleil Press, 1993.

Polking, Kirk. *Writing Family Histories and Memoirs.* Cincinnati: Betterway Books, 1995.

Poynter, Dan. *The Self-Publishing Manual: How to Write, Print, and Sell Your Own Book.* 8th ed. Santa Barbara, Calif.: Para Publishing, 1995.

Sturdevant, Katherine Scott. "Documentary Editing for Family Historians." *Association of Professional Genealogists Quarterly* 5 (Spring 1990): 3.

DOCUMENTATION, NUMBERING, INDEXING, AND STYLE GUIDES

Chicago Manual of Style, 14th ed. rev. and expanded. Chicago: University of Chicago Press, 1994.

Crane, Madilyn Coen. "Numbering Your Genealogy—Special Cases: Surname Changes, Step Relationships, and Adoptions." *National Genealogical Society Quarterly* 83 (June 1995): 84–95.

Curran, Joan Ferris. *Numbering Your Genealogy: Sound and Simple Systems.* Arlington, Va.: National Genealogical Society Special Publication, 1992; also available in *National Genealogical Society Quarterly* 79 (September 1991): 181–93.

Gibaldi, Joseph, and Walter S. Achtert. *MLA Handbook for Writers of Research Papers.* 3d ed. New York: Modern Language Association, 1988.

Hatcher, Patricia Law, and John V. Wylie. *Indexing Family Histories.* Arlington, Va.: National Genealogical Society Special Publication, 1994.

Lackey, Richard S. *Cite Your Sources: A Manual for Documenting Family Histories and Genealogical Records.* Jackson: University Press of Mississippi, 1986.

Mills, Elizabeth Shown. *Evidence: Citation and Analysis for the Family Historian.* Baltimore: Genealogical Publishing Co., 1997.

Turabian, Kate L. *A Manual for Writers of Term Papers, Theses, and Dissertations.* 4th ed. rev. and expanded by Bonnie Birthwistle Honigsblum. Chicago: University of Chicago Press, 1987.

Wray, John H. "Numbering Your Genealogy: Multiple Immigrants and Non-emigrating Collaterals." *National Genealogical Society Quarterly* 85 (March 1997): 39–47.

Index